BAGH.

Adventures of a truck driver

by

Kevin Noble

and

Chris Foote Wood

NORTHERN WRITERS

First published in 2006 by
Northern Writers
"Wor Hoos" 28 Cockton Hill Road
Bishop Auckland
County Durham DL14 6AH
www.northernwriters.co.uk

British Library Cataloguing in Publication Data

A catalogue for this book is available from the British Library.

ISBN 10 0-9553869-0-X
ISBN 13 978-0-9553869-0-9

Typeset in 10/12pt Garamond

Typesetting and origination, printed and bound by
Lintons Printers Ltd, Beechburn, Crook, Co. Durham DL15 8RA

www.lintons-printers.co.uk

"A truck is like a woman. When she's running well, she's a dream. When she's not, she can be a perfect bitch. Treat her well – keep her clean inside and out – and she loves it. Treat her badly, and she'll never forget it."

– Robert Hutchinson.

"The Middle East trucker can be described in many ways, from an adventure seeker to someone trying to get out of debt. They are all knights of the road, with many years and miles in the saddle, prepared to lay their heads on the block to better themselves."

– Kevin Noble.

"The first run was made around 1963, UK to Afghanistan. Slowly road transport came to be an efficient solution to take freight to Central Asia door-to-door. By the end of the 1960s, transport companies were sending their trucks to Pakistan. In the 1970s the economic expansion in the Middle East was so strong, the Arabs were buying just about everything. Harbours became totally congestion, so road transport was the only practical solution. Drivers were hauling their goods to Qatar, UAE, Kuwait. Within ten years the traffic was so intense, there was a non-stop flow of trucks between Europe and Asia. But by the mid-80s the situation in the harbours had improved, making the price of transporting goods by road more expensive than by sea. This put an end to twenty years of the most extraordinary era in the history of road transport."

– Ferdy De Martin.

"Like many other guys, I did this job from '74 till '86. We were all lucky enough to use the opportunity, as it will never occur again. This was a window in time that I was privileged to take part in. The world has changed a lot since then, and it's not possible to recreate the circumstances. I have enough memories to last me a lifetime, and I feel proud to have been one of the trucking pioneers who carved a name for English truckers across the continent of Arabia."

– Ian Taylor.

"There are a few diehards that still do it, but it's much more difficult now, and I wouldn't think half as much fun. There are many truck drivers who are still finding out about this period of modern trucking history and regret that they will never have the opportunity to go where no trucker had gone before. Many people can't get their head around the fact that a round trip to Qatar is the best part of 10,000 miles!"

– Ian Taylor.

"Turkish Tonka drivers are paid by the trip, and they are paid peanuts. So for them it was always rush, rush, rush…The more trips they made, the more money they earned."

– Robert Hutchinson.

"Pay up and smile." – Franklyn Wood.

Chapter One

Turkish Hospitality

Early evening was upon us before clearance was finally granted to enter Turkey. We'd been at the border for eight long hours, not helped by the squalid surroundings and the oppressive mid-summer heat. It had been a taxing day since leaving the Greek coastal resort of Kavala, hampered by the insistence of the Turkish customs to inspect every part of our cargoes. I was travelling at the rear of the three-truck convoy, expecting to be in Istanbul around ten-thirty.

Once parked up, I was eagerly anticipating a cool shower, a kebab and some ice-cold Efos beer. The two-lane highway was notorious for accidents, but surprisingly the traffic was light, considering it was the busy holiday period. Some sixty miles later we passed by the town of Inecik before heading into the darkness of the open countryside. My headlamps were focussed on the "Long Vehicle" signs of the trailer in front, which were prized as collectors' items among the Turkish and Arab truckers. Soon we would clear the city of Tekirdag, before skirting the shoreline of the Marmara Sea. There, the cooling breezes would be more than welcome in the stifling atmosphere.

Minutes later, the truck at the head of the column signalled his intention to stop, followed by the Volvo and myself. I was cursing our luck at such an unearthly hour, for what appeared to be a mechanical failure. After extinguishing the headlamps, ejecting the Abba cassette and switching on the interior light, I prepared to go up front to see what the problem was.

Suddenly, a gunman emerged from the darkness, armed with what looked like a small machine gun. With the window fully open he contented himself with standing on the cab step, holding onto the door with his right hand, whilst directing the gun with his left. Christ, we were being hijacked! He made a half-hearted attempt towards opening the door, but fortunately for me it was locked from the inside. I'd often heard about these situations, now I was facing the stark reality. But instead of ordering me to drive or get out of the cab, the gunman had other ideas.

"Pass-a-port!" he demanded in a deep, coarse voice. He was around thirty, heavily built, unshaven, with a large black moustache and shoulder-length hair. His breath stank of strong tobacco and garlic. His upper palate proudly sported two gold teeth, adding to his sinister appearance. "No passport," I replied, firmly but quietly. His dark eyes narrowed with suspicion, while searching the cab contents from the windscreen to the bunk. I was adamant he wasn't getting my passport cheaply, because without it I wouldn't be able to get out of Turkey, or move freely anywhere. It also contained my truck number within the transit stamp. First and foremost it was my identity card, my lifeline, and without it I was nothing.

"Man-ee-fest!" he shouted in his best pidgin English, referring to the documents detailing the goods inside the trailer. "No manifest," I responded, somewhat sheepishly, my mind still numb with the suddenness of events. The gravity of the life-or-death situation still hadn't quite registered. It was as if the whole exercise was nothing but a charade, despite me staring down the barrel of a gun.

We were parked on a slight bend in the road, restricting the visibility of passing motorists, with the constant tooting of horns no doubt directed at the "stupid foreign bastards!" I couldn't quite figure out why he hadn't stopped us in a parking area a few miles further on. Maybe that was too risky? The other drivers were in the same predicament, so my unwanted, gun-toting guest had to have at least two accomplices. As yet I was still rooted to my seat, unable to communicate with anyone. "Pass-a-port! Man-ee-fest!" he kept repeating in an agitated manner, the tone of his voice gradually increasing in volume.

"Caa-rgo, caa-rgo!" he barked, by now with much more menacing demands, gesturing with the gun barrel as if it was his finger. His knowledge of the English language appeared to be limited to three very effective words, but no doubt the word money would be the fourth. He would know I'd just crossed the border and would have all the documents he required, so I had to say something quickly to satisfy his demands. I could only hope and pray that he'd be patient.

"Shiza papier, ladung shiza papier," was my response in a stammering German dialect, as the gun was again thrust towards my face, prompting my heart to skip yet another beat. For a few seconds he seemed puzzled and confused, as he digested the conundrum as to why I would be transporting toilet rolls. He appeared to have no problem understanding the content of my reply. This wasn't totally unexpected, the majority of Turks being more conversant with German than English.

The truck's V10 engine was quietly idling under the

cab floor, this being the only sound to invade the tense atmosphere. But I knew I was running out of time and that if I didn't co-operate quickly it would be a bullet. My cargo was eighteen Leyland diesel engines, which I'd collected from Trafford Park international freight terminal at Manchester, destined for the Baghdad Bus Corporation in Iraq. It was quite possible that my assailant had inside information about the trailer's contents, either from unscrupulous border officials or government agents. After all, the engines were as precious as hard currency, especially to the various terrorist networks operating within the Turkish frontiers.

All sorts of things were flashing through my mind, the most important being not if, but when I was going to die. I had to act quickly. The gunman was getting increasingly impatient with my feeble explanations, and the last thing I wanted was to be ordered out of the cab to an uncertain fate. I'd always had reservations about travelling in Turkey during the dark hours, now it appeared I was about to become a victim of my own advice. "Moment, moment, passport, manifest," I cried, trying to defuse the situation. At the same time I reached over to the centre console, removing some papers from the tray, making it appear as though I was acceding to his request. Swiftly I handed him a football magazine encased in a Bulgarian map. The suddenness of events caught my tormentor momentarily off guard, resulting in the gun barrel deflecting away from me. In an instant I elbowed the bastard in the face as hard as I could, causing him to lose his grip on the door. He screamed as he disappeared into the darkness.

There was no time to waste. I'd committed the foul deed and had to get moving. I swiftly engaged gear and released the brake. Unfortunately, as my vehicle was right hand drive, the presence of the trailer in front meant my forward vision was virtually non-existent. Quickly I edged my way left to re-join the highway, making sure my passenger side rear view mirror showed a clear exit. At this point I was working the controls from a virtual standing position, leaning across the cab to observe any headlamps coming towards me. The thought of a head-on collision was inconceivable, as I battled against the added problem of sweat running into my eyes. Suddenly I was clear, then it was go! go! go! The manoeuvre took only seconds, but to me it seemed like an eternity.

By this time the rest of the bandits had emerged from the front of the convoy, alerted by their colleague's screams and the urgent engine noise. Three of them were standing in the middle of the road, brandishing their guns in the air for me to stop, but I was in no mood to accept their invitation. At the same time I was trying to keep my head as low as possible, just in case they got trigger-happy, but they quickly bottled out when confronted with thirty-five tonnes of truck hurtling towards them. The adrenaline was pumping rapidly as I quickly headed towards Tekirdag, hoping to alert the police or the military. Under the circumstances, anywhere would do. The army had regular security checkpoints, but even though my mind was working overtime I couldn't remember where.

After a few miles, flashing headlamps began to appear in my mirrors, ending my brief taste of freedom. I'd naively hoped that my assailants would have other things to take care of, but no such luck. After all, I was witness to their actions. They were indeed desperate people to give chase on a main highway, but there was no way they were going to overtake. I was leader of the pack and fully intended staying there. Every time they tried to pass me, I would veer the truck from side to side in a snaking motion. Drivers coming from the opposite direction had to take their chances.

Thankfully, my pursuers had no ideas about shooting at the mirrors, which would have made it impossible for me to monitor their movements. Even so, their blinding headlamps were a constant source of discomfort. By now I was dripping with sweat, my dashboard-mounted cooling fan having little effect. I then held a brief conversation with James Bond, wondering what he would do in my situation. He'd probably have machine guns mounted behind the long vehicle signs. Sorry Kevin, this is the real thing. Agent 007 is not available to help you.

There was only one person left who could save the day, and that was the Almighty. Although I prayed out loud and asked him for guidance, the good Lord probably had a lot more of his flock in dire straits. My pedigree of worship wasn't of the highest standing. I had to confess, since my days as an altar boy I had only been to the church for weddings and funerals.

I classed myself as being fortunate to get away, whilst wondering what fate awaited the other drivers. They'd probably be forced to drive their trucks to some obscure destination and I wasn't very hopeful of ever seeing them again. At least my destiny lay in the palms of my own two sticky hands. The road seemed endless, winding its way through the dark wasteland. Finally, faint flickers of welcoming light appeared in the distance, perhaps only two miles away. In the tense atmosphere, it was impossible to gauge the terrain or distances with any accuracy.

I was now feeling slightly more relaxed, but still keeping my speed at sixty miles an hour. This was much too fast for the road conditions, but circumstances dictated that the horses couldn't be spared. My eyes were glued to the road ahead, looking for potholes and abandoned vehicles. This only added to the drama in my rear-view mirrors. Surely the scum hounding me would stop shortly, not wanting any contact with the legal authorities.

Suddenly I remembered. The lights were from a restaurant on the outskirts of Tekirdag. It was a place I knew well, having passed there several times in daylight. At last, salvation was in sight. I decided to drive straight up to the main entrance. This, I hoped, would afford me better protection. So, without any indication, I braked violently, exited the highway and raced towards the restaurant. At this point I had expected that my pursuers would vanish into thin air, but no such luck. They were right behind me, determined to see things through to the bitter end.

Unfortunately, the area outside the restaurant had no concrete or asphalt hard standing, just loose rubble. No time for caution! I slammed on the brakes and the rig shuddered to a halt, amid much sound and fury. Moments earlier, the people dining outside had been enjoying a candlelit meal. Now, they were enveloped by a cloud of choking dust, caused by the appearance of a massive juggernaut next to their tables. I jumped from the cab and ran for the open door, not daring to look behind. I must have presented a rare sight for the restaurants guests, as I charged through the inside dining area, clad only in shorts and with my shaven Kojak hairline. James Bond-style, I dashed into the kitchen and rushed past the startled catering staff, searching desperately for a door, any door to the outside world.

I found the exit, but my passport to freedom was securely chained and padlocked. Seconds later it was all over. My heart sank and the adrenaline quickly drained from every part of my body. Gun barrels were thrust into the back of my head. Jubilant cries of "fuckin' Ingiliz!" echoed around the kitchen. Victory had been achieved. They must have left their other colleagues back at the crime scene, but no doubt I would suffer for my actions.

By now the restaurant was in complete turmoil, with diners and staff shouting and gesturing, all directed towards me. What my captors were screaming, I hadn't the faintest idea. They were no doubt pointing out the errors of my evil ways, with everyone of the opinion that I'd committed some sort of immoral act in their country. At one point the situation threatened to spill out of control, as the diners added their voices to the turmoil. The restaurant manager was waving his hands and shouting abuse to the point of hysteria, as I was forcibly manhandled outside. It was then the turn of the dust-covered diners to vent their anger, with the occasional slap to the face, accompanied by a constant volley of spitting. It was impossible to distinguish the spit from the sweat, as I was led to a dimly lit area surrounded by a copse of trees. Here I was away from prying eyes, and in the cast-iron grip of my jailers to do whatever they pleased.

My mood was one of anger and disappointment. Unless I could conjure something up within the next few minutes, the lucky breaks that had helped me along throughout life were about to come to an abrupt end. If only I could free myself from their forceful grip, I'd be prepared to risk a bullet trying to flee. Surely anything would be better than just waiting for the end. The chances of escape finally diminished to zero as my hands were roughly shackled behind a gatepost. For once I could imagine how the condemned prisoner must have felt on his way to the gallows, only I was the innocent party. I had one final throw of the dice. This might buy me a little more time, a commodity I was desperate to extend.

"American dollars," I shouted, "American dollars." Surely that would tempt them. Every man has his price.

Instead of turning their heads in anticipation of the spoils, they totally ignored my invitation, cursing me in their broken English and laughing loudly. Once I was out of the way, they would have a free hand to do whatever they wanted. They would know I was carrying enough money to pay for the round trip expenses, and would eventually find it when they ransacked the truck.

My mouth felt dry. Whether it was the hot evening or the fear of death, I couldn't be sure, as I resigned myself to the inevitable. With no reprieve in sight, it appeared as though my passage of time had run its course. This was it, the end of the road. The wheel had finally turned full circle. My thirty-six years had been most enjoyable, but I hadn't expected my earthly presence to be ending quite so soon, along with my lofty aspirations. Given the choice, I would have preferred a better time and definitely a better place, but is any time the right time?

At requiem mass, the Priest would always remark that the deceased was going to a better place. I had no desire to go to a better place. The one I was living in was fine, apart from one or two minor problems. My life started flashing before me. As the nightmare unfolded, I kept thinking of the devastating effect my death would have on everyone back home, especially my daughter and

Mother. I said one last hopeful prayer, as my Turkish guards, still laughing, retreated a few paces, guns at the ready. Be prepared to meet thy maker.

Seconds dragged into minutes. My captors appeared to enjoy putting me through some form of Chinese torture, probably hoping I'd break down and cry. They'd be disappointed. Not only was my body drained of moisture, but also of soul. It was while I was saying my final prayers for the umpteenth time that my fellow-drivers Errol Flynn and Taffy Davies suddenly appeared from out of the gloom. At first I thought it was fatigue playing tricks with my mind, until Errol, clearly annoyed, had his say.

"What did you fuck off for? They were only undercover cops wanting to check our documents." Errol's broad Scots accent was balm to my soul.

While I was still trying to come to terms with reality, it was impossible for a Turk to impersonate the man from bonnie heather country.

"How the fuck did I know who they were, all I was faced with was a gun!"

Taffy then had his say.

"We're all in the shit now, because you've broken his fuckin' nose and they're talking about locking us all up!"

This was all I needed. Not only were the Turks against me, but also my two companions.

"Never mind about that, untie my hands and get me a drink, I'm fuckin' parched."

I wasn't bothered about the prospect of prison, I'd just been spared a firing squad. I was ecstatic. Besides the adrenaline pumping once again, I cannot truly explain how I felt. It was similar to someone getting a reprieve on death row. The police still classed me as a prisoner and wouldn't allow my hands to be free, so Errol and Taffy had to feed me like a baby. The diners were licking their lips in anticipation. Hoping to witness a public execution.

More police arrived, this time in uniform. The ranks of lawmen swelled to around a dozen, as if they were investigating a murder or a major heist. Instead, I was in the frame, a humble Geordie bricklayer's son who had risked bullets rather than stop. The allegations against me were classed as being so serious, that the police had called for the British Consulate in Istanbul to attend the scene.

The last ambassador I'd met in Milan had given me twelve quid for a rail ticket to London, but somehow I doubted if there would be any repeat. Our man arrived within an hour, so I assume he lived close by. At least his appearance ended the non-stop abuse being hurled in my direction from the restaurant manager, who was all but ready to pull the trigger. After being untied I joined Errol, Taffy and the envoy at one of the outside tables that had earlier been covered in dust, along with a teapot, four glasses and some sugar cubes. The envoy was Turkish but spoke good English. I just told him the truth, that I was suddenly challenged by the gunman. What the hell was I supposed to do, other than try and make a run for it? Errol's version of events differed slightly. He'd been signalled to stop by uniformed police using neon-type hand lamps, before the undercover men assumed control. With me travelling about 150 yards behind him, I hadn't seen any of this.

The Embassy official then explained the reason for us being stopped. Certain cargoes transiting Turkey were disappearing, and the government was desperate to catch the perpetrators. Bogus Middle Eastern companies, using unscrupulous agents, were arranging arms shipments for use by terrorists, generating massive profits. Parts of military equipment, listed as machinery, were being carried in separate trucks to conceal their true identity, later to be re-assembled. After clearance at Turkish customs, instead of being transported across the country to the Arab states, the goods would get no further than a warehouse in Istanbul. The rigs were then hidden away for up to a month while false documentation was prepared, making it appear as if the cargo had been delivered to Iraq, Iran, Syria or Saudi. The trucks would then leave Istanbul to re-load in Europe, for another phoney journey to the Middle East.

The police were working incognito between the border and Istanbul, with me unfortunately being one of their prime suspects. The points raised were:

- Did I know the gunman was an undercover cop?
- Was I trying to hide something by driving away?
- Did I discard anything on the journey to the restaurant, perhaps drugs?
- Would I compensate the broken nose victim?

A search of the truck and trailer had already proved negative. If I'd been carrying drugs, it's most likely I would have been bringing them from the opposite direction to sell in Europe, not the other way around. I'd hate to think of the outcome had I been a regular grass smoker. Even carrying a small amount for my personal use would have meant a long stay in a Turkish jail and goodbye to my virgin arse. I'd already formed the opinion that it was accepted practice for the police to dabble in various forms of weed, but outsiders had to be made an example of. I also made the point about the undercover men's state of dress, which made Starsky and Hutch look top-drawer.

The official never doubted my story for one moment, but he would have to convince the Turkish authorities as to my sincerity. The Consulate and the legal powers worked very much hand in hand. When my predicament was fully explained, the police took it all in good spirit. After a further hour of haggling I was allowed to go without charge. There were nods and handshakes all round, except from the restaurant manager. We arrived at the Londra camp just after 3am. Notions of cool showers and refreshment were long gone. All I wanted was a few hours' sleep.

Two days later in Groovy Hasan's gift shop, I developed the shakes, which lasted until Baghdad. At first I thought it was a fever, before realising it must have been the after-affects of the trauma.

On arrival at the Baghdad Bus Company, I was greeted with cheers of delight. The engines were desperately wanted. They had been ordered for more than a year, and twenty per cent of the 600-strong fleet was waiting for spares. The Iraqis had run British-made buses since the year dot, but I got the impression they'd had enough, being unable to get spares through strikes and delays in the UK. German manufacturers MAN were being tipped to take over the lucrative export business. Not only would they supply buses on time, but guaranteed future delivery of urgent parts within twenty-four hours. Little did the officials of the Baghdad bus company know what I'd been through to get them their vital spares.

Chapter Two

Rebel Rouser

A February snowstorm signalled my arrival in 1944, in the coal-mining town of Crook in north east England. My Uncle Bernard escorted the nurse for three miles through the blizzard conditions, ensuring I entered the world in capable hands. While Dad was at war with Hitler, me, my elder sister Anne and our Mother "lived in" with my elderly grandparents in their large terraced house in Coronation Street.

Later that year the household was grief-stricken, with the tragic news that Mother's cousin, Peter Hill, had been killed at Arnhem. Pete, a 22-year old glider pilot, was a popular figure at the Tarrent Rushden aerodrome. He had been detailed to fly the famous writer, Ernest Hemingway, in one of the Hamilcar gliders when he was visiting the base. The previous year Peter had escaped death by only inches when attacked by the Luftwaffe off the Portuguese coast, ditching his glider into the sea. Luck finally deserted him on 25th September, when he was fatally wounded as British troops were retreating across the Rhine.

My early years were largely dominated by the staunch Catholic ladies of the house and their strict Victorian beliefs. Their favourite saying was "spare the rod and spoil the child," meaning I was forever on the end of thrashings. Grandad was in his mid-seventies, so our communication was somewhat limited. A native of

Galway, he came to Crook in his early twenties and served in the local constabulary for twenty-five years. Times were difficult, with frequent strikes and disputes. Well aware of the miners' plight, Grandad often turned a blind eye to poaching and petty pilfering. He had seen plenty of poverty in his native homeland. The majority of Crook's 16,000 population were people of Irish, Scotch and Welsh descent, whose forefathers had migrated to the Durham coalfields to mine the black diamonds.

When I was three I went missing, only to be discovered in the driving seat of a car belonging to a local businessman. My first encounter with a steering wheel.

Dad was finally demobbed in 1947. Having seen each other only twice in three years, we both had a lot of catching-up to do. He was a Tynesider, a true Geordie. He came from the Gateshead side of the Tyne, where life was much more hectic than the tranquil surroundings of the Crook countryside. Besides being gentle and warm-hearted, he was a simple-living type, with Woodbine cigarettes his only form of luxury. Had he been like Mother, or Gran, I would probably have gone missing permanently. Dad's first priorities were a job and a house, being fortunate to land both almost immediately. He found work as a bricklayer, and with his demob money and a little help from his in-laws, he bought a three-bedroomed terraced house in Grey Street, close to the town centre. The church tower was clearly visible from my bedroom window, while the Baptist Chapel was only yards along the street. Either way, God was our neighbour.

To supplement his weekly income, Dad would regularly work weekends. He would replace the old black-leaded kitchen ranges with the latest tiled fireplaces for just £2. Some people would pay five shillings (25p) a week, while others would always find an excuse not to pay, with a night on the drink taking preference. Dad had had a limited education. Living in an impoverished inner-city area, he would often attend school in his bare feet. Mother came from a better-off family, and was educated at St. Mary's Convent school at Berwick-upon-Tweed near the Scottish border. Her family and friends possibly thought she'd married below her station, especially to a Geordie bricklayer, although I was never made aware of it. They'd met at a wedding at St Mary's Cathedral in Newcastle. Had Dad not been a Catholic, then their relationship would have been doomed before it had even begun. In the eyes of the church, and my grandparents, you married one of your own. Mixed marriages were unthinkable, whatever the circumstances.

The Sisters of Mercy, who administered my early education, belied their name with their liberal use of the cane. The word compassion had no place in their vocabulary. Rather, they seemed to enjoy doling out punishment, of which I was a regular recipient. I could never understand the nun's motives or thinking. They were Irish, fully aware of the hardship associated with large families, unemployment, poverty and drink, yet never showed any understanding towards the victims of people with these problems.

Some of my most enjoyable childhood days were spent at Dad's former home in Gateshead, reached via a two-hour journey by bus and tram. I was made fully aware of the city's offerings, besides being a regular visitor to Newcastle's much-acclaimed Quayside market. One stallholder, no doubt once bitten, displayed a notice in bold print: *"God helps those who help themselves, but God help those I catch helping themselves!"* The sounds of the ships' sirens entering and leaving the Tyne at night fuelled my imagination, helping lullaby me to sleep. Tyneside was famous worldwide for its shipbuilding and heavy engineering expertise. Geordies adopted a work hard, play hard attitude, with Scotswood Road alone boasting fifty-six watering holes.

Joining the Cubs was a natural progression of excitement for most of us, also coinciding with my elevation to the Church altar and choir. St. Patrick's Day was a huge event, it being the only time I got to celebrate my confirmation name, Patrick. It held as much significance among the Irish population of the town as Christmas Day, whether you were part Irish, or had a second cousin from the Emerald Isle. Irish songs would be heard throughout the day, with the pub stragglers in full voice on the journey home. My favourite was "Galway Bay," probably because I'd heard it sung so often. Dad would pay tribute to Mother by singing, "I'll Take You Home Again Kathleen," a song she confessed to me many years later that she never liked.

The twice-yearly school plays and pantomimes were performed to packed audiences. We all thought we were the tops, parading around in our colourful costumes, in front of dazzling stage scenery. An elderly Irishman, Jim Sullivan, played the accordian. He made the instrument sound as good as a band, his fingers gliding across the keys at lightning speed as he played an Irish Jig. Jim was a regular visitor to Coronation Street, where he and Grandad would sit in the back kitchen, reminiscing about the old times in Ireland. Jim was from Belfast, and although they shared the same religion they tended to differ politically. After a drop of the hard-stuff, heated conversations would give way to some lively Irish songs.

My wanderlust showed itself at an early age. I collected foreign labels from packages and cans. These I took to school, pinpointing the various countries on a map, where the oranges, pears, bananas, dates and tinned meats came from. Missionaries would call at school to enlighten us about their work abroad, mainly the poor countries of Africa. One African charity we collected vigorously for was the "black babies." We were given a large card, which had to be covered with stamps costing 3d (1½p) each, with the completed card portraying a picture of the orphans.

The highlight of the week was the Saturday morning matinee at the Empire Cinema, as we eagerly awaited the next episode of Flash Gordon. The first priority was to get some sweets, for nothing if possible. "Tazis" (Taziolis) ice cream shop was next to the picture house. If young Joe or Gino were serving, we'd order a quarter of sweets from a jar on the top shelf. This required climbing a small ladder. Both sons were grossly overweight and less than agile. It took them an eternity to retrieve the jar, during which time we'd fill our pockets from the counter offerings. If Mrs Tazi was on duty, getting freebies was a problem, so "Woollie's" (Woolworths) was next on our list.

Then it was off to the flicks, with The Lone Ranger, The Bowery Boys and Laurel and Hardy among my favourites. The fun continued after the pictures, as the "left-footers" (Catholics) and "prodi-dogs" (Protestants) prepared to do battle behind the advertising hoarding. This was simple inter-school rivalry, nothing at all to do with religion. Skinned knees and black eyes were the legacy of our fun.

We'd end up at the colliery reservoirs in Kitty's

Wood, scouring the murky waters for a glimpse of the Messerschmitt that had crashed in one of the ponds during the war. We'd each claim anything below the water line as the remains of the plane, whether it was a rusting bedstead, a wheelbarrow minus the wheel or a bicycle frame. The pit yards were reserved for playing at the weekend when it was quiet. Here, we'd practice our skills at being a miner, pushing the empty coal tubs on the tracks outside, but falling short of venturing into the darkness of the pit. All these places were officially strictly off limits.

The disused quarries at Dovefold, overlooking the town, also provided a wealth of adventure, besides being home to gamblers and courting couples. It was there that our fantasies would be acted out, playing war heroes and cowboys, or spying on the gamblers and courting couples. At the entrance to the quarries were the Devil's Stones. They had to be circled three times, or the Devil would have his wish.

For the gamblers, the quarries provided an ideal haven away from the public eye, where they could enjoy their Sunday afternoon game of pitch and toss. We would lie on the grass at the top, keeping out of sight until everyone was assembled in the quarry bottom. They would then form circles (schools), with a "chucker" standing in the middle of each circle ready to toss the coins in the air. Once the games had started, we would bravely move forward on our bellies to look down on the action, with shouts of "heads a dollar" commonplace, a dollar being five shillings (25p). The atmosphere occasionally reached boiling point, with the losers, some fuelled by drink, cursing the lucky bastards who'd won. The next two hours would determine whether drink and cigarettes would be affordable until the next payday, and whether there'd be bread on the table in the coming week. The police usually turned a blind eye to these proceedings, unless they received a complaint from some irate housewife.

Our next-door neighbour, Tommy, was a partner in Crook's "Sound Service" shop, which sold all the latest wirelesses, radiograms and the new craze – television. Naturally he had a set, with the twelve-inch screen being in big demand by the street's residents, even to watch children's programmes. Tommy also had a guitar and would sing country and western songs, using a matchstick to strike the strings. This was the first time I'd actually seen a guitar "in the flesh", and I was impressed by the sound, if not with Tommy's yodelling.

To generate a few extra pennies, I ran errands after school for a retired haulier and also a second-hand furniture dealer. Both constantly reminded me to call at the cheapest places, so much of my time was spent window-shopping. On Saturdays, the haulier would give me a shilling and half a dozen pigeon eggs. He probably thought I looked undernourished. Occasionally, I'd sneak onto his allotment to sample some of his mouth-watering strawberries, which I reckoned to be better for my constitution. The other chap, Jack Turner, had a small saleroom near the town centre. His well-worn bright red face was always shining like a beacon, giving anyone the impression he'd been weaned on a whisky bottle. He must have been disillusioned with shaving, because I can never remember him having a completely clean face. Some days he would miss his chin, other days his cheeks.

The Central was the largest and most popular of the town's three snooker halls. Here the miners would meet up with their mates to catch up on the latest "crack," before dispersing to the bars and football matches. The saloon's décor advertised all the leading brands of cigarettes and sweets on mirrors around the walls: Woodbines, Players, Turf and Senior Service, all jostling with Fry's chocolate cream for the best positions. Comics and cowboy books were regularly exchanged, with the merits of the "Gunfight at the OK Corral" loudly debated. My parents strictly forbade me to visit any of these places, insisting that the only things I'd learn would be bad. Of course they were right, but I'd frequently chance my luck.

I was ten before I tried my first cigarette. Despite glowing reports, I must admit to being disappointed. After buying a Woodbine and two matches at Tazis for tuppence (1p), I attempted to join the big man's world in the back room of the Central. I was instructed by one of the proper smokers, a boy of twelve, to inhale the smoke. At this point I was nearly sick. The cigarette was then nipped (extinguished) until the colour had returned to my cheeks, thereby justifying the need for the extra match. Added to this were the regular exhibitions of "body blessings" in the school field, with some of the older boys comparing themselves as to who had the biggest appendage. Finally, after judging the best "tail", the proudly-displayed organs would be exercised to show us youngsters how to do it properly.

Football was our number one game. Cricket was played at school for a few weeks before the summer holidays, but wasn't taken seriously. It soon became crystal clear, that if you were no good at football, then your sporting aspirations were severely limited. There was also tennis and golf, which tended to be the leisure activities of the better-off, such as businessmen and colliery officials. They were joined by hangers-on and working-class upstarts who would vote Conservative after a few elocution lessons.

After a shaky start to the 1953-54 season, Crook Town FC finally found their shooting boots, progressing well in the FA Amateur Cup. Many a pound changed hands on match days, together with the occasional punch-up between opposing supporters. If Crook were playing away, we'd have our own game of football in the back street, with the winners claiming nothing more than bruises and ripped clothes. After the pubs had closed for the afternoon, some of the customers on their way home would join in the game, trying to demonstrate the skills and dribbling wizardry of Jackie Milburn and Len Shackleton. Most were unsteady on their feet after three hours of drinking, more often than not ending up flat on their backs after failing to connect with the ball. We'd be careful not to laugh, just in case we ended up the same.

The 1954 Amateur Cup final was between Crook and none other than their arch-enemies from six miles away, Bishop Auckland. There was bitter rivalry between the teams, much the same that existed between professional neighbours Newcastle United and Sunderland. By a twist of fate, they had somehow managed to avoid each other all the way to the final on Wembley's hallowed turf. Incredibly, this "local derby" between two small-town clubs attracted a maximum 100,000 crowd to England's premier stadium, with Crook eventually winning the second replay 1-0. Not to be outdone however, the "Bishops" won the trophy for the next three years in succession, staking their claim in history as the world's greatest amateur football team.

Joe French (Frenchie) was two years older than me and lived in the next street near the gasworks. He had crazy brainwaves from time to time, such as sailing bathtubs on the beck. This was another place strictly off limits, due to the dangers of rats and liquid waste from the coke-works. I was always the guinea pig for his experiments, but never complained, secretly loving every minute of it. My pioneering spirit usually ended up with a soaking, followed by a good hiding. It wasn't too difficult to fathom out who Frenchie got his ideas from. His dad was always experimenting with newfangled gimmicks. He bought two ex-army walkie-talkies from the Exchange & Mart. For weeks after, he and a mate would often be seen playing soldiers in the long grass. His dad also fancied himself as a handyman. In fact he was a jack-of-all-trades but master of none – or maybe one? He came up with the idea of installing an upstairs bathroom, but to us it was all hot air. However, within weeks, after much dust and hullabaloo, it was ready to use. Frenchie's dad held the proud distinction of being the first in the neighbourhood to have an upstairs bath.

Frenchie had a roving eye, and was a keen student of female underwear on the washing line. Betty the catalogue woman was a regular visitor to his house. Dressed in tight-fitting clothes, her shapely body drove us young boys wild with lustful thoughts. Betty's catalogue would be smuggled upstairs to Joe's bedroom as often as possible, allowing us to feast our greedy eyes on the women posing in bras and panties. It was our first sex book. Betty was most impressed with the bathroom, and it was only a matter of time before she was invited to use it. Frenchie had confided in me that he'd drilled some tiny holes in the wooden bathroom wall that were virtually

impossible to detect. Friday night soon arrived. The
excitement almost too much to bear, as we waited and
listened from the sanctuary of his bedroom. The sounds
of footsteps on the stairs, followed by the running of
water, quadrupled my heartbeat. Minutes later the water
stopped. I was absolutely terrified. With deathly silence
we tiptoed towards the bathroom, before taking up our
positions to view "what the butler saw." With such
facilities a rarity, the hospitality of Frenchie's mother
gradually extended beyond Betty, so we were visiting the
spy holes for months. I suppose you could say we were
true patrons of the saying, "the best things in life are free."

One of the scariest experiences with Frenchie, was at
Cala cave near the Dovefold quarries, allegedly the former
habitat of a hermit. The back of the cave seemed endless,
but we were determined to satisfy our curiosity. Judging
by the torches, ropes, heavy coats and boots that Frenchie
had commandeered from his father's works van, it
appeared as though we were going to tackle Mount
Everest. As per usual I was allotted the task of explorer,
with the back of the cave revealing a long straight tunnel.
The further I progressed communication became
impossible, with the walkie-talkies crackling non-stop.
The air was cold, with noises in the distance sounding like
dripping water, but I couldn't be sure. What made things
worse, were the stories from years before about German
prisoners who'd escaped from nearby Harperley Camp.
Maybe it was them making the noise? What if they
caught me and I was their prisoner? I didn't need much
convincing to make a swift return to the daylight, so at
least the German prisoners would have no chance of
being discovered by a frightened schoolboy.

Failing the second part of the scholarship brought me

down to earth with a bang. I'd been hoping to go to St. Aidan's grammar school at Sunderland, but those hopes were now dashed. I classed myself as just an average scholar, but failure was still hard to accept. Advised to find a school with better facilities than those available at Crook, my parents sent me to St. Leonard's Secondary Modern in Durham City. The school was a large Victorian mansion, originally built for a gentleman called Joseph Love. He was reputed to have been England's first self-made millionaire, having made his fortune in coal mining. Maybe my parents were expecting their son to follow suit? It was only a matter of days before the bullies surfaced, with the older boys determined to stamp their mark on the new recruits.

Michael Mallin was fourteen and fancied himself as the king of the castle. He and his cronies populated the outside toilets at break times, making life hell for us young pupils. He would wait until you were having a dribble, then push you forward, causing the front of your trousers to get wet, besides demanding money for cigarettes. I didn't say anything to my parents, not wanting to worry them, but it got to the point where I dreaded walking up the school drive every morning. I could use my fists in my own age group, having been in lots of scraps, but taking on someone a lot older and bigger would prove to be a problem. It got to the point where I was nearly a nervous wreck, before finally deciding I'd had enough, come what may. After plucking up the courage to refuse his demands we both ended up battling on the ground, unleashing the anger that had been building up inside of me for weeks. By the time the prefects broke up the fight we both had bloody noses. The tough-talking junior "Teddy Boy" was disappointing with his fists, considering the age gap. As far as I was concerned his bullying days were over, but for others who were quiet by nature, and not inclined to "have a go," the pain continued.

Uncle Bob lived in the Southwick area of Sunderland. A fitter and turner by trade, he was a mild-mannered chap, with none of the vices of drinking or smoking. He was a keep-fit fanatic. He'd won numerous bodybuilding competitions, and had been a Mr Great Britain finalist. Uncle Bob's party piece was walking on his hands, no mean feat for a man in his fifties. Over the years he taught me a lot, most notably swimming. He had a passion for the outdoors, much the same as myself with the scouts. On visiting the Lake District, we'd pitch the tent and have a quick cuppa, before tackling his favourite mountain, Helvelyn. His only negative aspect was being a skinflint, with not the slightest chance of an ice cream or a bottle of pop.

The "Teddy Boy" fashion was becoming commonplace. The long, colourful Edwardian-style knee-length jackets and "drainpipe" trousers were exhibited nightly in the bars and snooker halls. The "Teddy Girls" were also something special, their flared skirts and tight-fitting jumpers revealing all that was on offer. Saturday night at the Elite dance hall was a popular venue for the "Teds." There were the inevitable bouts of disorder, due to rival tribes, booze and girlfriends. Crook had just experienced its last influx of Irish migrants from Donegal to work in the coal-mines. They liked nothing better than a good scrap, so the Teds and the Paddies would be at it tooth and nail.

When the film, "Rock Around The Clock" was being screened at the Hippodrome, I begged my parents to let me go to the Sunday night viewing. After much persuasion they relented, provided my elder sister Anne accompanied me. What happened that night was frightening. As soon as the singing started, the Teds and their girls began jiving in the aisles. The management, unable to come to terms with the latest craze that was sweeping the nation, switched on the lights and threatened to stop the film. Order was briefly restored until Bill Haley again broke into song. After more dancing and more threats, the police finally arrived to calm things down. I only saw half the film, but witnessed the first picture-house riots in my home town.

Being on the perimeter of the Durham coalfield, Crook was classed by many as the last outpost. Every town and village has its fair share of eccentrics, and Crook had more than most. There was even a resident tramp, Maurice Pybus, who lived in the piggery at Peases West on the outskirts of town. There was always plenty of excitement on offer for us young tearaways, with Sammy Johnson's redundant garage near the gas works a prime target. It was a refuge of junk, an Alladin's cave, with us always hopeful of finding a pot of gold. The problem was old Sammy's monkey, appropriately named Samson. It had the run of the place, treating the garage as its own private jungle. It was far worse than a dog for biting, besides being able to move quickly. Samson caught me twice, letting out shrieks of delight, while leaving painful marks on my back and legs. Excursions into the garage were limited to the summer months only, when the monkey was tied up during the day.

Summertime was also good for scrumping apples. Just after dark, four of us entered the orchard of a retired doctor in St. Mary's Avenue, an upmarket part of town.

Almost immediately the outside light came on, followed by shouting and dogs barking, the signal for a quick exit. In those situations it was every man for himself. If you got caught the only thing to do was to cry, say you were sorry, and plead with them not to get the police. It nearly always worked, the culprit(s) let off with a stiff lecture. However, if you and your pals had left the orchard bare, there was no reprieve. A visit from the police, followed by a good hiding from your father, would be the order of the day.

Next we tried the priest's garden. Considering the four of us were Catholics, it wasn't very patriotic stealing from one of our own. Surely the priest wouldn't mind sharing with his choirboys? Inside the greenhouse, the grapes were begging to be picked. Unwittingly, we took more than we could eat, proving that our eyes were bigger than our bellies, leaving the priest barely a few morsels. Over the following days we all suffered from diarrhoea. Was this a sign from up above? Had we been caught, we'd have been condemned to Hell by special dispensation, besides being ordered to say ten Hail Mary's and ten Our Father's, three times a day for the rest of our lives. The Priest never attended to the vines ever again, making me feel guilty for many years afterwards.

I'd assist Dad as a junior labourer as often as he'd let me. People craved the independence of the motorcar, and Dad was much in demand to build garages to house them. Much to my annoyance he would limit my work to a few hours, insisting that I enjoy myself as much as possible. If I'd had enough money, that would have been all well and good, but I wasn't a saver, preferring to live for the day.

I'd been told by one of my classmates, that if a woman drank plenty of milk she'd have a baby. This must have satisfied my curiosity until the word Durex surfaced. Snooker hall education gradually taught me, that playing doctors and nurses without the aid of a Durex would have far-reaching consequences. These much talked about "French letters" could be purchased at Jimmy Thexton's barbershop. They would be ordered when the haircut was nearing completion, being signalled by a nod, grunt or movement of the eyes. The small packet would then be discreetly slid under the apron into the hands of the customer, similar to a secret service operation. The "university of life" was beckoning, but I would have to learn many lessons and endure many disappointments before graduation day.

A few of us young lads wanted guitars to copy our idols, thinking that after a few weeks we'd all be rock 'n' roll stars. The new sounds emerging were mainly American, leaving Tommy Steele, Frankie Vaughan and the skiffle of Lonnie Donegan to fly the flag on the home front. I pestered Dad for months, eventually being rewarded with a second-hand instrument. I really looked the part, posing in front of the sitting-room mirror. I could play a mouth organ, as could Dad. The guitar however was a different proposition, with sore fingertips another painful issue.

We budding musicians first got together at the home of Gordon Crawshaw, who for some strange reason was nicknamed "Korky." This large residence previously housed his father's dental practice, the former surgery ideal for us to practice our rock star ambitions. Gordon attended St. Aiden's grammar school, and for his academic achievements had been rewarded with a new Hofner electric guitar. It was the first electric guitar I'd ever had the pleasure of holding, making the hairs stand up on the back my neck. To simulate the sound of a double bass we used a tea chest, while a washboard borrowed from Gran acted as a good substitute for a drum kit. Frenchie wasn't musical, in fact he was tone deaf. This possibly explained why he liked the record his father regularly played, "Shifting Whispering Sands," knowing it word perfect.

Mother had studied the piano as a girl, and much of her "tinkering" involved Irish songs and melodies. There were three songsheets on the music rest that I remember her playing occasionally: "St. Theresa of the Roses", "The Wild Colonial Boy", and a rather unusual choice, "The Man from Laramie." "The Wild Colonial Boy" told the story of a teenager who'd left Ireland in troubled times to seek fame and fortune in Australia, only to fall foul of the law. I couldn't help but glance at it when tuning my guitar.

"There was a wild colonial boy, Jack Duggan was his name, he was born and raised in Ireland, in a place called Castlemaine. He was his father's only son, his mother's pride and joy, and dearly did his parents love the wild colonial boy."

Mother's favourite saying, especially when I'd been in hot water, was that I would end up either a "priest or a pauper." She often remarked that she would have doubted my lineage had I not been born at home. This stuck with me throughout adolescence and beyond, being branded as the only "mischievous element" in the clan. I believe that in younger brother Leo, a quiet no-nonsense boy, she saw someone who would fulfil her desired objectives.

When I reached thirteen I had more than one reason to be cheerful. Not only was I introduced to long trousers, I was also promoted to the backbenches of the church choir. Religion was the hub of my upbringing, and just about every room in the house carried some memento of the faith, either in pictures or statues. At the bottom of the stairs was a verse, woven in green silk thread onto Irish linen, reading "May you be in Heaven an hour before the devil knows you're dead." I didn't think for one moment that all Catholics were do-gooders. To me, they had just as many drunks, wife-beaters and corrupt people as other religions. What made us different and in a sense unique, was that we could go to confession and wipe the slate clean, giving us the license to start all over again.

After nagging Mother for two shillings, I acquired a large map of the world from the church jumble sale. She thought I was losing my senses, buying what she termed a useless piece of junk. I could now pinpoint all the places of interest in the world, even though it was forty years out of date. Besides portraying a united Ireland, it also featured Persia, Siam and Manchuria. Nevertheless I was fond of it, with the old names sounding much more charismatic.

The school bus from Durham would periodically carry the odd sailor who'd docked at the Tyne. They were usually the worse for drink, but kept the passengers entertained with tales of places you could only dream about. I would always make a mental note, checking the countries they'd visited as soon as I got home. Top of the pile were the Commonwealth destinations of Malta, Gibraltar, Hong Kong and Singapore. Tales from America were very scant indeed.

During the summer months, Saturday mornings meant trips to Durham Baths. We used the narrow back alley at the bottom of Silver Street as a shortcut to Elvet Bridge. It was quite obvious that Moatside Lane was used for more things than shortcuts, due to the masses of discarded "French letters" and betting slips. Swimming was followed by a mooch around the city, always taking in the music shop window. Even though rock'n'roll was stamping its authority on the country's teenagers, the shop tended to cater more for the student jazz-lovers. After checking if the statue of Lord Londonderry's horse in the Market Place was still minus its tongue, we'd call in at Lipton's store for a tuppenny (1p) bag of broken biscuits. I had a crush on a blonde girl working there, thinking of any excuse to prolong our stay in the shop. Elsie was sixteen, but after months and months of admiring glances, and bag after bag of broken biscuits, she let me down with a bang. My little world suddenly fell apart, when I noticed her near the bus station "linking" a lad of eighteen. Silly little boy – keep dreaming.

Frenchie left school and started work in a brickyard. His earnings rocketed to over £5 a week, whereas the income from my paper round and odd jobs barely totalled eleven shillings (55p). The gangster films were still firm favourites of ours, and we would mimic the accents of Al Capone, James Cagney and Humphrey Bogart. The main recipients for our hoodlum impersonations were the Tazioli brothers. Besides being overweight, Joe and Gino tended to perspire heavily, making them perfect "victims."

At school, I constantly diced with authority. Speaking out of turn resulting in my near permanent place at the front of the class. Strangely enough, it had a huge positive influence on my interests in history and geography. Miss Lucy Cullen, the form teacher, once viewed me with suspicion when I excelled in an English exam. How can you cheat at English? My reputation even preceded me into the dining hall, where discipline was administered by Mr. Ryan, nicknamed Buck. When punishment was ordered, my pleas for sympathy fell on deaf ears. "Buck" Ryan would flex the cane between his huge hands, preparing for the kill. The gleam in his eyes convinced me that I was about to make his day. So it proved, his arm coming over quicker than Freddie Truman ever bowled a cricket ball. My hand still tingled two hours later. Even though the lessons were painful, I continued to live life on the edge, often straying into troubled waters.

Frenchie's next brainwave saw the arrival of an old, non-running Austin Seven car. He'd bought it off a workmate for a few pounds, but within days the ignition problem had been solved and the car was ready to roll. Frenchie was only sixteen, but that didn't bother him in the slightest, having had plenty of practice since the age of twelve.

We decided to broaden our horizons with a Sunday outing to Whitley Bay on the north east coast. Minor details such as having no tax or insurance, and driving under the legal age didn't bother us. On top of that, the car was the oldest on the road by at least ten years. Frenchie had been growing a moustache to enhance his appearance by a year or two. With this, his black shirt, white tie, Brylcreemed hair and cigarette drooping from his mouth, he looked more like a city "spiv." I still kept sampling the odd cig, trying to copy the pose of Robert Mitchum, even though I'd only been in long trousers for a little over a year. Three miles from Whitley Bay the engine developed a knock, giving us all cause for concern. After checking the oil and water, Frenchie decided to "nurse" the car seawards for the remaining three miles.

Suddenly there was an almighty bang, accompanied by clouds of steam, as the car shuddered to an abrupt halt. We all looked at each other in total silence, and I must admit to instigating a laughing spree with the back seat passengers, much to Frenchie's displeasure. His spiv-like appearance quickly reverted to that of a humble brickyard worker, as the car was left on waste ground with a gaping hole in the side of the engine. We'd driven around the big wide world for thirty-three miles, ending our bid for glory with a bang and a puff of steam.

My parents finally succumbed to the pressure of their three children by getting a television. Now I could experience the "Six-Five Special" rock'n'roll show in the comfort of my own home. The medical profession was of the opinion that watching too much television would affect our eyes in later life, having also said that about playing "pocket billiards" too often. The only lessons that could be deduced from our learned friends, was that the good things in life were bad for your health.

I was getting itchy feet, due to everyone around me working, and school was beginning to be a drag. One day I was summoned to the headmaster's office to account for my dismal disciplinary record. Mr. Mulkerrin was a quietly-spoken man and easy to talk to. I'd possibly had more contact with him over the past four years through various misdemeanours than anyone else in the school, including the teachers. The meeting between us was to be our last. I stood perfectly still while he sat at his desk, quoting from the records, before asking what my intentions were on leaving school.

"An electrical engineer or a rock and roll star, sir."

I immediately realised I shouldn't have said the latter. I was trying to add a touch of humour to the conversation, only for it to backfire. After remarking that the guitar was the instrument of the devil, he promptly removed his spectacles and rose to his feet, ushering me towards the large window at the front of his study. For a few seconds I was bemused as to his intentions, until he pointed out a building, asking if I knew what it was? I didn't recognise it, but was assured it was Durham Jail. He then continued with the warning that if I didn't alter my ways, then the inside of the prison would beckon in years to come.

Despite high hopes of becoming an electrician, I started work as a motor mechanic on October 18th 1959, at the recently-built Smith's Prompt Service Depot (Park View Garage) in neighbouring Willington. My wage was £2-18-6 (£2.92½p) for a 44-hour week. On my first day I was given tuition on how to light the pot-bellied workshop stove. Later I was to cheat slightly to save time, using a dangerous mixture of paraffin, petrol or thinners. Sometimes it had the adverse affect, resulting in a minor explosion, singed hair, missing eyebrows and a black face. Mother had secretly been hoping I'd follow grandfather into the police force, referring to the conditions and pension, but to me that held no attraction whatsoever. Anyhow, what 15-year old jack-in-the-box was interested in a pension?

As the months progressed I saw very little of Frenchie. On one of our last get-togethers, he introduced me to the "drink of the devil." My only other experiences had been a glass of sherry or ginger wine, when I was "first-footing" on New Year's Eve. The Catholics held regular social evenings, encouraging young and old from different parishes to form new and lasting friendships. Everyone enjoyed a knees-up, with music provided by an accordion, fiddle and drums. We only knew the barn dance, but that was enough to get us an introduction to any promising "talent." Besides, my parents wouldn't be there, so I could have a sly cigarette. Frenchie suggested we call at the Balaclava pub at the bottom of Church Hill on our way to the social. This was to summon up some Dutch courage, but would I pass for eighteen? After much deliberation I agreed to wear one of his father's trilby hats, which still rested on my ears, even after some minor adjustments. We proceeded to the room at the rear, which was occupied by three pipe-smoking pensioners playing dominoes. Frenchie, as confident as ever, wandered over to the small serving hatch and ordered two pints. I nervously lit a cigarette, but my heart missed a beat when he returned empty handed, explaining that the landlord would bring the drinks.

Moments later, two large black shoes appeared in the doorway. I lifted my head slightly to observe light-coloured trousers rising from the shoes, two arms carrying a tray of drinks, and a black waistcoat behind the arms. My appearance must have given him the impression that he was confronting a youthful Humphrey Bogart. Much to my amazement, he deposited the beers on our small round table, followed by three bottles of Guinness for the domino players. The beer tasted awful but I put on a brave face, more so, when three of Frenchie's under-age workmates appeared. One pint increased to two, three and even more, accompanied by jokes and juicy tales. The band's accordion was belting out an Irish jig as we entered the school hall, heading for the bottom corner among the other unattached males. This was an ideal vantage point to eye up the visitors, with everyone preparing to stampede across the floor if they knew the next dance.

Within half an hour, my aim of "clicking" with some sumptuous girl had totally disappeared, as I began to feel increasingly unwell. When Frenchie remarked that my complexion had turned a deathly white, it was my cue to make a quick exit to the playground. Almost immediately, I discharged the evening's intake of Strongarm beer into the drainage system, washing my shoes and trouser bottoms in the process. After wandering around for two hours I returned home, swiftly retiring upstairs, only to experience the ceiling spinning around. My only thought was "never again!"

The one thing on my mind when I reached my sixteenth birthday was to get a motorbike. The latest purchases were on show outside the Continental coffee bar, ranging from the small BSA250 to the highly-powerful Triumph Bonneville. I managed to secure a small machine for a bargain £20. Taxing and insuring it would account for my spare cash, but I would have to ask Mother to lend me the money to buy it. She detested motorbikes, as did most mothers, but she was the only person in the household who could lay their hands on that kind of money. Our relationship was still as cold as ice, but after promises regarding my future conduct she came up trumps. With the quality of the bike usually dictating the pecking order of the dames, I had no intentions of taking it to the Continental, where it would struggle to attract a suitor.

Every second Saturday in July, the miners from the north-east coalfields converge on Durham for their annual gala, known as the "Big Meeting." Thousands of miners, their families and friends attend, showing loyal support to the trades union movement. The shop windows are boarded up for protection against the swarming masses, with scenes reminiscent of a huge street party. I'd never been to the Big Meeting before, so I arranged to meet some Technical college classmates at the Angel Inn at eleven. Even at such an early hour there was the odd person the worse for drink, giving some indication as to what was in store for the rest of the day. The atmosphere was electrifying, with the dense crowds taking you along with their every movement. We weren't interested in the speeches from the various politicians and trades union activists, just what was on offer at the showground.

After some hair-raising rides on the waltzer and dodgems, we ended up in the boxing booth. There, the promoters were offering £10 to any person still on his feet after three rounds. There was no shortage of takers, especially among the powerfully built, well-muscled pitmen, some of whom had trained all year for the event. There were also the others, who'd trained on a few beers and fancied their chances, with the bookies doing a roaring trade. The boxers were all ex-pros, who, whilst not making the grade at the professional game, still had a few tricks up their sleeves. For most of the fight the miner had the upper hand, with shouts that the pro was past his best. The packed audience would be licking their lips in anticipation of winning a few quid. With seconds remaining the boxer would deliver a swift blow to the miner's chin, leaving his stunned opponent lying flat out on the canvas, and it was all over.

With all the excitement I found myself separated from my pals. It was then that I took the unusual step of getting my fortune told by the "world famous" Gypsy Rosalee. After checking my palm, my Romany friend assured me that I was going to live a long life, travel the world and have a large family. I agreed wholeheartedly with the first two appraisals, but the last left me in doubt. It was there that I struck up a conversation with Marian, another of the Gypsy's customers.

After watching the odd scuffle between drunks, we headed for the coolness of the beer tent. Marian was quite tall, around five-nine, and probably five years older than me. She'd come from Sunderland with her boyfriend. He had hit the whisky bottle on arrival, and was now sleeping it off on the far side of the racecourse. I conveyed my sympathy, while at the same time praying that the bugger didn't sober up quickly, call in the beer tent and give me a good hiding.

Marian suggested we move on. I wasn't quite sure what her intentions were, but mine were to gaze at her minus her clothes. By now the drink was pickling my brain, causing the adrenaline to spiral out of control, as we settled for a comfortable nest near the rugby club. I explained to Marian that I hadn't done this sort of thing much before, feeling more like a Friar Tuck than a Robin Hood. My fears were totally unfounded, with my lady leading the way like a guiding light. All those words of vigilance, from preachers, parents and honourable people were surely untrue. The fairground music was playing Elvis Presley's "Surrender," while I was enjoying my boyhood fantasies with Maid Marian. Durham Big Meeting was my first introduction to the "golden rivet."

After wallowing over all the musical publications and stargazing at the TV, I finally got the chance to see one of my idols. Billy Fury, Liverpool's answer to Elvis, was appearing at Spennymoor Rink, only five miles from my home town. It was a breathtaking experience. Billy's singing was top dollar, but his gyrating body movements threatened to cause pandemonium among the suitors of the swooning girls.

In March 1961, just after my 17th birthday, I was given the chance to learn to drive. The boss offered me the use of an old Morris car that had been part-exchanged against a new mini. It was taxed and insured. All I had to do was supply the petrol and a qualified driver. On Whit Monday I drove to Weardale with Frenchie alongside, while two of the "gang" took up the rear seat. The weather was hot, so we combined the lesson with a swim in the river. On returning to town the recently-appointed Sergeant Elliot challenged us, demanding our driving licences and car ownership details. The majority of people called him the fat sergeant due to his bulging waistline, but we nicknamed him Elliot Ness, after the man who caught Al Capone. The problem was that Elliot wasn't after gangsters, he just liked putting the shits up people. He had a lady friend in Willington who bought her cars from Smiths. It was only a matter of days before our confrontation came to the boss's attention. He immediately withdrew his offer, maintaining that the car was strictly for learning and not for the pleasure of others. Sadly, my driving aspirations were put on hold.

Smith sold his garage to the oil giant, Texaco, transferring his business to the former Empire picture house in Willington town centre. The cinema was just how it had been left after the last performance. According to the posters behind the ticket office, the films "Spartacus" and "Some Like It Hot," had brought the curtain down for the final time. It had originally been built as a theatre, with the dressing rooms underneat the stage shortly to house tyres and spares. I couldn't help but think that I was standing on the same spot as many famous people of yesteryear. The moving pictures had caused the demise of the local theatres, now television was closing the picture houses. The Railway Tavern, a drinking house for more than a hundred years, was nearby. It too would succumb to the needs of the sixties, being converted into a car showroom with residential flats above. Next to the tavern was Angelo's coffee bar, where the local talent would be rocked by the jukebox or cherished by any new additions that came through the door. Further down the street was Billy Cottle's pub, the liveliest spot in town, where admirers of the local girls would regularly punch seven bells out of each other.

A blanket of snow greeted New Years Eve. By late evening the celebrations in the Queen's Head were in full swing, with Chubby Checker's "Let's Twist Again" blasting to the heavens. Men of all ages, some carrying sprigs of mistletoe, were eager for a festive kiss from the girls and women they had a fancy for. Occasionally they would end up with a black eye, broken nose, or both for their troubles. I was just feeling my feet with a certain young lady, when big Billy Plews, the landlord, came across the room to have a word.

"You can drive, can't yer, Kevin?" said Billy, putting his large hand on my shoulder.

"Yes Billy," I replied, while thinking it a most unusual question at quarter past eleven on New Year's Eve. It transpired that his brother's mate had to get to Witton le Wear, with the buses having been withdrawn from service due to the wintry conditions.

"I wonder if you could do me a favour and drive Tommy home?" said Billy, while confirming that cars were indeed still travelling the roads.

"Whose car are we using?" I asked. "Mine" said Billy.

I didn't even know Billy could drive a car, never mind own one, but it must have been a long time since his sixty-inch waist was behind a steering wheel. I was then introduced to an elderly Austin Sheerline limousine, which would have been more suited to an old-type gangster film. When it was new, its surroundings would have been one of stately homes and people of means. Now it was relegated to a dingy garage behind a beerhouse. Judging by the feathers and dust, the rear seats must have been home to some form of livestock. I was unable to contain myself at this point and burst out laughing. Billy not in the least amused that I was taking the piss out of his pride and joy.

I knew Tommy had been drinking for most of the day. Totally inebriated and unable to stand, he was helped onto the back seat by three lads of a similar disposition. Billy's brother Stan sat alongside me. After travelling only a few minutes the snow started falling again.

What I'd said about being able to drive was correct. The only problem being, I didn't have a licence!

To enter Witton village, we had to descend a steep hill, the only means of turning around being the wide entrance to the cemetery halfway down. As I pulled into the entrance, fearful of being stuck for the night, the chiming of bells in the distance signalled that 1962 was already upon us. Tommy was still out for the count, snoring away in the back seat, so I suggested to Stan that we carry him to his house further down the hill. Stan, keen to get back to the Queens, shook his head.

"There's no fuckin' way I'm carrying him Kevin, the fucker must weigh sixteen stone," he argued.

"We can't leave him here Stan, he'll fuckin' freeze to death," was my reply.

"If he does, they'll not have far to carry him," quipped Stan, as we both laughed at his motionless body.

We got Tommy out of the car, sat him down on a rubber mat and wedged him between the wall and the cemetery gates to prevent him falling over. A search of the car revealed cardboard and papers which we used to cover him up. Hopefully, he'd awaken with the cold and find his way home, with the snowflakes by now heavier then ever. The hefty weight of the car helped it to chug its way to the top of the hill, where we both breathed a huge sigh of relief before wishing each other all the best for the New Year. On arriving back at the Queen's, most of the guests, including my intended hot water bottle, had departed. By two o'clock I was ready to call time.

The town's Royal Hotel and Post Office corners were the main rendezvous points for the latest gossip. It was there that the unemployed bar-room lawyers would deliberate on the nation's affairs, before taking up residence in the pubs, clubs and snooker halls. Prime Ministers would be told how to govern, with the Chancellor forever being accused of inflicting hardship on the working classes. In addition to the usual assembly one day was Vic Owens, a flamboyant character, who'd just returned from a life on the ocean waves. The focal point most of note was the ring in his left ear, Vic having been caught up in the latest craze to sweep Miami. My only other sightings of male earrings had been in the cinema, on pirates. If it was all the rage in America, then I wanted to get on the bandwagon in my part of the world.

Stan Crosby, usually referred to as Bing, sold jewellery, repaired watches and pierced ears, but was rather taken aback with my request. He took some convincing as to my sincerity, finally telling me to call after-hours on Saturday afternoon so there would be no interruptions. My guess was that he didn't want to be seen fondling male ears. Another mate, Bob "Nobbler" Emmerson, agreed to be the other guinea pig. Bing got his four quid for his part of the action, but for me the joy would be short-lived. Dad seemed to have doubts about my gender, with the word "puff" repeated on several occasions, while Mother was in a state of shock. At work I was banished to the rear of the workshops as if I was a leper, besides being forbidden to come into contact with customers.

The only problem with being an apprentice was empty pockets. Even though I was working as much overtime and spare time as possible, I was barely keeping my head above water. Insofar as transport was concerned, I was limited to the two and three wheeled varieties. Owning four wheels was out of my grasp, especially on earnings of less than five pounds a week. Hopefully I would reap the benefits once I'd reached the magical age of twenty-one.

A secret agent, 007 James Bond, was thrilling us all in the cinemas, whilst also exhibiting the latest hi-tech gadgets. Little did we know that this was just the start of the entertainment explosion, both on stage and screen, and with the sounds from Liverpool shortly to rock the world. While the sixties were proving to be good for the younger generation, they were proving equally devastating for the Durham coalfield. The announcement of yet further mine closures added more doom and gloom to the town. Some of the pits had been in production since the 1840s, employing generations of the same family name, until the powers-that-be classed the coal as being uneconomical to retrieve. Only six years earlier the lads from Donegal had arrived with high hopes of a secure future, but the pits were closing, and closing fast.

Day-release took me to Darlington College, with Durham not catering for the two-year Technicians course. A good knowledge of the technical side was essential if the practical side was to be totally efficient, but I never knew anyone who topped the ratings in both.

"Those that can, do it, those that can't, teach it."

The Turk's Head pub in Darlington's Bondgate was always advertising its delicious meat and potato pies. The landlord also looked like he was getting his fair share, being a dead ringer for Billy Plews. The manager of the nearby Doggart's shop called in for his usual midday drink, informing the landlord of a break-in at the premises the previous evening. Surprisingly, nothing had been stolen. The manager, a solemn-faced chap in his fifties, said all the police found were finger-marks on the dummies arse! I couldn't help but laugh, while the manager's face still retained its deadly serious expression. However the best was yet to come. The fat landlord replied that the thief must have had a good sense of imagination. Tears of laughter started running down my face, as the pub erupted in uproar. The manager, fuming with anger, beat a hasty retreat, muttering under his breath about us silly buggers not appreciating the gravity of the situation.

The limits of my involvement with the opposite sex tended to be brief affairs. The first women in my life, Mother and the Sisters of Mercy, had all given me good hidings, so maybe I was fearful of the fairer sex in case the punishments continued. By now I was a bass guitarist with local rock group, "The Gravediggers." This helped the finances enormously, allowing me to upgrade to four wheels. On finishing playing one hot summer's night I took to the road with a lady friend. We stopped on the edge of Crook at the five houses, a spot favoured by courting couples. Needing more space to make ourselves comfortable, I removed the drummer's kit from the van. We were just settling down into our new surroundings, when flashes of lightning lit up the sky, followed by claps of thunder and torrential rain. This left me facing the problem, as to who or what would be first to stop, me or the rain?

Chapter Three

Pommie Bastard

My first venture abroad was to take an assisted passage to Perth in Australia. I was seeking fame and fortune, or maybe just fortune. I'd tramped around most of Britain and Ireland with long-time pal George Hopper, but Oz was the big one. Talk of golden sands and sun-tanned girls had been more than enough to convince me to tick the box in the newspaper ad.

It's quite possible I had a predecessor of the same name who'd been a wicked bastard, with me being charged for his misdeeds. Or maybe it was divine intervention, to stop me pressing the self-destruct button. Whatever it was, five weeks after arriving in Oz I got a letter from my girlfriend. She was pregnant. Could I come home as soon as possible?

Unfortunately, or fortunately as the case would be, I just happened to meet the right girl at the wrong time, four months before departure. During my final stint with "The Gravediggers," an attractive blonde with an unusual spiky hairstyle, more suited to Chelsea's King's Road than a mining town, suddenly caught my eye. This chance meeting was the start of a whirlwind romance, leading to much soul-searching and anguish as the day of departure loomed. Do I go to Australia, and then send for Ann? Do I not go? From being a kid I'd dreamt of travelling to faraway places. Was my dream going to be shattered forever?

I can't remember what my reaction was to reading Ann's letter: shock, joy, sadness, probably all of them. A sense of numbness engulfed me. I read the letter over and over again, hoping its contents would somehow change. A visit to the doctor had confirmed the inevitable, with the baby due in early October. My mind was working non-stop, searching for a solution. I was chain smoking to keep myself calm. What do you do from 10,000 miles away?

Just at a time when the pieces were gradually falling into place, my whole world had suddenly collapsed. I hadn't the stomach to eat, so after collecting my thoughts as best I could, I showered and retreated to the beerhouse. The terms of the immigration agreement specified that I had to stay for a minimum of two years. Even if I had the money, which I hadn't, I still couldn't leave the country, having forfeited all travel documents and my temporary passport on arrival at Perth.

The two-day flight from Heathrow had indeed been an eye-opener. At Istanbul, our first refuelling stop, the Turkish police looked menacing with their side-arms. After further calls at Baghdad, Karachi and Colombo, we endured a nail-biting eight hours in Singapore. Finally, after two unsuccessful attempts to repair the engine problem, the Britannia aircraft took to the skies for the last leg with all four propellers functioning properly. Most passengers were families, excited at the prospect of a rosy future.

At the "welcome to Oz" meeting, everyone expecting to get a rapid suntan was given a lesson in the harsh reality. The climate proved to be the biggest obstacle, with mid-summer temperatures of 90F (32C) and more a regular occurrence. Some years previously, two newly-arrived Scottish lads had ignored the warnings, exposing their bodies to the sun's inviting rays for many hours on the beach. They suffered severe burning, and had to be suspended in nets at the hospital while the skin pealed off them. They died.

Only hours after arriving, I'd been fortunate to secure a job at a Land Rover garage in the suburb of Subiaco, allowing me to leave the hostel in record time. Subi was a delightful place, only minutes by train to the city and the beach. Ma Cooper's rooming-house at the bottom of Rokeby road served my most basic needs, its dark hallway and high ceilings also offering some respite in the boiling atmosphere. It was home to many permanent guests, mainly retired chaps who lived alone, either through choice, divorce or bereavement.

Within days I was greeted with the typical Aussie saying of "pome (pommie) bastard." One of the residents, Lance, an ex-naval officer with a false leg, informed me that "pome" stood for "Prisoner of Mother England." These letters had been tattooed on all transported convicts as a means of recognising them if they escaped. Lance would also reflect on the weather.

"When English women come to Australia and get the sun on their backs, they're like fires. If you don't stop home and poke them, they go out." He was a funny old bugger and was probably speaking from experience.

When I asked Lance how to get rid of the mozzies (mosquitoes) he just laughed, telling me that eventually I'd get used to them. During the night, the familiar drone of these winged pests was non-stop. I was the target of countless bites. I tried all sorts, even closing the window and spraying the room and myself with insect repellent, but without success. As a recipe for a good night's sleep, I was advised to work hard, drink plenty of beer and leave the window wide open. It worked.

Besides its California climate, Perth showed much American influence. It had freeways, highways, drive-in movies, barbies (barbecues) and the recently introduced currency, which had seen the pound give way to the dollar. Australia was a new country, full of go-ahead people, without centuries of tradition to hinder progress. I had my brush with Americanisms in a Murray Street store. After buying some shorts and a pair of thongs (flip-flops), I asked the assistant for three vests. He returned with three waistcoats and a bemused look on his face. At that point I realised my mistake, only by having watched American movies, with a waistcoat being termed a vest. For a while the store was in humorous uproar as I made the point, before the assistant gladly showed me their range of singlets.

The hotels and bars enjoyed all-day licensing hours. Swan lager was the standard drink, either on tap, or in bottles or tins. Back home we had pint and half pint glasses, whereas the Aussies tended to measure their drink in ounces, ranging from a glass (seven) midi (ten) schooner (15) to a jug (40).

The nearby Cottesloe beach basked on the shores of the Indian Ocean. Its panoramic beauty extended far beyond my wildest dreams, similar to a tropical island. After two hours I decided to leave, not wanting to gamble with the sun. What I wasn't prepared for was the hot sand on my bare feet, with the soles of my feet feeling like they were treading on red-hot cinders. I hopped, ran and shouted my way off the beach, much to the amusement of all present, who must have thought I'd had one too many.

Besides the unrelenting daytime temperatures, the nights could also be hot. Occasionally I'd sleep in a sitting position in the shower cubicle, with a cool drip from the leaking rose offering some slight relief. I still felt terribly lovesick and homesick, which was about as sick as you could get. Now I was suddenly faced with my biggest problem ever, making everything else appear totally irrelevant.

First I would have to send a sympathetic letter to the immigration department at Canberra. The Australian government had subsidised the £10 fare, so no doubt would be seeking some form of recompense. My ambitions of travelling the country had instantly evaporated, along with any ideas of meeting my great uncle, Michael Burke, in Sydney. We must both have had the wanderlust fever in our veins, which not only spelt freedom, but the excitement of not knowing what was around the next corner. The sins of the flesh had landed me in a situation that society was gradually tolerating. If Uncle Michael had been in a similar predicament fifty years earlier, he most likely would have found a resting-place at the end of a gun barrel or rope.

No doubt there'd still be tinges of adventure in the coming months, but my future in Oz would not be dissimilar to that of the convicts transported a century earlier. There'd be no ball and chain, and I'd be free to roam as I pleased, but accumulating the amount of money needed to free myself of the shackles would be difficult. Christ, I thought the poor bastards who couldn't speak English were handicapped, but at least I had that in my favour. Maybe it was time to heed Mother's farewell words of advice, by visiting the local church getting down on my knees.

My purse totalled 145 dollars (£60), a lot less than I'd anticipated. Saving 17 dollars (£7) a week was no good anymore. I had to make a lot more money if I wanted to return home quickly. The daily paper carried ads for singers and guitarists for local groups, but I didn't want to get on that bandwagon again, along with all the baggage that went with it.

The asbestos mines at upstate Wittenoom Gorge paid good wages. I mentioned this to Lance, who told me in no uncertain terms to give the place a wide berth. "It's a hellhole." He then mentioned the large construction firms that had been advertising work on iron ore developments in the north of the state. Three months earlier, nearly a thousand workers had left Perth, bound for the outback and the megabucks of Dampier. He advised me against that also.

"Spend another summer in the city to acclimatise, before heading into the bush." Unfortunately, time wasn't on my side.

Every morning I made a beeline for the "situations vacant," without giving the rest of the newspaper a second glance. There were plenty of positions on offer in the city and suburbs, but precious little elsewhere. Even the jukeboxes and radio stations kept reminding me of my responsibilities, with "Homeward Bound" riding high in the charts.

When the news finally broke back home the tongues were wagging non-stop. The general consensus of opinion was that I had dumped my girlfriend and fled to Australia. I felt terribly guilty about the prospect of Ann having to face people alone, while my folks were in a state of shock and disbelief. This was followed a few days later by a letter from Dad. There were no chastisements or shouting on paper, just plain honest, understanding words, asking how much money I needed to get home. I felt dejected after reading it, regretting over and over again the distress my actions had caused to him and Mother, as well as Ann's parents. There was no way I would take a penny off a 57-year old who'd worked hard all his life. I'd got myself into trouble and would get myself out of it. It was big thinking from a man who'd took to the drink of late, having walked out on the garage job. I immediately replied to his letter, trying to sound as upbeat as possible, besides offering a thousand apologies and hoping to be back later in the year. They had enough problems with the scandal of their first grandchild being born out of wedlock, without worrying about me.

One morning, after counting the coins and looking through the haze in the mirror, I decided it was time to have a meeting with myself. Either that, or keep going on the booze and self-pity journey to nowhere fast. Thinking positive was always difficult, especially when alcohol was a factor. People back home were relying on me, but if I didn't buck the current trend I would shortly be a party to Mother's" pauper" outbursts. I couldn't let her win at any cost. It was time to put idle hands to work, but not in a garage. I wanted a new challenge. There was casual work being offered at the Labour Exchange, so I tried that. It turned out to be wise move, with plenty of variation, ranging from gardening and painting, to removing minor glazing problems in piss-pots.

On returning from work one day, the letter rack contained a brown envelope bearing the official insignia of the Australian immigration department. My pulse rate instantly quickened. While they sympathised with my plight, the rules had to be strictly adhered to. Should I fail to stay the specified term of two years, they required a payment of 420 dollars (£175), with a passport issued upon receipt. Excellent news, even though I'd been secretly hoping that my sorrowful letter would have been rewarded with an amnesty. Now I knew what was needed, around 1,300 dollars (£540) to repay Canberra and for the flight home. At the current rate of saving I would be here two years, without the need to repay Canberra.

A firm operating small drilling rigs was advertising for labourers, with 95 dollars plus free tucker and accommodation for six days' graft. It appeared to be a family concern, the address being a large bungalow in the affluent Mosman Park district. The rigs were working east of Kalgoorlie bordering the desert regions. The owner noted my knowledge of mechanics, which was a huge plus. But I also had a much bigger minus – being a recent migrant. The last newly-arrived pom he hired had suffered from severe nosebleeds in extreme heat, so it was "sorry mate, no job."

In April, Ma Cooper broke the news that I was to have an English roommate. My initial thoughts were, here we go again. The previous lodger, Rod-the-conman from Melbourne, had absconded owing everyone money, including me. I was greeted by my new compatriot, Raymond Nicholson, formerly of Gladstone Street, West Gorton, Manchester.

"How are ya, Kevin?"

"I'm fine thanks, Ray, apart from being in the fuckin' shit right up to me eyeballs!"

My reply caught him slightly off guard. I quickly put him at ease, briefly outlining my predicament of failing to keep my horse in the stable, before suggesting we call at the bar after showering.

Ray was ten years my senior, five foot nine, stocky, with thinning fair hair. He was another "ten-pound pom," having previously worked for Ferranti in Manchester, following a stint in the Merchant Navy. Our stories had a familiar ring, the problems being self-inflicted insofar as the pleasures of the flesh were concerned. We were both desperate to get back home for different reasons. Ray wanted to see his elderly parents, after promising to visit them for the past two years. At the moment he was down on his luck, but not broke, having been both winner and victim of the fairer sex.

A fitter and turner by trade, Ray had worked around Perth for three years before taking up an appointment at Koolan Island in the northwest. Eighteen months later and £2,000 richer he planned his return. Before flying home, he and a work-mate, "Coventry Johnny," decided to spend a week in Perth. This resulted in Ray falling head-over-heels for a good-time girl. He missed his flight and sold his return ticket for peanuts.

For the next six weeks Ray lived life to the full in the Savoy Hotel, spending lavishly on his new-found love. When the pennies ran out, so did she. His last abode was a fleapit near Perth railway station. We laughed when comparing Ma Cooper's to the Savoy, but at least it was clean and cheap.

Ray confirmed what everyone else had said, that the only mega-money was in the bushlands of the north. There, the construction boom was at fever pitch, creating new townships and port facilities to cater for the country's newfound wealth, iron ore.

"The biggest problem in the north is the year-round high temperatures, coupled with periods of torrential rain in the summer months. I've been here five years and still find the bush climate merciless, so it will bring you to yer knees!"

The wages were triple those of the city, with the added incentive of special tax allowances in areas bordering the twentieth parallel. Even though money was the number one priority, our objectives were slightly different. I just wanted enough to pay Canberra and the flight home. Ray couldn't arrive in Manchester on the breadline, after being in the land of opportunity for five years. That night I slept better than of late since arriving, feeling as though the tide was finally beginning to turn.

For many of the bush workers visiting the city for a brief holiday, as in Ray's case, it tended to be the familiar vices of drink and wild, wild, women. The exceptions were the migrants from mainland Europe, predominately Italians and Greeks, who would shudder at the thought of wasting their hard-earned cash. The good-time girls knew you had money-a-plenty if you had worked in the bush. They would attempt to entangle you in their web, spinning tales of love, or rustling up a convincing sob story. Alien accents, sun-blackened bodies and lily-white ankles, were the tell-tale signs that meant you were easy prey. It was a long-standing joke, that you could always recognise a pommie by his white ankle marks, this a reference to where the chain shackles had been attached to transported convicts. In the case of the bush workers, it was a result of having to wear safety boots which blotted out the sun.

Besides being the hub of activity, the Savoy Hotel in Hay Street also offered a well-presented buffet selection from midday 'til two, when for the set price of a dollar you could eat your fill. It had also accommodated the British Lions rugby touring team, with the high-spirited players ripping a few doors off in the process. Tony the barman greeted Ray like a long lost brother. He probably hoped for a fat tip, which undoubtedly would have been the norm when Ray was the hotel's best customer. As the night wore on, I got the feeling Ray was secretly hoping to catch a glimpse of the girl who broke his heart, a chick by the name of Sonya.

Beatlemania still engulfed the city, the Beatles' second film "Help" playing to capacity audiences at the nearby Plaza. It made me realise just how big the group had become since I saw them making their Sunderland Empire debut. Then they were billed as a minor act on the Helen Shapiro show, being introduced by Dave Allen the compere as "four lads from Liverpool, who we think will go a long way."

Gradually, very gradually, the mind was beginning to adapt, helped enormously by the newcomer from West Gorton, whose sense of humour undoubtedly lifted my spirits. The heartache was still there, but the father-to-be situation and my determination to succeed were now overtaking it. Ray had travelled extensively and didn't appear to have a care in the world, but under his brave exterior he had been a victim of life's ups and downs from time to time. He also had a slight medical condition with his back. It was covered with carbuncles (large boils), necessitating the wearing of a shirt at all times.

I'd promised Ann that on a certain day and time, I'd telephone the hairdressers where she worked. On the day in question I chickened out for one reason only – money. I could think of all sorts of excuses, but the sad fact is I let her down badly, instead of giving the £5 phone call top priority. This must have put further doubts into her mind, besides those around her, as to whether my intentions were indeed honourable.

Despite scouring the "situations vacant" in the West Australian newspaper, and countless visits to construction offices of the firms working up north, it was the same old answer. No vacancies, but we'd be notified by telegram of any developments. That could be next day, week, month, anytime. It got to the stage where our faces were as recognisable as wanted posters, besides us knowing every face that mattered. This prompted us to move digs to the city itself, in order to keep in close contact with prospective employers. From the time of stating our intentions of working up north, we made it abundantly clear, that should the opportunity present itself to either one of us, it had to be seized with both hands.

The bubbling personality of Mrs. Theresa O'Neil welcomed us to her imposing Victorian house close to Mount Street. Our large first-floor room was furnished more lavishly than what we'd been used to, with carpets, wall lamps and a spacious balcony. It transpired that Mrs. O'Neil's parents were from Galway, accounting for her slight Irish brogue.

Within days we had our first break in the bread and butter stakes, but the close camaraderie that existed between the Mancunian and the Geordie would be tested to the limit. Among the many vacancies listed in the Labour Exchange was one for labourers to lay railway tracks, with top wages for top men. Australia was converting part of its railroad system to one-size standard gauge of 4ft-8½ins, which was common throughout most of Europe and America. Sizes ranging from 3ft-6ins to 5ft-3ins were widespread within Oz, creating difficulties travelling overland. This meant, that anyone travelling from Sidney to Perth, a distance of 2,800 miles, could be inconvenienced by having to change trains up to four times.

Joe Robson was paying 84 dollars (£35) for six shifts on the eastern line towards Midland. We bullshitted regarding our status, just in case he wanted bona-fide labourers – which he did. Joe's workforce was mainly Italian, with a mixture of Slavs, Greeks and Brits. The groundwork had been prepared, with new wooden sleepers in position on top of the ballast. We worked in a gang of eight. The first part of the operation was to lift the rails, stacked alongside the track, onto the sleepers. Each man then had to hammer his quota of steel pegs into the sleepers to secure the rail. The whole operation, timed to the minute, was virtually non-stop.

The first week was a "killer." The biggest problem was blistering on our hands, caused by the constant sliding of the hammer shaft between the palms. Nightly doses of methylated spirits helped to harden the skin. Vaseline, another essential, was applied to the eyebrows to prevent the salty sweat entering our eyes. Drinking water was contained in canvas bags mounted on tripods. Even though it was warm it was a godsend, with lemon added to disguise the taste.

Occasionally I'd have a lapse of concentration, resulting in me hitting the rail instead of the bolt head. This had the same effect as hitting a cricket ball with a piece of hardwood, causing the body to tingle and the teeth to chatter. We would joke that we were working on the chain gang, in the same torturous conditions employed a hundred years earlier, but without the shackles. Some of the other contractors engaged further up the track were more mechanised, with mobile compressors and jackhammers, but I guess it was all down to price. All we were interested in were dollar bills, crisp, crumpled or dirty.

Our other gang members were "Eyeties", their knowledge of the English language limited to the basics of yes, no and of course dollar. As with the garage in Subiaco, the majority hailed from southern Italy, where wages were little more than a pittance. Every Friday afternoon, Joe would press a wad of dollar bills into their hungry hands, making them feel like millionaires. Their hard-earned cash was not wasted. It went towards buying property, or a business. The Brits tended to work hard and play hard, while the Italians worked hard and saved hard. Their only fault was jealousy, always of the opinion that the English-speaking races were getting extra favours.

Inevitably, there was the occasional trouble, with too much firewater turning the mildest of men into would-be bare-knuckle champions. If I'd been handy with my fists, I'd have made my living as a boxer, not laying railroad tracks. The "pommie bastards" term would surface from time to time, but with much more intent. You'd just brush it aside as the words of a drunk, but if the situation became intolerable, then the pair of you would have to settle your differences. If your opponent was built like Mr. Universe, or acting like the devil possessed, you had to find something quickly to even up the odds. You would either hit him with a brick, throw dust in his face, or kick him in the balls. If all else failed, then you got the hell out of it, or hoped someone stopped the fight before you were badly marked. In the movies the good guy always wins, but in real life this is rarely the case.

If you were a teetotaller when you arrived in Oz, the conditions dictated that the pledge would soon be broken. During the hot weather, Sunday afternoon drinking on the beach was a law laid down in stone. Each person contributed a slab of "tinnies" (24 cans) and an icebox (esky). Warm beer was worse than a mortal sin. I'd never seen beer (grog) in a can before, and with no ring pull to open it, how could we have a drink? The first can was opened with a coin or a key. When empty, the tin was folded. The "V" created by the fold opened the other tins with a blow from the hand. Simple, until I tried it. Practice makes perfect.

Then Sonya surfaced, something I'd been secretly dreading. After work we would always wash our throats in the Station Bar before dining, and we were halfway up William Street when our paths crossed. I must admit she was a stunner. Tall and slim with shoulder-length dark hair, Sonya had a slight resemblance of Liz Taylor. I guess she'd been around the block a few times and broken a few hearts along the way. I left her and Ray in deep conversation and was showered and ready to eat before Ray emerged, acting like a boy who'd just found a lost toy.

It didn't matter a fuck to me what he did. It's just that it was strikingly obvious he and Sonya weren't made for each other, and I was afraid he'd pay dearly once again for the pleasure of taking her pants off. If she expected him to have a fat wad of notes then she was sadly mistaken, but no doubt she'd be digging her heels in. From that day on our relationship began to crumble, as I prayed like never before for the telegram boy to deliver some good news. Ray and his new-found love proved to be inseparable, but the only word I could see looming on the horizon spelled "disaster," in letters the size of HOLLYWOOD.

Ray never turned up for work on Monday. I blamed too much water for giving him the shits, but Joe tended to think that too much grog was the problem. Seven of us had to do eight men's work that day, resulting in us being on our knees at the end of the shift. The following Monday was a repeat, Ray's absence almost causing steam to emit from Joe's nostrils. In Ray's defence I have to say, that in different circumstances I couldn't have blamed him if he'd had a bedroom lock-in for weeks on end, she was that tasty. His actions reminded me of miners back home, who would constantly miss a Monday shift due to the weekend's excessive drinking. But instead of suffering from a hangover, Ray was getting his conkers oiled!

One morning at the smoko break, in my haste to finish the last slice of toast thieved from the breakfast table, I bit heavily on a hard corner and broke a rear tooth. Later in the day it began to ache slightly, gradually worsening as the week progressed. A small bottle of liquid purchased from the pharmacy instantly eased the pain, but as it began to lose its effect, a visit to the dentist became priority. After the gum was injected I was again at peace with myself, until he tried to extract the remains of the tooth, the pain suddenly returning with a vengeance. Apparently an abscess had formed around the gum, causing me to endure a further week of discomfort while I undertook a course of antibiotics. The final bill for treatment was 55 dollars (£23), plus three hours leave of work. It was an expensive piece of toast.

One night, as Ray was preparing to meet Sonya, I asked him to look in the mirror.

"What's wrong Kevin?" said Ray, moving his head from side to side, expecting to see a hair out of place or a mark on his face.

"Keep looking in the mirror Ray, and tell me if you see Tony Curtis, Sean Connery or Errol Flynn? Sonya can get any man she wants, milk them dry then spit them out, with you already bitten once."

I must have hit a raw nerve. Ray rushed out of the room and slammed the door. I was powerless to do anything, but I didn't want to witness a man throwing away his hard-earned dollars on a good time girl. At the time I was reading Errol Flynn's biography "My Wicked Wicked Ways." Although Flynn was a star of the forties and fifties, his name regularly cropped up due to his gifted manhood. Good-looking and with an athletic build, Flynn boasted of having bedded thousands of women. I never realised he was Australian from Tasmania, always thinking him Irish. At least Flynn could claim grandfather rights to the Emerald Isle, but never for one moment did I ever imagine that I would meet his namesake years later.

Despite a final warning, Ray let the team down once again and was dismissed. This made me wonder if he was as committed as I was to get home. Why should he be? Sure, he wanted to see his folks, but he'd already had the money and failed, and judging by recent events was going to fail yet again. Whatever the outcome, it was all being decided over a bit of pussy. Within days he'd left the digs and moved in with Sonya, so I assumed he would return to casual work.

The dictionary offered five possible explanations for the word "love," ranging from cupid to a score in tennis. If the academics didn't know, what chance did we have? Love is a thing that men have travelled the world for, fought and died for, yet it still remains a mystery. The travelling sounds fun, but I'm not so sure about the dying.

Days turned into weeks but the notice board remained bare – still no telegrams. Mrs. O'Neil's favourite saying was "maybe tomorrow." It reminded me of Billy Fury's record of the same name, and I would attempt to sing a few lines, if only to make her laugh.

I was showing 340 dollars (£142). It was time to forget about the big bucks, it just wasn't going to happen. The way things were shaping up it looked as though Mrs. O'Neil's lodge would see out my two-year term in Australia. It wasn't a question of failure. It was the unexpected occurrence of having to plan my return home within weeks of arriving. I was just a victim of life's problems that happened to most people, with the best-hatched plans kicking you in the teeth occasionally. But you still had to have hope, something to cling on to, dreams to fulfil, or what the hell was life all about? I'd already accepted that getting a telegram was a damp squib. A more likely scenario was my voice going hoarse singing "Maybe Tomorrow."

Most nights were spent in my room, writing letters or reading, gradually accepting reality. I was dreading breaking the news to Ann, feeling as though I'd let everyone down, after promising her the dizzy heights.

When Mother named me after an Irish Saint, I reckon some of his good luck charm must have rubbed off on me. Within days, the doom and gloom that had engulfed me receded slightly. In mid-June, among several positions being advertised by the Western Mining Corporation, was one for a diesel fitter and another for a machinist at Port Hedland, 1,100 miles north of Perth. I remembered from my schooldays that it was 1,000 miles from Land's End to John O'Groats, but it was a distance that was impossible to comprehend insofar as going to work was concerned. I'd studied the geography of the country back home, but in reality hadn't realised just how

big it was. The huge landmass of the western state was
nearly six times larger than the United Kingdom and
more than three times the size of Texas. Yet despite its size
it had only one million inhabitants.

I quickly located Ray at Sonya's North Perth flat,
much to her disapproval. He had no problem with the
machinist position advertised, but my only diesel
experience was limited to minor maintenance jobs. What
if I failed, what then?   Next night we met up in the
Station Bar.

"What's the news Ray?" I asked. "The news my
friend, is that we both have an excellent chance of getting
the jobs. And guess what – the personnel officer's a
Geordie!" We both punched the air, accompanied by
whoops and yipees.

Within seconds of entering the offices of Western
Mining, I was talking to the man who would either make
or break my immediate future. He was a chap formerly
from Bishop Auckland of all places, who'd migrated some
fifteen years earlier. The majority of the interview was
taken up talking about the great games between the
Bishops and Crook, especially their Wembley epic. He
was also greatly impressed with my qualifications and
references. It was then that I decided to come clean, not
wanting to let him down should anything backfire. I
explained that I'd only worked on a few diesels, mainly
servicing. His reply caught me totally off guard.

"If you're not sure, just bullshit your way through
until you get into the routine."

After more reminiscing, he confirmed not only my
job but also Ray's. My wages were 148 dollars (£62), a few
quid less than the machinist's position, but I wasn't
grumbling, I was ecstatic. Meals were to be taken at a

hotel and deducted from our wages, and the airfare repaid over six weeks. Before I could say another word he arranged our tickets for Saturday's midnight flight. Outside the office my heart was pumping overtime. At last, at last, this was the break I'd been so desperately wanting. I could now plan my return, month by month, week by week, day by day. What had happened in the past was history, with no way of righting the misdeeds or reliving the pleasures. My honeymoon with Perth would soon be over - the price to pay for those extra dollar bills.

Before going our separate ways, Ray begged a favour. A loan of 200 dollars plus my suitcase, the handle on his having departed long ago. He needed to buy a few things, but I had a sneaking suspicion that the majority would be for Sonya's benefit. Even though I was leaving myself short of cash, it was worth it to get him out of the clutches of his long-nailed gold-digger. By the time I'd topped up my wardrobe I would be left with only 70 dollars, and would need every cent I possessed until my next payday. The landlady wanted 32 dollars on Saturday, but the unexpected turn of events had caught me slightly wrong-footed. I was in a quandary. Mrs. O'Neil had been good to me and I didn't want to let her down, but it looked as if I was going to have to, albeit temporarily.

On the Friday night I couldn't get Mrs. O out of my mind, awaking nearly every hour as I hatched my cowardly exit. Next morning I breakfasted early complete with work clothes, giving the impression I was going to be a busy bee. After making my way to Subi, I called in at the Greek woman's shop to hock the overcoat and three-piece suit I'd arrived in, casually mentioning that I was moving to warmer climes further north. She excused herself for a moment, returning with a small photograph, explaining that her husband of twenty years had suddenly left and believed him to be upstate. Quite clearly she was upset, but hopeful, handing me the photo and her phone number, plus ten dollars for the clothes. Unfortunately, the Greeks I'd come into contact with looked much the same as the photo. Black wavy hair and olive coloured skin.

Glancing back at Ma Cooper's rooming house from the rail platform, I briefly relived the past events. It being rather ironic that my two biggest heartaches had occurred at places of no fixed abode, Durham Station and room number 7 on the other side of the world. In her latest letter, Ann was preparing her bedroom for the new arrival, with the cot and pram already purchased. As yet, her hopes and dreams lay in a faraway land. Even though we had the comfort of each other's writings to carry us through troubled times, my right hand was also a regular source of satisfaction in times of need.

My next call was the huge GPO building near Perth Railway Station. If you were moving accommodation, you could have your mail forwarded c/o GPO Perth, with the government offering a free service for new migrants and travellers. After dining on hot dogs and beer, I bought a large sheet of brown paper and ball of string, wrapping the new suitcase to camouflage its appearance. I then wrote Mrs. O'Neil a letter, apologising most sincerely for my actions, while spitting fire at Ray and his two-bit floozie. All day I'd had to play a game of cat and mouse, over a lousy 32 dollars. I left packing my belongings until the last minute. On the stroke of eight, and under the shroud of darkness, I began my sneaky undercover operation. Most of the other guests were already downtown. I then doubled the string and fastened it to the suitcase handle, before lowering it from the balcony onto the garden below. After muttering a fond farewell I made my way downstairs, tiptoeing through the darkness of the dining room and depositing the letter and the room key on the kitchen table. By now my heart was pounding fifty to the dozen. I then went out through the front door and around the side of the house, collecting the case before proceeding to the front gate.

"Good evening Kevin, are you leaving us?" called a voice from out of the darkness.

No one could mistake the sound of Mrs. O'Neil. I stood rooted to the spot for a few seconds, hoping that the ground would devour me, before walking back down the path to face the music. I could feel myself burning up as I stood face to face with the kind-hearted lady, preparing to go out for the night with a gentleman friend. I honestly didn't know what to say or do, other than ask her to wait a few moments while I retrieved the letter from the kitchen.

I felt so ashamed, besides cursing Ray and Sonya into hell for the umpteenth time. There wasn't much point going into all the sordid details, the damage was done. I'd been caught red handed. After reading the letter in the lobby Mrs. O emptied both barrels into me, far worse than the headmaster at St. Leonard's, leaving me feeling lower than a snake's belly. She was most disappointed that I was leaving in such an underhand manner, and had expected that with our common Irish alliance that I would have been more forthcoming. With that we both left, and once out of the gate headed in different directions. If I'd carried the case downstairs, I would have been away before she emerged from her ground floor quarters. God loves a trier. Maybe I was trying too hard.

The Savoy was thronged with "talent" and deafening music. I eventually found Ray sitting at the bar, alone. Where was Sonya? They'd spent the day shopping, arranging to meet up later, with Ray trying to appear his cheery upbeat self.

"She'll be coming," he kept assuring me, but as the night wore on it became increasingly apparent, that she wouldn't be joining the company of a man down to his last few dollars. It's probably just as well he was nearly broke, because I wasn't at all convinced whether the job would have taken priority had his wallet been healthier. The fuckin' bitch, letting him down at the final hurdle when he most needed her. Even so, my exit from Mrs. O'Neil's brought the best laugh of the evening. We were now on the first leg of our journey into the back of beyond. Next stop, Port Hedland.

The majority of the Fokker Friendship's passengers, possibly forty in all, were returning home from either business or pleasure in the city. The flight was uneventful apart from a few take off and landings, probably because I was asleep most of the time. We touched down just as dawn was breaking, and were greeted by the driver of a pick-up truck. The sun was a rising ball of flame in the sky, the landscape a rich reddy-brown, barren apart from sprinklings of scrub. Ray knew what to expect, but for me it was new territory. As we were driven to the firm's premises on the fringe of town, the clouds of red dust generated by the truck's wheels on the dirt road was our welcome to the outback. It was still only seven o'clock, with no visible signs of life apart from the barking of dogs.

This was my first experience of a bush town and quite honestly I was taken aback. It was as if we were going back in time. The paradise we'd left behind seemed part of another era, another planet. The town had many Victorian features, especially the hotels, with wooden sidewalks and upstairs verandas. They reminded me very much of the western films, the only missing character being the hombre from "A Fistful of Dollars." Perhaps we'd get lucky later in the day.

The port, dating back to the gold rush days of the 1880s, was home to a thousand people. Now its principle export was iron ore, the covering of red dust the price to pay for the town's new-found wealth. We were only 120 miles from the former gold mining town of Marble Bar, where a cold beer was once valued more than gold. It was on record as being the hottest place in Australia. In 1924 the temperature never dropped below 100 degrees (38C) for 161 consecutive days. The conditions must have been torture for the early pioneers, always hopeful that a lucky strike would get them out of "hell." At least we had the benefit of refrigerated coolers for our food and drink. Some hotel lounges and dining areas even had the added luxury of air conditioning. We were also within sight of water, so at least we could look out to sea and psychologically feel cooler. Ray would regularly relive his experiences of working 600 miles further north. The hot humid conditions testing peoples resolve to near breaking point. The drink served as both demon and saviour.

At nine we were welcomed by the general manager, who promptly showed us around. He seemed friendly enough, but I got the impression that he wasn't keen on two poms joining his Aussie workforce. He also remarked about expecting someone older for the diesel fitter's job - a good kick in the balls. A few truck and drag combinations were parked up, predominantly Leyland

and Scammell. These were used to haul the iron ore from the firm's inland mine at Mt. Goldsworthy to the port, for shipment throughout Asia, mainly to Japan. The only other large trucks I'd seen around the state were Queensland-based Theiss Bros, which carried the American Mack badge.

The sleeping quarters left a lot to be desired. They resembled an open house free-for-all, with three bodies snoring away sleeping off the grog. With the windows and doorways permanently open, privacy was an impossible luxury. At least the steel-framed beds had springs. Mattresses weren't practicable, due to the dusty conditions, heavy perspiration, bed pissing, or a combination of all three. By midday there was a noticeable rise in temperature compared to Perth, with local estimates in the eighties – not bad for the middle of winter. All meals were taken in the kitchen of the Esplanade Hotel, starting with a late breakfast of generous portions that would see you through the day.

Next morning I was introduced to Saul the foreman. He was the first Saul I'd met, but remembered the religious teachings about Saul of Tarsus, later St Paul. Whether Saul was a Christian or an atheist was of no concern to me. My immediate priority was the initiation test, which would decide my bush status. When a vacancy is created in any walk of life, the successful applicant has to prove he's worth his salt. My first task was to fit a diesel injector pump. This was where my many hours of practical instruction at Darlington Tech paid dividends. Once everything had been timed and tightened the truck burst into life. Welcome to the bush.

The mozzies were still in full flow, enjoying their nightly meal. It was just a question of having to grin and bear it, along with drivers coming and going at all hours to and from the mine. The sleeping quarters were really for their convenience, not ours. The only alternative was to fork out more money for a hotel room. Along with the outside showers and toilets minus doors, this was ideal for curing masturbation problems, the chance of a "jerk" being as remote as hen's back teeth. The only crumb of comfort was that it would help delay the wearing of glasses.

Sunday was the only time possible for a dip in the sea. Although inviting, it was much too dangerous. Sharks, sea snakes and stonefish all lurked beneath the surface. On receiving my first pay the immediate priority was Mrs. O'Neil. I could easily have ignored her, but that wasn't my stamp. I sent her 50 dollars by special delivery, the extra money for a treat.

We'd have a regular chinwag in the hotel bar with Old Bill, one of the other fitters, whose spare time and money was taken up with booze and gambling. Bill saying he never did get back to the old country, made me think he'd come to Australia as a young migrant. When I asked him how old he was when he left England he looked puzzled.

"No Kevin, I'm Australian, but my grandfather came from Gloucester."

He jokingly added that all of us "pommie bastards" came to Oz to eat all the white bread and shag all the black women. Like so many of the older generation, Bill still referred to England as the old country. Then, the grandfather of your typical Australian most likely arrived as a tradesman, miner, shopworker, domestic servant – or in shackles!

Australians tended to think that you were familiar

with everywhere in the UK. Distance was something that didn't mean a thing to them. They would drive hundreds of miles to meet friends. Back home, even travelling 60 miles to Leeds was classed as a major event. Insofar as dialects were concerned, the Aussies all sounded the same to me, as opposed to Geordie and Cockney. One of the company's drivers was ex-Merchant Navy. Besides reminiscing with Ray about their time on the high seas, he would often mention his trips to England, especially the north-east port of Hartlepool. He always enjoyed the Strongarm ale, along with the ladies of the day, but could never understand why the English served warm beer.

The hotel was also the drinking den for the lads loading iron ore at the jetty. Their dusty faces had the appearance of having been coated in red oxide paint, except black-faced Noel, whose face resembled that of a coal miner. His dockside navvy was steam-driven, the smoke from the damaged chimney blackening his face. On going down to the dock I could hardly believe my eyes. Standing there in all its glory was an early 1900s Ruston-Bucyrus loading shovel, still performing its daily duties, a fitting tribute to the brilliant engineers of days long past.

Like so many other bush towns, Port Hedland had lost a lot of its young people to the city. Perth and the suburban areas accounted for three-quarters of the state's population, so it was fair to assume there'd be plenty of one-horse towns. Even though the locals weren't as streetwise as the city dwellers, they were a tough bunch of characters, and not to be crossed. Nearly all had British roots, which probably accounted for us being made welcome.

The port was also my first hand experience of "Abos"

(Aborigines). Other than the odd Asian bus driver in Newcastle, my only other sightings of coloured people had been in Birmingham and Oxford. There was an Aboriginal community on the edge of town, with a few of the girls on domestic duties at the hotel. The females were termed "gins" while the men were called "black fellas." People in general shunned Abos as second-class citizens. Abos weren't allowed to buy or drink beer in the hotels, but they still managed to get it, besides other ways of getting "high." When Ray was feeling his feet regarding the "sheilas" (young ladies), old Bill suggested a gin. Ray shook his head, adding that he didn't really fancy a black woman. The old timer's remark, "the longer you stay up here the whiter and whiter they look," was greeted with a huge roar of approval. I sympathised with their plight, reminding those at hand that the Abos were the first to populate the continent, but my opinion definitely wasn't encouraged.

Rosie worked in the hotel kitchen. She always laughed at my Beatle impersonations, even though my accent tended to be more "brummie" than "scouse." Although Rosie was little more than a schoolgirl, I could tell Ray fancied her, no matter what he said to old Bill. The two of them always found time to natter, and my suspicions were confirmed when Ray asked me to buy some bottles of beer for her father. I blamed the mozzies for keeping me awake, but old Bill and the jetty boys weren't at all convinced that I was drinking them as a nightcap. I told Ray to be careful, but I guess it was a case of a standing prick having no conscience. He was twice her age, and the last thing we wanted was to be drummed out of town by a group of irate Abos. During our walkabouts we'd pass the settlement where Rosie lived. It was little more than a collection of corrugated tin-sheeted shacks, just slightly better than our accommodation, with vicious looking dogs roaming around to deter intruders. Their abandoned vehicles were home to most forms of livestock, reminding me of the old Sheerline car in Billy Plews's garage at Crook. As yet, MOT tests hadn't reached that part of the world, so broken windscreens, damaged lights and missing doors, were all part of normal everyday life.

Sunday July 31st was a day for celebration, even though we were the only poms in town. England had won the World Cup, defeating the old enemy, Germany. We'd received some sort of signal around midnight from the world service, but as the game gathered momentum so did the bottles of grog. As far as the Hedlanders were concerned, the only sports of note were horse racing and footy (Aussie rules). Football was a big favourite of us both. Ray was a staunch Manchester United fan, while I would remind him of Newcastle's three FA Cup triumphs a decade earlier. The World Cup-winning Charlton brothers were also Geordies, although I had to concede that one of them played for his idols.

The next World Cup competition was to be held in Mexico, so we toyed with the idea of going there, as England would automatically qualify. Ray confessed that it could be a slight problem for him. During his navy days ten years earlier, his ship had docked near San Diego for temporary repairs. His brother, who was married to an American girl, invited him to stay at their home near Los Angeles. Ray was so captivated by his new surroundings that he stayed eighteen months. After being caught up in a cathouse brawl at Tijuana in Mexico, he was handed over to US customs and deported. He arrived in

Manchester complete with poncho, cowboy boots and stetson.

Heat can affect people in many ways, especially when mixed with alcohol, creating a lethal cocktail. One unsavoury incident involved a welder from the machine shop, a quiet Perth family man in his early thirties. After finishing work on Saturday he headed straight for the hotel, and was well pissed by closing time, still in his work clothes. Even though it wasn't his usual stance we thought nothing about it, thinking he was either celebrating or drowning his sorrows. Next morning, the stray dog that normally roamed around the site was lying dead near the workshop entrance. With no visible signs of injury, poisoning seemed the most likely cause of death. All was revealed later in the day, when the welder admitted killing the dog, saying it had attacked him as he went to the toilet in the early hours. It was a rather timid excuse, but what was even more bizarre, was that he'd strangled it! We came to the conclusion that he must have received some disturbing news from home.

Rosie's family must surely have been aware of her relationship with Ray, but seemed content to accept the bottles of grog, which I joked was an ongoing payment for a shagger's licence. One of the settlement's elders, her grandfather, was confident he could cure Ray's carbuncle problem. The old man prepared his own concoction of ointment. By now Ray's back was beginning to look unsightly, with puss constantly marking his shirt. I told him to use the magic potion sparingly, just in case he ended up with pimples on his "john thomas." The old man claimed it would cure almost anything!

Chapter Four

Highway to Hell

Six weeks after arriving in town we received two redirected telegrams from Mrs. O'Neil. Our presence was requested at the offices of Utah Engineering and Construction in Perth, regarding vacancies at Dampier. This was only a few "Irish" miles to the south of Hedland, with a phone call to their Perth office confirming our appointments. The money was better, with the added bonus of free accommodation and tucker. Saul was disappointed but not surprised that we were "shooting through." By contrast the manager was like a raging bull, full of hell about the way we were treating him. He insisted we work our notice until Saturday afternoon or forfeit a week's pay. Seemingly he'd forgotten about wanting an "older man" for the diesel fitter's job.

Rosie cried. I'd warned Ray that he was getting in too deep, but who was I to advise anyone? He took a room in the hotel for the final days, with the timid excuse that he was having trouble sleeping due to the heat, but I reckon a certain young lady would cause the room temperature to rise even higher. The jetty boys were also aware of his movements, but he just laughed off their suggestions. It was bad enough being called a "pommie bastard" without the handle of "gin shagger" attached. Noel also noticed I never bothered with the sheilas, so I gave him a brief account of my dilemma. I had enough problems of my own, without a family of Aborigines chasing me around

Crook market place. My trusted right hand was the only friend I could truly rely on, although its action was still severely limited.

There were daily flights to Dampier, but with huge excess charges for my tool-boxes. Rosie's father offered us an old Holden sedan "banger" for fifty dollars. At least all the windows and doors were intact. On the Sunday morning, our quest for more money continued as we drove out of town, embarking on what can only be described as the journey of a lifetime. The temperature was nudging 90F (32C) as we headed south, with 125 miles of dry, dusty roads to negotiate. I'd been advised to keep my speed around 50mph, allowing the car to ride over the small stones with a cushioning effect. Travelling fast or slow would cause debris to strike the underside of the vehicle, sounding like a hammer hitting a bathtub. It was impossible to monitor anything behind, due to our slipstream of dust. The sparse landscape was little more than a wilderness, with the odd dead beast and dried up creeks (riverbeds). These would transform into raging torrents when the summer storms vented their fury.

After travelling fifty miles the gearbox developed a grating noise which gradually worsened. There was nothing I could do apart from check the oil, pray, and head slowly towards the nearest point of civilisation. Within three miles the problem rapidly escalated, amid further rattles and bangs, leaving the contents of the gearbox on the northwest coastal highway. This was a similar scenario to Frenchie's car at Whitley Bay, only this time there were no bouts of laughter. Now what? All we could do was dig a hole to hide my tools, then start hitching. The nearest town was Roebourne, thirty miles to the south. Sunday was proving to be a quiet day, with traffic virtually non-existent. Those that did pass were going the other way, leaving only a mouthful of dust as a calling card. The blazing sun showed no mercy. I shielded my head and shoulders with my long-sleeved shirt. We had no drinks, no food, no hats or boots. My paper-thin shoes were little better than slippers. We could have found some shade and waited for a lift in due course, but at least by walking we were getting nearer our objective, slowly but surely, carrying our suitcases.

Around five all we wanted was a drink, any drink, hot, cold, clean or dirty. At the sound of an engine we'd perk up, following its dust trail towards us, but the odd vehicle that did pass showed no signs of wanting to take a chance with two strangers. By now the sun had lost its venom but it was still hot. We struggled along until dusk, but in the cool night air we began to feel the effects of too much sun and shivered uncontrollably. This only added to the problems of our aching bellies and parched throats, as we prepared for a long night by the roadside. Dampier was the furthest from our minds, with visions of a hearse for two more than a distant reality. Hopefully we wouldn't be burdened with snakes or dingoes. Even though we covered ourselves with everything available in an attempt to keep warm, the shakes continued until dawn.

Once again the sun took its seat in a cloudless sky, as we prepared for another scorcher. Ray's face had a peculiar look about it. The sun had affected it to such a degree that his eyes were like slits. I joked about him looking like Charlie Chan, the famous Chinese detective, but in the absence of a mirror he was unable to see the funny side. By now the soles of my shoes were completely worn through, and I had to rip my trouser-legs into pieces to act as cushions for my blistered feet. It was late morning before a cocky (farmer) finally liberated us from our walking hell. Climbing into the back of his ute (pick-up) was a painful operation in itself.

Aussie bush towns certainly knew how to satisfy their customers. There might have been a shortage of petrol, or even females, but they always had a good watering hole. How we appeared to people passing by, god only knows. Penniless drifters, trudging along covered in dust. As we passed through the open doors of the Victoria hotel, the bar's elderly occupants gave us more than a casual glance. Sipping the cold beer created a burning sensation in the gullet, as it gradually found a way past our chapped lips. It was fully five minutes before we were able to come to terms with tasting liquid again. The barman was constantly scrutinising our every movement, as were the other customers, but nothing was said. They stared at the latest high noon arrivals, badly affected by the sun, carrying suitcases that had seen better days. One with no bottoms in his shoes, and the other fucker looking like a Chinaman.

I ordered another jug of beer, some food we could easily digest and a room for the night, but not before the barman insisted on seeing the colour of our money. I could see his point of view, because anyone's first impressions wouldn't have expected us to muster one dollar between us. It was impossible to speak properly due to my tongue being as rough as a badger's arse. The locals were bemused by my "old country" dialect. Roebourne was the bygone capital of the northwest, its history spanning a hundred years. It had many colonial-style features, the heritage of the earlier boom times of gold fever and pearling. This was similar to my birthplace, with everything dependent on the earth's offerings. In

Durham it was coal; here it was gold, iron ore, copper and asbestos. The industrial bush towns also provided "pleasures of the flesh." However, the therapy house would have to wait until we were ready and able. The flesh was weak, and the spirit weaker still.

We needed at least two days to get ourselves back into shape, with a visit to the pharmacy first on the list. We stayed indoors for most of the time, having had enough sun to last us a lifetime. We declined an invitation to a kangaroo shoot. Thought by people outside of Oz to be man's best friend, kangaroos are a constant scourge to farmers and motorists. Coming into contact with a fully-grown male weighing up to fourteen stones, a vehicle could be extensively damaged. This was the reason for the heavy-duty roo-bars (bumper bars). Basically, a kangaroo shoot was a piss-up. At closing time the participants piled into jeeps and headed for a billabong. It was then a deadly quiet waiting game. Once the roos had amassed around the water, powerful spotlamps illuminated the way for the guns.

By midweek I could still only walk about fifty yards. It was pointless limping into Utah's office, when they were expecting fit young bucks champing at the bit. Ray got rid of the Chinese detective look, but our faces were still a mess. Bush hats and sunglasses helped to camouflage our appearance. It made us realise that anyone exposed to the sun for long periods, without adequate protection or water, would surely perish.

Early on Sunday morning, one week later than planned, we finally arrived at Dampier and headed straight for Utah's portable offices at King Bay, overlooking the Indian Ocean. The sea was as calm as a millpond, like a sheet of glass, with not a breath of air to ripple the waters. Hundreds of static caravans were dotted across the landscape, giving us some idea of the size of the operation. Dampier was an area that was being transformed into a community and major port to despatch the iron ore from the mines inland. Although Port Hedland was a town of modest means, it boasted traditional roots of seventy years. Dampier was a coastal wilderness that had been home to a few Aborigines, before earthmoving machinery had invaded its tranquillity.

I later found out that it was discovered and named after the buccaneer William Cecil Dampier, a Somerset man. He was the first Englishman to set foot on Australian soil nearly three hundred years earlier. Later, his travels of the world inspired the writing of the books "Robinson Crusoe" and "Gulliver's Travels." In 1699, Dampier had deemed the land too barren to be of any use, but now it was serving the needs of the twentieth century.

Ray was detailed for machine-shop duties, while I was offered only a labourer's position. Due to my late arrival, the fitter's vacancy had already being filled. One thing for sure, the work couldn't be harder than the railroad, only hotter. We were issued with a round red tin badge, with the words Utah-Dravo boldly written across it in white letters. This was to be attached to your clothing at meal times, being a type of identification pass to prevent outsiders having the luxury of a free meal. Seemingly, there'd been cases where workers from other firms were using the facilities, plus drifters looking to be fed and watered. Utah was based in Salt Lake City, whereas Dravo was another American conglomerate, with varied interests in mining and construction.

The vans were arranged in holiday camp formation, with Ray and I allotted to different sections of the site. Two sharp knocks on the van door were greeted by the voice of an Irishman. Once inside, the coolness generated from the air-conditioning was immediately apparent, with the mozzies' nightly meals banished forever. I was then introduced to Pat, Ivan the Yugoslav and an Aussie named Fraser. The English-speakers of the trio were relieved to hear a Geordie accent, the last worker having been Polish. I was on a top bunk with Fraser underneath, while Pat occupied the other top bunk. Top bunks weren't favoured, due to the risk of falling out after a night on the grog.

Each van was mounted on four concrete blocks, with heavy wire ropes attached to the blocks from each corner of the van. The coastal stretch from the North West Cape (Tropic of Capricorn) to the far north of the state, suffered periodical tropical storms and cyclones during the summer months. It was essential to fasten down anything prone to movement in the high winds and incessant rain, which could flood the area within hours, continuing for days on end. Depending on the time of year; it was either hot and wet or hot and dry, but at least the crocodiles were further north. I wondered if Slim Dusty, the famed Aussie singer, had any experience of bush life. The lyrics of his song "A Pub with no Beer" must have echoed true on many occasions, particularly during the "wet," when roads were impassable due to flooding. Torrential downpours in temperatures over the ton, with not a cold beer in sight – it doesn't get much worse.

For those who didn't have to work on a Sunday, the usual routine was football on the beach, followed a swim, a few beers, then dinner. In the afternoon you could laze around, catch up with the mail, or whatever took your fancy, all of which suited me fine. The football teams were made up of various races and creeds, reminding me of some of the old war films where the POWs would play each other. My feet were still sore, so I gave the game a miss. The Italians took their football seriously, even sporting the Azzuri's colours. I was warned not to rub salt in their wounds regarding their early exit from the World Cup at the hands of minnows North Korea. They were still the masters of ball control, demonstrating their skills for all to see, which was the cue for Pat's temper to surface.

"Get on with the fuckin' game instead of showing off. If you were any good at football you wouldn't be working in this fuckin' hell hole." With their limited vocabulary, I very much doubt if they understood a single word he said.

A small area of the beach had been prepared for safe swimming, with steel nets attached from the seabed to the surface as protection against unwelcome guests. The nets still had to be checked at regular intervals, due to the sharks' insistence of trying to enter the arena. Even though the sea was inviting, the limits of my trustworthiness allowed the water line to my shoulders only. The occasional funny guy had been known to attach a fin to his arse then swim underwater close to the surface, causing a few hearts to miss a beat. I'd only known Pat for a little over two hours, but long enough to realise he was totally unconventional. At the football game everyone was wearing shorts, whereas he wore long trousers. For swimming, Fraser and I had bathers, while Pat dropped his pants and ran towards the surf in his birthday suit, proudly showing off his one-and-a-half knackers.

Part of a warehouse had been converted into a makeshift bar, where Ivan was sat playing cards with a group of his fellow countrymen.

"Ivan's got a bit of a problem with his waterworks, occasionally pissing the bed," declared a smiling Fraser, "that's why Pat sleeps on the top bunk."

I was always one for a good yarn, with Fraser's definitely worth ten out of ten. Ivan had arrived six months earlier, with the two of them helping him through his homesickness. Pat was eager to continue.

"Three times the fucker gave me a shower during the night, with the piss coming through the mattress onto me below. This is the thanks you get for helping a man from a foreign country to settle in. He repays your kindness by pissing on you while you sleep." By this time we were all creased up with laughter, not daring to look in the direction of the man from Zagreb. The giggles continued for a little while longer, as we listened to the Irishman's account of replacing the wet mattresses by raiding one of the other vans. Much to Pat's amusement, I informed Fraser that I'd been known to piss the bed on the odd occasion. This caused him to go quiet for a few moments until I put his mind at rest, assuring him that my bladder problems had been dormant for quite a while.

"There'll not be many people in this world who've gone through life without pissing the bed, that's for sure," concluded Fraser.

On entering the canteen you were greeted by two large stainless steel urns, containing gallons of ice-cold orange and grapefruit juice. There were tables of food, catering for all the tastes: steaks, chickens, hams, fish, salads, pasta, salami, eggs, ice cream, cakes, and so on. I'd never witnessed such a grand spread. There was no limit to what you could eat, as long as there was no waste. Notices were prominently displayed, warning of the consequences of over-indulging. Apparently, there'd been instances of people taking advantage, resulting in as much food being thrown away as what was being eaten. Salt tablets were also freely available, along with the warning that anyone contracting illness due to lack of salt intake would be instantly dismissed.

After the meal I left the boys to reflect on the day's events, with the thermometer on the office wall registering 88 degrees (31C). Maybe I could plan my return home earlier, but I wouldn't disclose anything to Pat or Fraser until I had their confidence.

We worked a six-day week, ten hours a day, starting at seven and finishing at six, with an hour break. After breakfast we were driven to the worksite in a semi-articulated trailer which had been converted to carry around eighty people. One of the main projects was the construction of a huge pelletising plant, to process all the iron-ore waste. The work involved preparing a series of large foundations, measuring approximately thirty feet by eight, by six feet deep. The hard ground meant constant blasting. Our job was to remove all the debris from the holes with shovels, picks, and crowbars. It was impossible for the dust to escape in the calm conditions, which meant that our sweating bodies attracted all the unsavoury elements, with flies another constant source of irritation. The temperature in the holes was unbelievable, with even the pores on my little fingers emitting fluid.

The only essential luxury we enjoyed was the non-stop provision of water. It was much the same as the railroad, but of a better quality, and colder. It was advisable to limit your intake to avoid getting crook (ill), but that was easier said than done. The smoko break was strictly limited to ten minutes for the five-hour morning and afternoon sessions, the powers-that-be being of the opinion that the slaves were being well paid and cared for. My other workmates, apart from Pat, were members of the "no speak English club," with a Pole, a Portuguese and two Italians, so at least we couldn't get accused of talking on the job. It was only then that I realised that the Australian Governments ten-pound assisted passage scheme must have covered most of Europe. There was no sign of our neighbours across the channel. Maybe they preferred French-speaking territories.

Patrick Carragher was an inch or so under six-foot, of slim build with dark, wavy hair and pale blue eyes. He'd left his homeland at fifteen, seeking his fortune on the motorways of England with McAlpine's fusiliers before migrating to Sydney. There, he worked on the Snowy Mountains hydroelectric development before moving west. I mentioned my brief visit to Blackrock when hitching around Ireland, and Pat rekindled his childhood memories of travelling to the coastal resort during his school holidays. His family still lived in the border town of Newry. The palms of his hands were so rough, it was like shaking hands with a sheet of sandpaper, so God help any woman he ever came into contact with. His feet were also a classic example, as tough as leather, along with scars and toenails missing. According to the Irishman, anyone suffering with a cough, cold, blisters, or indeed a dose of the clap, would all be termed as having the "barcoo-rot." It was an Aboriginal saying, adopted by the early settlers to describe the problems encountered with malnutrition and scurvy.

Fraser's non-stop smile and happy-go-lucky approach

to life were a tonic. There were a few Aussies on site, but most preferred to work in or around Perth. The large majority would venture no farther than the coastal resorts, classing the back o'Bourke (back of beyond) as a "no-go" area. Pat chipped in with his explanation as to why there was a noticeable lack of local labour.

"The Aussies would rather stay in Perth working for low wages, so they could shag all the women whose husbands were up here grafting their balls off."

It was a common occurrence for marriages to break up due to husbands working away for prolonged periods, but this was the price you had to pay to accumulate lots and lots of paper. Dampier was an excellent opportunity to save money. After working there for two years, you could buy and furnish a new home outright, with money to spare.

Planning my return, I needed a passport photograph. Whether from north or south of the border, the Irish have a common allegiance to the words Pat or Paddy, irrespective of religion. My mentor Pat introduced me to Paddy, a "gofa" for the surveying team, whose hobby was photography. From one of the prints he cut a small picture of my head and shoulders, which I sent to Canberra, along with 430 dollars.

Things were finally happening. Next target, Heathrow.

After calculating all the "ifs and buts" I reckoned I could be home by December. I would probably arrive back with only a hundred pounds to my name, with no chance of ever again of saving mega money. Broke or otherwise, my first loyalty was to my future wife and yet-to-be-born child.

One of the office clerks, John the pom, formerly of

Leicester, asked if I'd served in the armed forces, which I found a rather puzzling question. Government legislation required all firms to give details of workers on the payroll, should they meet the criteria for possible military service in Vietnam. Whether this applied to other European nationals, or only those from Commonwealth countries I don't recall. Potential fighting men were selected by a ballot system. When I enquired as to the distance from Australia to Vietnam, John pointed across the ocean in a northerly direction.

"About a thousand miles north of Singapore."

He was of the opinion, however, much the same as his overseers, that the war would be over in a matter of months. Hopefully I wouldn't have to return home via Vietnam.

All construction work was on behalf of the Hamersley Iron Company, who owned the mines inland and probably all the land around, so I was indirectly indebted to them for my meal-ticket. When vast reserves of iron ore were discovered in the Hamersley mountain ranges it was like the gold rush days all over again. A new railroad was nearing completion from the port to the mines, a distance of 190 miles, to accommodate two huge diesel locomotives and an endless train of ore-carrying trucks. Laying the track meant toiling in constant high temperatures, so the contractors were keen to hire people living in similar conditions. Their chosen recruitment spot was Thursday Island in the Torres Straits, off the northern tip of Queensland, 200 miles south of New Guinea. Dormitory-style accommodation was provided for the islanders.

They were the first people I'd ever witnessed swinging a hammer in searing heat, clad in coats, large hats and trousers to keep the sun at bay. Working long hard hours was something that the TIs (Thursday Islanders) had never experienced, and within weeks speculation was rife as to the wisdom of their appointment. Even though they were getting a king's ransom in wages, it was a totally different situation living in the conditions compared to working in them. The Aborigines were a typical example of people not wanting to exert themselves too much when the sun was in full bloom. Knowing what the job entailed I didn't envy them one little bit, with working in the salt mines, rowing in a slave galley, or building the pyramids to compare.

Countless problems occurred, mainly accidents due to carelessness. Many of them were experiencing white man's liquor for the first time. We'd glance around their quarters occasionally, with the new building reminiscent of a disaster zone. The spew and piss-covered floor had to be hosed down every morning. Like the Slavs, the TIs were also prone to flashing a blade when under the influence of grog.

At a quarter of a million tons, the huge ore carriers calling at Dampier were the biggest in the world. Dredgers constantly kept the coastal area free from debris. One such dredge was named "De Grey," after a river north of Port Hedland. The other was the "Alameda," after the city and county bordering San Francisco Bay.

Utah tried to make our stay as comfortable as possible, but unlike Port Hedland and Roebourne there were no females to keep the lads happy. The gold mining town of Kalgoorlie was noted for its brothels, and I got the feeling that it wouldn't be too long before the fair ladies of Perth were heading north, keen for their share of dusty dollars. Open-air movies were held in a clearing alongside the vans. Western or gangster films were the main features, the same film being shown for three consecutive nights in English, Italian and German. There were no organised seating arrangements, you just took your own chair and sat wherever you fancied. Sometimes I'd go on the other nights, with the German language definitely not suited to spaghetti westerns.

On October 9th Ann gave birth to a baby girl, Lynda, weighing in at a hefty 8lb 8ozs. Even though the celebrations were fairly muted, I was quietly chuffed with the choice of gender, not wanting to be held responsible for a wild, reckless son. Ann had kept working to within a few weeks of the birth. It couldn't have been easy having to stand all day. My lovesickness had never diminished, and the latest events left me deflated for a few days.

With the onset of summer, the temperature was constantly in the nineties (34C). It made life hard for us fit young lads, never needing an excuse to down an ice-cold Swan. Fraser and I were briefly promoted out of the hellholes to do other jobs, mine being to assist a surveyor. He was a recent pommie arrival, but only talked to give me instructions. He wasn't interested in wasting his breath on a common labourer from Durham who couldn't even speak the Queen's English properly. Instead, he would save his patter for the beerhouse, pissing up the backs of them that mattered. Fraser had previously worked for the firm of steel-erecters he was helping. Their foreman went by the handle of Heavy, and was some 20-stone plus. His light grey, two-piece overhauls made him appear larger still. Heavy's leisure activities were strictly limited to exercising his right arm in the bar. We got talking about the TIs and where they were from. Heavy was more than familiar with the area due to his war years in New Guinea. I mentioned Errol Flynn's early years there, working on coconut and tobacco plantations, as well as prospecting for gold.

"That lucky bastard must have screwed nearly every dame on the island, judging by the Flynn look-alikes among the natives," replied Heavy, as we joked about one of Australia's famous sons who made it big time. It appeared that Errol was sowing the seeds of love long before his arrival in the glitter world of Hollywood.

The new VC10 "whispering jet" was operating on the London route, with us both excited at the prospect of flying in a plane without propellers. Ray had pencilled in November 21st as the most likely departure date. I felt it was now time to tell Pat and Fraser of my plans, but the initial shock left them reeling.

After my week-long stint with the surveyor I was again asked to help out, this time driving a dump truck. It had the words "El Diablo" painted in large black letters above the cab. To the Italian and Spanish workers this was "the Devil." If looks could kill, I wouldn't have lasted a day. The original recipient of the painter's wrath must indeed have been a bad bugger. There was an impressive line-up of muck moving machines. Besides Le Tourneau and Euclid dump trucks, there were the dozers, scrapers, loaders and graders bearing the Caterpillar and Gallion names, along with the Marion draglines. The workhorses used by the white-helmeted chiefs were Japanese-manufactured Toyota Crown pick-ups. I'd never seen or heard of them before, but they were most impressive. Similar in design to the American utes, they stood up to the rigours of the bush with ease.

Ivan was leaking about once a fortnight, the tell-tale sign being a strong ammonia smell next morning. One

Sunday after dinner, I accompanied Pat to thieve a mattress from one of the new vans that had been delivered. There was a shock in store. We were confronted by two workers enjoying each other's pleasure in one of the bunks. One was an air-track driller around my age, the other being a foreman in his early forties, both from the city. If that was their scene, good luck to them. One of our favourite sayings was that Dampier was a good place for a queer or a preacher, or a queer preacher. Back home we called them homos or puffs. The Aussies elaborated further, terming them puffters. It reminded me of a story Uncle Bob used to tell Dad when I was a youngster. When Greek ships called in for repairs at Swan Hunter's shipyard on the Tyne, the firm's apprentices would be ushered out of the way of the visiting crewmen. Just in case the seamen had any ideas of "your turn in the barrel tonight!"

In the West Australian newspaper, I noted that an Italian ship, Achille Lauro, was leaving Fremantle on November 1st bound for Southampton. The basic price was 509 dollars (£212), which seemed good value for money, compared with the 855 dollars (£356) for a flight. Everything was provided on board, including meals, recreation facilities and entertainment. If the salty air was to be my preferred option I could leave Dampier three weeks earlier, and be back home only ten days later than travelling by plane. I had already paid Canberra and my passport would be arriving soon, so the maximum I would need, including the flight from Dampier to Perth, would be a thousand dollars (£416). The sea voyage fuelled my imagination. Besides, it would be a fitting end to an extraordinary adventure. Sharing a twin bunk cabin with no sea view was all you got for the basic price, but I wasn't bothered about the view, having worked within sight of water for the majority of my time in the western state. Ray was deeply disappointed, having expected us to walk across the tarmac at Heathrow together, but understood my need to cut costs. Another crucial factor that had some bearing on my decision was Ray's past record with Sonya. The plan was to stay in the airport awaiting the London flight, but if Ray got a hard between his legs, there was nothing I could do to stop him short of chloroform.

As my days as a bushman drew to a close, my only major concern was my missing passport. I had no choice but to telephone Canberra. It was a mammoth task just locating the correct department. I was on the phone line for over half an hour, only to be told my passport was still being processed. I also stated my new departure date, along with Perth GPO as my future mailing address, before being presented with a hefty bill for the 2,500-mile call. I could have applied for it a month earlier. I had the money, but wanted to be sure there would be no last minute hiccups. My application also had the added problem of having to be referred to other departments for clearance. All my previous plans had tended to blow up in my face, but this time there was little room to manoeuvre. Everyone back home was banking on me to deliver.

Although I'd worked in Dampier for only three months, I felt as though I was betraying the company's trust in me by walking out on them. Western Mining and Utah would never understand how much I appreciated the break they'd given me, after I'd virtually resigned myself to completing a two-year term. On the Saturday night we got into party atmosphere. Pat and Ray's rendition of Danny Boy frequently changed key.

Back in the city, it was noticeably cooler than a thousand miles north, but still hovering around the eighties. The bustling port of Fremantle was my final stop. I opted for an old Colonial-style boarding house close to the harbour. After removing the basic essentials from my case, I was devastated to find that I had left my travel clock behind. It was a farewell present from Ann. The clock had been my constant companion through thick and thin, but would now remain part of the van's furnishings, along with Pat, Fraser, Ivan and their new companion. Next morning I headed back to Perth and the GPO, but still no passport. Disappointment was a word I'd forgotten about in recent weeks, but it was rearing its ugly head again. After yet another expensive long-distance call to Canberra, I was brought back down to earth with the news that it was still being processed. No-one was interested that I had an important appointment next day with a ship. I tried all ways to get aboard, even offering to telephone Canberra from their office and have the passport forwarded direct to London, but their message was clear. You can't leave the country without a passport.

Next day, nothing. Worse was to follow, with the news that 150 dollars was being deducted from my refund as compensation to the shipping line for my last-minute cancellation. My predicament was not classed as exceptional circumstances. In my last letter to Ann, I'd said that when she read this I would be riding the ocean waves. Unsure what to do, I decided to say nothing until I had one foot on the gangplank, not wanting to convey more heartbreak. Later that afternoon I hung around the dock, watching the passengers embark. Then, amid much fanfare and tears, the majestic-looking liner slowly made its way into the Indian Ocean, leaving me with an empty, helpless feeling. So near, yet so far away.

The passport arrived one week later. During this time I'd been making inquiries as to the possibilities of working my passage home on one of the many cargo ships departing the port. After first discussing the latest music scene with a Scouse crewman, he sounded out the problems. It wasn't easy to get to England, on account of two things. A seaman's ticket could possibly be arranged, but what would be the ship's destination? Once his ship had finished loading grain it was bound for India, but then might have to return to Oz for another cargo. I could always leave the ship in India and try my luck from there, but the idea of being landed in Asia, rather than Europe, didn't exactly appeal to me. My days as a seafarer ended on dry land, without me having even got my feet wet.

Another Italian ship, the Galileo Galilei, was sailing to Genoa in northern Italy on Nov 22nd. Prices ranged from 437 dollars (£182). By sheer coincidence, that was the day after Ray's flight to London. The ship, only four years old and named after the famous Italian astronomer, was the ultimate in sea-travel. With the latest technology in stabiliser systems, it offered high standards of luxury for the 156 first class and 1,594 tourist class passengers. Its top speed of 27 knots had taken it from Genoa to Australia in a record-breaking time of 23 days, compared to the usual month-long voyage. Genoa wasn't a million miles from England, so if all other avenues failed, it looked like I could be heading to a Catholic country. That would definitely please Mother.

Meantime, I tried for some casual work to help top up the funds. I only managed to get five days, and I had to fork out more money to buy work-clothes and boots. As the days passed it looked as though the Italian adventure was about to become reality. Five days before departure I booked a basic tourist class passage. I was that fed up with hanging around I would willingly have travelled in a rowing boat. I also needed some travel clothes, which would have to be cheap. There was a huge choice of suits and uniforms on offer at the second-hand shops, ranging from Al Capone to a Japanese general, although the majority smelled of foist or mothballs. I could have tried the Greek woman's shop in Subi, but, not having spotted her husband, I didn't want to distress her even further.

My final visit to the GPO was rewarded with a letter from my sweetheart and a photograph of a chubby infant with masses of black hair. My daughter was now five weeks old. It was a moving moment, much too difficult to grasp from the other side of the planet. Then I had one last task to perform that would make me either ecstatic or sad. I'd had plenty of ups and downs over the past months, so another one either way wouldn't make much difference. The London departure from Perth airport left at one-thirty. Ray would be on that flight.

On entering the Savoy I was greeted by Tony the barman, who inquired about the work up north, and Ray's welfare. Those last few words satisfied me immensely. I felt as though a huge burden had been lifted from my shoulders. What Ray Nicholson did for me was immeasurable. His happy-go-lucky approach had helped ease my heartaches and torments. I often wondered if the dolly birds were in cahoots with the barmen. Were they being tipped off about the big spenders? On leaving the lounge I just happened to glance in the dining room.

There, sitting among a table of four was none other than con-man Rod. They were in deep conversation amid a table of drinks. I was within a few feet of the table when Rod recognised me. He instantly turned to one side to engage one of the other chaps in conversation.

"How are ya, Rod? Long time no see," I greeted him, whilst at the same time tapping him on the shoulder to command his attention. He turned and looked me straight in the eyes, his reply being loud and to the point.

"I'm sorry, you must be mistaken. My name's not Rod."

His three companions were dying to laugh at the pommie bastard, who'd probably had one too many and was getting his faces mixed up. I wasn't having it.

"Unless you've got a twin brother lurking in the shadows, then I'm the silly fucker who bailed you out of the shit a few times. Whatever your name is doesn't interest me, but it's pay-up time, to the tune of seventy-five dollars."

The mood of the table suddenly changed, the others sheepishly looking at each other wondering who to believe. Going off Rod's past record, I knew there wasn't a cat in hell's chance of getting paid. To me he was just scum, not even having the courtesy to acknowledge I existed. Whatever the outcome, I was going to have my pound of flesh one way or another before the ship weighed anchor. One thing that caught my eye was the jacket on the back of his chair. In one swift movement I grabbed it and ran towards the door, catching everyone by surprise, before turning to Rod.

"I'm taking the jacket as part payment for what I'm owed. Anything in the pockets will be left downstairs at reception. I'll wait there for two minutes. If you want your jacket you'll have to fight me for the fucker."

Rod stood across the room, cursing me into hell and warning of the consequences, more so to impress his colleagues rather than me. On heading down the stairs, I removed a wallet, handkerchief and pen, but kept the cigarette lighter. Even though I was conceding two inches in height and more than a stone in weight, it didn't bother me in the slightest. The mood I was in, I would have fought anybody. Rod was probably wanted for petty crimes by every state in the land, so I knew he wouldn't call the police. This was the reward for helping people who were down on their luck. Not only do they drop you in the shit, they also rub your nose in it. Five minutes on I was the only one gracing the foyer, Rod being a typical coward.

After donning Rod's jacket, which fitted where it touched, I spent the rest of the day viewing the sights. Sadly, it was too late to appreciate the surroundings, in the city responsible for breaking a few hearts, whilst illuminating many more. The early settlers must have been mightily impressed by the tranquillity of their new abode, even if some were in chains. The views from King's Park, overlooking the city and the Swan River, were truly magnificent, along with all the colours of mother nature. I felt guilty about not visiting Ma Cooper and Mrs. O'Neill, just to let them know I'd made it. Back in Fremantle, I spent my last night on Australian soil quietly, Jim Reeves and his "Distant Drums" wearing out the jukebox in the nearby bar. My main concern was the sixty dollars (£25) I had left, which was barely an allowance of one pound a day until Genoa. I had hoped for £150, but with the lost deposit and three weeks' B+B, the pot had rapidly diminished.

At four in the afternoon I walked up the gangplank and was directed to my quarters below. Camelo, or Charlie as he preferred to be called, was occupying the bottom bunk, at least until Sicily. The small cabin contained a washbasin, wardrobes, table and chairs, while the showers were further along the gangway. Later I joined Charlie on deck to witness the departure. The Italian goodbyes seemed to have more emotion than those of the Brits, with lots of tears, gesturing and shouting from both the ship and the dockside. I stayed around until the mainland lights were merely a twinkle, before tearing the photograph of Greek woman's husband into small pieces and despatching them over the side. I didn't want to create the wrong impression by carrying a photograph of a man on my person. The Greek lady was so full of hope and expectation. Possibly the north thing was her husband's excuse to put her off the scent. I hope he came back.

Maybe I hadn't fulfilled my dreams, but I couldn't help but reflect on how lucky I'd been in so short a time. If I hadn't been forced to chase the big bucks and work in the outback, I would never have got the chance to meet the Aborigines and bush people, who lived a totally different life to the city dwellers. After all that was the true Australia, where the early pioneers had earned their corn. It had also been a refreshing experience toiling and living with different nationalities, in circumstances that I wouldn't wish to repeat. I was now on the first leg of my final destination, but would it go according to plan?

Farewell to the sunshine city of Perth, a pure gem. Farewell to the hot dusty highways. Farewell to the land of opportunity.

Chapter Five

Welcome to Milan

On heading down below, I found Charlie lying on the bunk with tears in his eyes. I excused myself, telling him I was going to explore what the ship had to offer, returning close to midnight. Next morning it was Ray who occupied my thoughts. The VC10 "whispering jet" would at any time be setting down at Heathrow. I felt proud that he'd finally reached his objective, thinking of the time we met in Ma Cooper's, when we were both one step away from the gutter. In a few weeks I'd be back home, with nothing but memories. In the meantime I would enjoy my last taste of adventure as a single man, albeit with a depleted purse.

Charlie was also returning home. He had worked in Australia for nine years, first arriving on its shores at the tender age of eighteen. He was blessed with thick, curly dark brown hair and large brown eyes, but was carrying an extra stone or two for his short frame. He always appeared sad, which I guess was understandable. His father had just died, and he was leaving the country he'd grown most fond of, possibly forever. As Charlie was now the family breadwinner, it was his duty to provide for his mother and grandparents, besides a brother and sister still at school. How did the shipping company manage to accommodate an Englishman and Sicilian together, with probably the most tearful hard-luck stories you'd ever want to hear?

The majority of passengers were Italian, returning to their roots for an extended holiday, with a small sprinkling of Greeks, Slavs, Germans and Brits. As usual, the Eyeties were exhibiting their football-juggling skills at the side of the swimming pool to impress would-be suitors. If you wanted to use the pool or play on-deck games, it was best at meal times. The deck would be almost deserted, while the dining area resembled a free-for-all. Within minutes of opening, the dining room looked like a swarm of locusts had swept through the area. Everyone jostled for the best delicacies, even to the point of hands and voices being raised. I suppose it was human nature to grab all you could as long as it was free. At the end of the sitting the place resembled a bombsite, with wasted food everywhere. It was indeed an eye-opener to obscrve self first, second, third and fuck everybody else. Charlie and I were allocated the same table as his fellow Italians, but there was no love lost between the neighbours from across the Straits of Messina.

Some took bottles of free plonk from the dining room into the lounge, playing board and card games before retiring for the night. It was then that I would write a few lines, using the free picture postcards advertising the fact that we were sailing the high seas on the latest technology. I'd been fortunate to stock up with a few before they went the same way as the chocolate treats. They madc a welcome change to the by-now boring paper thin airmail letters. At least the postman would be kept up to date.

The Italian language lessons were held in the small compact cinema. This was the only time I got the opportunity to rub shoulders with a few of the first class passengers. For once we were all on the same level, rich or broke. I'd always had the notion that it was possible to explore the ship inside out, but sadly that wasn't the case, my ramblings strictly limited to the working classes. The cinema was also host to John Wayne, who seemed more comfortable mimicking a Latin tongue than Clint Eastwood had been with German.

It took two days for the Brits to surface. There were eight in all, with a Welshman and a Paddy leaving the ship at Singapore. The lad with the goatee beard from Port Talbot was travelling to Thailand. He peddled aspirin as a health cure, but I reckon he was only looking for cheap thrills. He always appeared to be on cloud nine, giving the impression he'd been puffing "happy-backy", or dabbling in something stronger. Brendan had worked around Melbourne, before moving west to the Kwinana oil refinery, fifteen miles south of Perth. The quietly-spoken Corkman was chasing yet more money, hoping to land a job on Christmas Island, with the interviews being held in Singapore. We'd just past the island, so if he got the job he would have to about turn. Next day we celebrated crossing the equator with an on-deck party, the offers of free drinks from the Captain much too good to refuse.

Bren asked me if I'd accompany him to the interview. The ship was in port for the day, and it would satisfy my curiosity as to the wages being paid. Walking down the gangplank, we wished the Welshman "bon voyage" on his quest into the unknown. He was carrying only the smallest of holdalls, no doubt full of the magic pills. He'd have to be careful, especially with Vietnam close at hand. John the pom had talked about the war being over shortly, but according to the radio and newspapers, the situation was only getting worse.

After travelling by trishaw for two miles, we arrived at what appeared to be a small church. Stale and dusty inside, it gave the impression of having been closed for some time. Interviews were conducted near the altar. About thirty shabbily-dressed locals were seeking labourers' positions. Surely it must have been cheaper to recruit in Jakarta, only a stones throw from Christmas Island? We were directed into a side room, where an Irish representative of Bannion Brothers warmly greeted us with the usual safe journey patter. It was quite amusing to hear the native tongue of both men, taking me back to my childhood days, listening to grandfather and other elders of the church. A desalination plant, to purify seawater into drinking water, was being constructed on the island. Bren, also a former member of McAlpine's fusiliers, was applying for a plant operator's job.

Within minutes he was signed up, then it was my turn to be offered a job, paying twenty-percent more in wages than Dampier. Naturally I had to refuse. Why the hell couldn't I have been offered this sort of job when I was desperate? I guess it's either the feast or the famine. The boss wasn't too forthcoming about the accommodation. Knowing the Paddies, Bren would probably be sleeping in a tent, with the thought of air-conditioning further away than the Blarney stone.

The rest of the morning was spent sightseeing. We had several proposals of illicit activities, before finally arriving at Bren's hotel, courtesy of his new employers. The trishaw rider was paid five Singapore dollars (37½p) for his four hours' work, having given us a brief insight into the world of them that have, and them that have not. Before he left, the rider advised us never to wear white shirts on future visits to Singapore. They were the giveaway that we were tourists. No wonder the girls were saying "Johnny, this" and "Johnny, that" on every street corner we stopped at.

Two of the Brits were returning home with their boyfriends to celebrate a double wedding, before flying back to Adelaide. That left Chaz, a lad from Leamington Spa, a Londoner and myself as the remaining single species. Chaz would mix in with the banter before retiring around ten. Once the lounge had emptied we'd have a bit of a singsong accompanied by a harmonica, courtesy of our Leamington Spa colleague, with us both imitating a few rock and blues greats before lights-out. He surprised me, not appearing to be the type. Then again, you can't tell a book by its cover.

Returning to the cabin late at night was always a daunting experience. Charlie would be snoring loudly, his bunk curtains drawn and the main cabin light blazing away. The procedure was to remove my shoes before entering, quietly undress, put the light out, and then gently climb up the ladder to the top bunk. Halfway up the ladder his curtains would suddenly open, accompanied by the shouting of a Latin tongue, with Charlie being covered in sweat as if he'd just awoken from a nightmare. He nearly gave me a heart attack the first time it happened, but eventually I got used to it. The most logical thing would have been to change bunks, but Charlie wouldn't hear of it, besides being totally unaware of his nightly outbursts.

Charlie was an early-to-bed, early-to-rise man who neither drank nor smoked. I also classed him as honest and caring. I didn't venture into details of his love life, but would imagine that any future bride would already have been arranged. The Italian family life possessed something that the English didn't; a closeness that included children, parents, grandparents and relatives. The Greeks were very much the same.

On entering the Arabian Sea the sun was showering us with affection. Unfortunately, due to my limited funds, the ice-cold water fountains had to substitute for the occasional bevvy. I was eagerly looking forward to the Indian experience, but Bombay proved to be a bit of a culture shock. Cattle were herded through the streets, along with smells of all descriptions. What was impossible to project in the cinema or on paper was the smell, mainly of sewerage, making you realise the necessity for typhoid, cholera and yellow fever vaccinations. In Bombay there was no confrontation from the ladies, just non-stop hassle from the males, desperate to peddle their wares. On returning to the ship I was alerted to the possibility of more dangers lurking ahead, this time at the Suez Canal. Since leaving Fremantle, we'd been fully aware of the imminent explosive conflict between the Arabs and Israelis. If the tensions suddenly escalated out of control it could result in possible closure of the canal, leaving us with no option other than to sail around Africa.

In different financial circumstances I'd have been in total agreement to visit Cape Town, along with the other refuelling ports. As things stood, I was having to penny-pinch on a daily basis, so an extra week on the journey would be disastrous. None of the Brits were aware of my circumstances, so I didn't want to suffer the humility of getting caught with empty pockets. Looking at a map of the world outside the Purser's office gave me other options, should we be diverted around the Cape of Good Hope. Once we'd rounded Africa I'd jump ship in Tangier or Gibraltar, assuming we stopped there. Then I could make my way up through Spain and France, instead of spending the remaining days sailing around the Mediterranean en-route to Genoa.

My fears were unfounded. We were greeted at the breakfast table with the news that we were on course for the Red Sea. After anchoring off Aden to take on fuel, the Captain announced that anyone wanting to go ashore did so at their own risk. That part of Yemen was ending its days of British occupation in volatile fashion. No passengers ventured ashore. We were all quite content to listen to the sporadic gunfire from the safety of the ship.

The Suez Canal was most impressive. It was quite amazing to think that the majority of the 110-mile channel of water was man-made. From entering the canal at Suez to leaving it at Port Said, the ship's speed was restricted to little more than walking pace. In the wider central areas, remnants of sunken vessels were clearly visible above the water line. Travelling slowly meant we were being constantly invaded by the Arab traders and their giveaway bargains. It was easy for them to pull alongside in small boats, then shimmy up ropes that had been fastened to the deck rails. All this activity was of course illegal, and the goods most likely counterfeit. I rewarded my beloved with a small wristwatch in the shape of a heart, while for my folks and future in-laws I bartered for a few small presents, mainly trinkets and the latest type of Ronson cigarette lighters. Compared with the gunfire at Aden, the passage through the Red Sea and the canal was relatively quiet. On entering the Med, everyone breathed a huge sigh of relief. The weather was noticeably cooler as we headed for Greece, with long trousers and jackets replacing the casual attire.

After nearly three weeks at sea, the first passengers

disembarked at the Greek port of Piraeus. During the ship's stay there, I briefly explored the ancient city of Athens in the bright winter sunshine, with the Acropolis and the old Olympic stadium my main objectives. An inspection of the back pocket revealed a cash balance of two pounds, plus some small coins. I had already resigned myself to taking a casual job for a few days in Italy or France. Even though I'd cut expenditure down to the bone, the money had gradually been frittered away. You can't travel around a city all day without spending something, besides wanting to digest as much information as possible. Those wasted weeks in Fremantle and my lost deposit would have helped enormously, but I wasn't worried anymore now that we were back in Europe. By contrast, Charlie wouldn't have spent more than five pounds during the entire voyage, never once leaving the ship to see what was the outside world had to offer.

Next stop was Sicily and Charlie's home port of Messina. For the past days he had been quiet and withdrawn, the puffy bags under his eyes telling their own story. As we entered Messina, Charlie waved frantically from the deck to his relatives on the dockside, tears running down his cheeks. He lived in a village ninety miles inland and would now have to revert to permanent residency at his former home. We enjoyed a long handshake and a hug, knowing there was no chance of our paths ever crossing again, and with that he was off down the gangplank. I watched them all embrace before heading towards customs, with Charlie looking up one last time and giving me a farewell wave. About the only thing we'd had in common during the entire journey, was being seasick between Bombay and Aden.

By late afternoon we were in the Bay of Naples, its houses nestling along the coastline looking very picturesque in the setting sun. Nearly three-quarters of the passengers disembarked, accompanied by shouts and cheering. Two members of the clergy appeared. They wore round brimmed hats and were dressed in black from head to toe, apart from a striking crimson waistband. As soon as the last person stepped off the gangplank they stepped on. It was immediately apparent that they intended to take full advantage of the ship's fleeting visit. Swiftly they moved up on deck, introducing themselves by thrusting a small card of the Madonna and Child into the hands of everyone present. Then there was a slight pause as they eagerly awaited our response to the brown leather money pouch produced from inside their vestments. I had just over a pound left in the entire world, a mixture of sterling and Italian lira, and reckoned my needs were greater than those of the Lord's. Even so, feeling more than a little guilty, I gave the holy men all the small change I possessed, a little over a shilling (6p). I was then showered with prayers and absolution, which I took to be the Italian version of "bless you my son, your sins are forgiven." I would savour the moment for Mother, telling her how her pauper son had given money to the priest.

On departing Naples, I had to plot my next course of action for when the ship finally docked in its home port of Genoa. Once on terra firma, the rest of the Brits were travelling to Milan, then joining the overland boat train to London's Waterloo Station. They insisted I join them for a farewell drink in the lounge after the evening meal. That proved to be a problem, because I fully intended landing in Genoa with my one remaining pound still intact. That night I was first to eat, being in and out of the dining hall within minutes, complete with a bottle of vino taken from one of the prepared tables. Next morning at breakfast, they were disappointed that I hadn't kept the date, the chef getting the blame for giving me the shits. When my compatriots enquired as to whether I was taking the train to Milan, I rustled up a story about visiting someone in Genoa whom I'd worked with in Perth. I was more than relieved when they left the dining room, leaving me to scavenge the leftovers. An hour later my epic voyage was at an end. While the Galileo prepared to return to the southern hemisphere with many more hopeful migrants, the route for me was north. The experience had been fantastic. I had witnessed a similar culture to England on the other side of the world, with all the different races, dress and languages on the return journey.

Once everybody was well clear of the port, I bartered with a taxi driver to take me to the Milan road on the outskirts of the city. The weather was cold and foggy as I started out on the 90-mile journey. It was a far cry from Roebourne, with a busy road and good footwear to help me along. The final part of the journey was a bit of a hair-raiser. I could have sworn the driver had been drinking, even though I couldn't smell anything. Instead of appreciating his driving skills, I was more concerned about possible "brown trousers," as we flew along the road and round the bends at breakneck speed. My only interest was the kilometre signs, the numbers of which were rapidly depleting by the minute. At least he looked after my welfare, taking me to the exact place I wanted to be, Milan Central railway station. I hadn't been aware of the overland service to London until the Brits declared their intentions.

The night train departed in a little over four hours, with the basic non-sleeper fare being £12, of which I was £11 and three shillings (£11.15p) short. It was quite clear that the fruits of my brief Italian lessons were not being understood in any shape or form, only realising later that the talking had to be accompanied by movement of the hands.

"Hey presto," a middle-aged lady suddenly emerged from the ticket office knowledgeable of my native tongue. Her husband had originated from Derby.

"Would the Railway be willing to issue me with a ticket, to pay for when I got home?" I asked.

"I'm sorry, no."

I wasn't too disappointed. After all, £12 was a lot of money for them to take a chance with a stranger, especially not one of their own. Plan B would now have to be activated, as I consulted a wall map near the booking office. It was pointless trying to hitch at night, especially in a foreign country, so I would use the station facilities for my first night under the stars. At least there'd be no mozzies, just icicles. Early next morning I'd head west to Turin, then into France. Heading north to Switzerland was a no-go. I'd heard reports about the Swiss authorities clamping down on hitch-hikers. Once in France I'd have to pick up some casual work en-route to a channel port. I was prepared to do anything, short of hiring out my arse! The distance from Milan to Crook was less than that of Perth to Port Hedland, with the added bonus of a tarmac road all the way, apart from a 25-mile strip of water.

It was time to eat. The few pieces of rock-hard toast covered in marmalade and a drink of tap water were a poor man's substitute for the previous weeks of luxury.

My interpreter again appeared. She mentioned the British Embassy as a possible means of getting home, having dealt with them for a marriage permit and work visa for her husband. I'd never even thought such a place existed in Milan, being of the belief that all top-level government business was conducted from Rome. Begging from the government had never been a consideration, chiefly because I never saw them fitting the role as moneylenders. I guess it was worth a try, especially with their hours of opening extending to twenty-four. Shortly after seven I arrived at a large house in Via San Paolo, not far from the station. The nameplate proclaimed that it was indeed the place I was seeking. The butler enquired of my business before showing me into a room off the main hallway.

Judging by the amount of books present, it appeared to be the study. Almost immediately I was greeted by an official-sounding gentleman in his early fifties. Besides having a pleasant mannerism he spoke with a perfect English accent, making it impossible to detect what part of the country he hailed from, other than the south. He gave the impression he was nobody's fool, and that if he'd suspected me to be a drifter, I'd have been dispatched to the footpath post-haste. At first he found my story of passion and adventure difficult to accept, until I backed it up with letters from Canberra and Ann, and the shipping ticket.

In government service for longer than he cared to remember, he had witnessed many tales of woe, but never a one as rueful as mine. Not only did he grant my request to be repatriated, but also gave me a month to redress the balance on my return. I then boldly asked him for an extra £3 in order to complete the journey to Durham, but unfortunately that wasn't possible. His jurisdiction was strictly limited to landing me on the mainland, which in my case was London's Waterloo Station.

He then summoned the butler, gave him some lira for my ticket, and instructed him to drive me to the station. Even though the Ambassador was completely satisfied with my story, he was still hedging his bets against me disappearing with the money. He then shook my hand, wishing me God speed and a rosy future, while I again expressed my humble gratitude. As he closed the door behind me he was smiling, no doubt with a good story to tell at the dinner table. I was also smiling, along with Lady Luck. The entire business was concluded in half an hour. It was a fine example of British hospitality, albeit in Italy.

The next thing I remember was waking at dawn, being greeted by open fields, and later entering Paris. Calais was my first sighting of the English Channel, where I braved the chill winds on the ferry deck to take full advantage of the occasion. Once the mainland was sighted I kept thinking about Vera Lynn singing "The White Cliffs Of Dover." In years past it must have been a welcoming sight for all the returning war heroes. On arrival at Waterloo my pocket totalled eight shillings (40p), which was enough to buy two cheap meals. I was left with two stark choices, as a means of ending the journey that began in Fremantle 25 days and 10,000 miles earlier. Either take a bus to the north of the city then start hitching up the A1, or try riding the rails without getting caught. After weighing up all the pros and cons I opted for the train, gambling for the last time that fortune would favour the brave – and the poor – for the final 260 miles.

At King's Cross Station I was juggling my route with the platform timetable, with trains stopping at Durham few and far between.

"Hello Geordie, what are you doing here?" said the voice behind me, instantly recognisable as that of the Leamington Spa harmonica player. "I thought you were staying in Genoa for a few days."

After recovering from the shock of being rumbled, I expressed delight at seeing him once again, while thinking of my next excuse.

"When I eventually found his house there was no one to be seen, with a neighbour saying that they were in Rome visiting relatives."

He conveyed his commiserations, making me feel as guilty as hell. Maybe I should have been in Rome also, to get my sins forgiven by the Pope. My friend was travelling to Peterborough to collect a car before continuing on home, so when he suggested we join forces on the train I was again caught with my pants down. My train wasn't until after five, whereas there were two trains to Peterborough leaving within the next twenty minutes. The only plausible excuse I could think of was that I intended taking in the sights for an hour or so, whilst praying that he didn't suggest accompanying me, or else I would have to spill the beans. He must have thought I was crazy, having travelled halfway around the world then wanting to go sightseeing in the middle of winter. I hastily forced the issue, extending my hand and wishing him well for the second time of asking.

It was possible that the rail authorities would issue me with a ticket, to pay for when I got home, but if they refused I had no chance of sneaking on unnoticed. At five

I retrieved my case from the left luggage counter and sat near the end of the platform. As soon as the train's engine started to rev, in tandem with the guard blowing his whistle and waving his flag, I made my move for the rear carriage.

There were seven carriages to move around in, beyond them being the restaurant car and first class. The only disappointment was the number of empty seats, especially with it being a Saturday. We were well under way before the cry of "tickets please" could be heard. Slowly I rose from my seat, casually heading in the opposite direction, finally disappearing into a toilet on the next carriage. I didn't lock it, wanting to give the impression it was "vacant." Once the coast was clear, I retreated to another carriage, repeating the operation an hour later. The remains of my money bought two sandwiches and a cup of tea from the trolley service. Now I really was a pauper.

So far, so good. After two hours, gradually heading north, my biggest problem was trying to keep awake. The next visit to the toilet was definitely for a call of nature, coinciding with the announcement that we would shortly be stopping at Doncaster. As soon as the train was mobile I vacated the toilet, coming face to face with the ticket inspector who'd just boarded the train. Fuckin' hell!

"Tickets please," was the dreaded sound coming from the man I'd been hoping to avoid, with a genuine visit of convenience having backfired on me big time. The inspector stood his ground, repeating his request.

"Could I see your ticket please, sir?"

"Err, err, I'm afraid I haven't got one," was the only answer I could think of. Furthermore, it was the truth, which made a change to recent events.

"You haven't got a ticket, where have you travelled from?"

"London." I should have said Grantham, but the mind was still in a state of shock after being rumbled. The glee in the inspector's eyes was a sight to behold, whilst trying to conceal the fact with some hard-hearted talking.

"London? Do you realise it's an offence to travel without a ticket, and you could face a fine or imprisonment?"

I just nodded my head, eyes downcast, hoping for some crumbs of sympathy. It appears I was the inspector's prize catch for the day, with him acting like the Wild West sheriff who'd caught a bandit. He had an audience of course, the passengers in the near vicinity enjoying every minute of it.

"Would it be possible to pay for a ticket at a later date?"

"No," was his short, quick-to-the-point reply. He ushered me to a nearby seat, warning me to stay there until he returned. He must have thought I was going to do a Houdini disappearing act, or a James Bond-style jump from the train. Later, for the further amusement of all within earshot, the jubilant inspector informed me in his loudest possible voice that we would be shortly arriving at York, where the railway authorities would very much like to see me.

In the station-master's office I was greeted by two officials, the inspector and I making up the foursome. I got the same briefing, only this time I had a sheriff and two deputies. To them the Australia thing was a load of shit, until I backed up my words with correspondence from the Milan Consulate, the shipping receipt and my passport. For a few moments they found it hard to accept, that the man in their midst had arrived back on these shores penniless, after being in the land of opportunity they'd heard so much about. Their usual clientele riding the rails, were drunks, students and drifters, with me citing personal reasons for my swift return. Before anything was decided, they asked what I would do if they refused to grant me a travel permit. I courteously replied that I would have to find my way to the A1 Great North Road and try my luck from there.

I was 60 miles from home. The darkness would prove to be a handicap insofar as getting lifts were concerned, so I was keeping my fingers crossed and acting with piety. I suppose they had to show us train-hoppers that our actions wouldn't be tolerated, whilst at the same time judging each person's circumstances differently. Maybe I passed the test as being a genuine case? Maybe they had a soft spot for me? Whatever it was it worked, so for the second time in a little over twenty-four hours I was being issued with a bill of payment, this time for two pounds eight shillings (£2.40p). They even gave me a pot of tea to wash down the remains of a sandwich I'd removed from the case, before giving me the thumbs up. The next train stopping at Durham was the Newcastle-bound sleeper, seven hours away, so I killed time around the bright coal fire in the platform waiting room. Unfortunately, it also acted as a haven for drunks and deadbeats, with one eye sleeping and the other on my case. I was hungry and tired, but happy. Congratulations extended to British Rail, the Milan Embassy and last but not least, Canberra.

Before I had time to fully reflect on the day's events we were in Darlington, the birthplace of the world's first passenger railway, with George Stephenson's famous train

"Locomotion," taking pride of place on the main platform. It was also a reminder of my days at the Tech, and William's music shop, where I'd bought my fiddle-shaped bass guitar, the one that was stolen. Next was Durham, for me the end of the line. Only a handful of passengers left the train, all being met by family of friends, whereas I was not expected back until days after the ship docked in Genoa. When the train's red light finally disappeared into the distance there was a deathly silence. I gazed across the tracks at the southbound platform, the scene of our tearful farewell. It had been a wonderful adventure, albeit with more problems than most, with "plan" a four-letter word I would be wise to avoid in the future. I was returning home poorer than when I left, but a lot richer in thoughts and experience. The only visible signs of travel being a deep suntan.

As I made my way down from the station, Durham Cathedral and Castle looked as majestic as ever, silhouetted against the early morning sky, guardians over my favourite city. The clock on top of the Essoldo picture house was showing 5.30 as I got into my stride, preparing for a 10-mile hike. If I hadn't bumped into the keen-eyed inspector, I'd have been back at ten, but better late than never. At Neville's Cross, I was more than surprised when the driver of the first car that came into view acknowledged my waving thumb. More so, when it transpired that the early bird was Mr Myers, the headmaster of Crook junior school. What a stroke of luck!

Chapter Six

Off-White Wedding

Outside the house there was a deadly silence. Only the light from the street lamps penetrated the cold, early morning darkness. Two sharp knocks on the front door, a deep breath, and I was ready for the hangwoman. I was more than nervous. I was terrified. Although it seemed an age, within seconds the hallway was illuminated. Half asleep, Dad gave me a muted greeting. As I stepped inside, my hopes of retiring to my former room until later in the day were instantly shattered. There was Mother, primed up and ready to greet her prodigal son. Before I had time to even lower my case to the ground, she set about me with all guns blazing.

I'd brought disgrace on the family. She was ashamed to meet her friends. I was the talk of the town. Such was the enormity and extent of my mortal sins, I would rot in hell forever. I offered no defence, with sorry a poor excuse. Now I was being made to realise the anger and torment my parents had endured since day one. Mother continued to blow off steam, Dad doing no more than nodding his head when required to do so. Mother continued. After blotting my copybook forever, I should have stayed in Australia. It would have suited her even more if I'd hidden away in a cupboard, never again to see the light of day again. From that day on our relationship deteriorated even further, if that were atall possible.

Eventually the shouting gave way to questions. When

are you getting married? Where are you going to work? Are you going back to Australia? One point I was adamant to get across was that I hadn't returned out of duty, I had come back for the girl I loved. That seemed to convince them that the sun had indeed melted my brain, with Mother raising her eyes to the heavens and sighing. Within eleven hours I'd been interrogated twice for being a naughty boy, with Mother's fiery tongue far worse than that of the rail inspectors. I'd have a word with my brother Leo once the dust had settled. I would imagine that his activities would have been well and truly curtailed, just in case he got any ideas other than looking at young ladies. Now that I was back under Mother's roof, I would have to abide by the rules of the house. Welcome home!

After some shut-eye, my first priority was to visit Ann and Lynda, the paltry sum of sixpence bus fare to Willington being the biggest obstacle. It certainly wasn't the time to be asking for money, so I walked the three miles. It was bitterly cold, my missing overcoat in the Greek woman's shop in Subiaco. My reunion with Ann was almost as tearful as our parting, but at least they were tears of joy. We had to remain rather formal in the presence of Ann's parents, who must have thought they'd seen the last of the hell-raiser. I was then introduced to a bubbly infant with masses of curly hair, curious to find out what all the fuss was about. It was such a strange feeling holding my daughter for the first time. Even though I'd prepared for the moment as best I could, it would take a while to adjust to the role of being an instant dad. I placed myself in Dad's position, not for the first time, but at least I didn't have the scars of battle to banish from my mind.

I was warned there was some animosity between the two sets of grandparents regarding Lynda's upbringing. Mother had insisted she be baptised in the Catholic Church. My future in-laws had wanted her christened in their local Church of England, so to keep all parties happy she was baptised twice, lucky girl. Little did everyone know that I was absolutely skint. Ann wasn't surprised in the least, she was just over the moon that her prayers had been answered. Once we were alone, she removed a tin of cash from the bedside cabinet drawer, money that she'd saved for our future. This caused me to feel more than a little embarrassed, especially with me looked upon as the breadwinner.

It was fully a week before I was able to have a quiet word with Leo. He re-lived the night Ann and her folks called at the house to say she was pregnant. In a small town like Crook news travels fast. The patrons of the local gossip-houses, cafes, shops and pubs had already sharpened their knives, convinced I would never return. With three mouths to feed, and Christmas just around the corner, I was fortunate to find work straight away as a machine operator in a local factory. Getting my first pay, I promptly sent a postal order to British Rail.

Wanting to get hitched as quickly as possible, we gave the authorities the required three weeks' notice. Mother dashed our hopes of a low-profile register office ceremony. She had already spoken to the parish priest, Father Lowrie, about a church wedding. Fully aware of the situation, he was all in agreement. However, many parishioners were of the opinion that we were making a mockery of the church's beliefs. We didn't want to cause further distress. If it made everyone happy having a church wedding, then we'd go along with it. Insofar as getting engaged was concerned, we'd do that the unorthodox way, leaving it until after the wedding.

Christmas was a very special occasion, with everything revolving around our little bundle of happiness. For me it was too much to absorb. I was still re-living the events of the past year, while trying to focus on the job in hand. Welshman Tom Jones was tugging at everyone's heartstrings with his chart topper "Green, Green Grass of Home." For the past three years the Beatles had occupied prime position over the festive period. Their last release "Yellow Submarine/Eleanor Rigby," creating another record of eleven No.1 hits in succession. On the last day of the year I got a letter, postmarked Manchester. I instantly recognised Ray Nicholson's handwriting.

"Hi Kevin. Thought I would drop you a line to let you know I made it and didn't get stuck in the Savoy, but after being here a week I wish I had. Hope you had a good trip home, I have sure felt the cold with flying. Have just wrote to my mate for the return fare, he said he would lend it to me when I wanted to go back, which would be tomorrow if it were possible, didn't think I would get fed up this fast.

Been telling the family about you and some of laughs we had, hope you can make it for a couple of days, although it may be awkward for you. Expect you will be getting married shortly, so would like to wish you all the very best and a happy marriage, which I'm sure you will have, I have never met her, only by the photos and she looks very nice. Also know that she is getting one of the best for a husband, after the few rough times we had together. Many is the time when I think back to Ma Cooper's and have a good laugh over it. Well Kev, I think that's all for now, so will close and hope to hear from you and see you in the very near future. All the very best, Ray.

PS A happy new year, hope it is better for you than this one."

According to his letter, Ray had only been back a week, so he must have left Perth a few days before Christmas, a month later than planned. He mentioned "Coventry Johnny" lending him the return fare. How come he was broke if he'd worked at Dampier until December? Or had he fallen victim once again to Sonya's charms or some other bimbo prior to his flight? I felt sorry for us both, momentarily re-living all we'd been through. Yes, our objectives had been achieved through grafting our balls off, but judging by his letter and my financial circumstances, we hadn't two halfpennies to scratch our arses with. No doubt Ray would have been the centre of attention in Manchester, with family and friends expecting him to throw his money around like confetti. I sure hoped "Coventry Johnny" turned up trumps, before Ray had to confide in everyone that his gold mine was in fact worthless. My demands were not so much the extravagance of an air ticket to Perth, but £14 to buy a wedding suit.

We used Ann's Dad's mini as our passion wagon at every opportunity. It was only natural that we couldn't keep our hands off each other. The rear seat was perfect for all our immediate needs, apart from the cumbersome floor-mounted ashtray. The car's interior designers decided for some unknown reason, probably cost, that the rear passengers should share one ashtray. Earlier models had enjoyed the luxury of two foldaway types in the side panels. This blasted central ashtray caused my knees no end of problem, but I don't suppose the designers would have thought for one moment that hot-blooded males would want to kneel on them.

I sent another postal order, this time for £12, to the

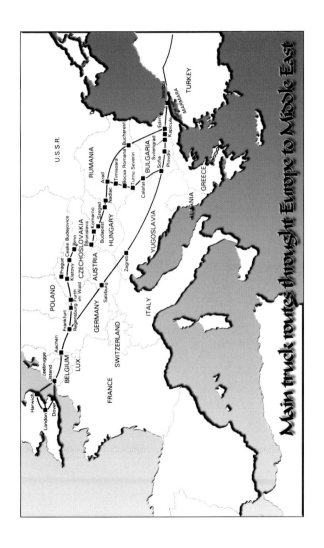

Map supplied by Ferdy of Toprun.

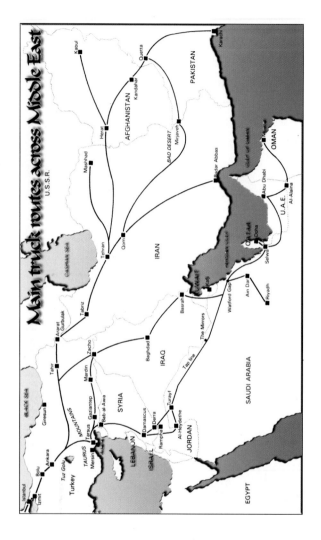

Map supplied by Ferdy of Toprun.

Overturned German Magirus truck, Turkey.
Photo supplied by Ferdy of Toprun.

Trailer crash. Photo supplied by Ferdy of Toprun.

Early picture of Port Hedland, western Australia.

Savoy Hotel, Hay Street, Perth, western Australia 1930s.

Abo women – a "gin" and her daughters relax at Mulyie,
Port Hedland, western Australia.

Camel skeleton in the desert at Nambi Station,
western Australia.

above: Early days at the Elite Dance Hall, Crook (1962). I am in the middle, between the girls (of course!).

right: My "Beatle-type" Hofner fiddle-shaped bass guitar, sadly stolen.

My daughter Lynda, growing up quickly.

Me in a German lay-by.

A Carmans Volvo F88 de-training, driving off the "piggy back" train in Cologne, Germany. © Ian Taylor.

Traversing Austria. © Ian Taylor.

Ruined Crusader fortress near Adana, southern Turkey.

Having a beer in Venice with Northampton John. I'm on the right in the Tyrolean hat.

Ted Hannon, Eastern Turkey (1977) with Mt Ararat in the background. The truck is in the Davies Turner livery.

Bulgaria-Romania ferry. © Ian Taylor.

Dardanelles Ferry. © Ian Taylor.

Bosporus Bridge, Istanbul, view from Beylerbeyi village
on the Asian side.

Looking across to the "patchwork quilt" fields of Syria.

Spectacular scenery in central Turkey. Two Carmans
Volvos parked up. © Ian Taylor.

Black Sea, Turkey. © Ian Taylor.

Old Turk with laden donkey, Pozanti, near Tarsus, southern Turkey.

Abu Ghraib tea house. The men take it easy while the women load wood onto the trailer.

Crashed truck near Istanbul.
Photo supplied by Ferdy of Toprun.

A burnt-out Guy Big "J" at Kapikule on the Turkish
border.

The five young Iraqi boys who helped offload my
first delivery in Baghdad. I supplied the lad on
the right with his "new" suit.

Staff at the Airport Hotel, Baghdad, mainly Kuwaitis.

Kavala, northern Greece
(l-r) Errol Flynn, Barry
Bradshaw, Taffy Davies.

Drivers Jimmy Richardson
and Gorden Crisp (right)
take their ease in Bulgaria.

Stuck in the snow at Leskovac, Yugoslavia.

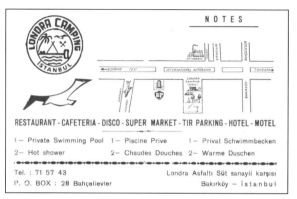

Londra Camp, Istanbul. Swimming pool and showers in three languages! Photo supplied by Ferdy of Toprun.

With my "Kojak" hairstyle, I look suitably menacing on my passport photo.

RAF mug, Habbaniya base, Baghdad.

British Embassy in London, freeing me of my shackles once again. The only thing I had to prove that I'd been to the other side of the world was my Canberra-issued passport. Nothing else, not even a dollar bill.

The morning of our wedding, January 28th, was blessed with brilliant sunshine. The only downside was the absence of the organ or bells, making the coughs, footsteps and whispering much more pronounced. I'd asked Father Lowrie about the possibilities, but there were to be no frills for a "mixed marriage." Had I not been a former altar boy, I doubt very much if we would have been granted the honour, more so if he'd ever found out I was a member of the quartet who stole his grapes. Six months earlier, our big day had been little more than a pipe dream. We'd made it against all the odds, even though our highly publicised affair would only be news for another seven days, before being relegated to the annals of statistics. What uncles, aunts and cousins thought beggars belief. The reception in the Uplands Hotel catered only for immediate family, twelve in all. This suited us fine, not wishing to advertise the fact of the cart arriving before the horse. In the lounge I raised my glass to Ann, wishing us happiness forever, just as Englebert Humperdink began singing "Please Release Me" on the background speakers. Good timing, Kevin!

Buying a house was a must. Even though my in-laws were helpful in every possible way, I saw myself as the burden that had suddenly turned their idyllic lifestyle upside down. There was also a night-time problem, with some of the beds advertised on the TV not exactly living up to their "silent" qualities. Two months later, a two-bedroom terraced property came onto the market in the west end of Willington for £1,275. £150 deposit and monthly mortgage repayments of £15 ensured my pockets were empty once again, but we were ecstatic.

The only slight problem I had, was my liking for a beer. Some landlords extended closing time by up to an hour, allowing you "one for the road," then another one or two to "help you along the road!" In Oz the heat was a major factor, but I couldn't blame the English climate for that. I don't know from whom I inherited my habit. Dad was only a moderate weekend tippler. I wasn't aware of any lovers of the bottle on Mother's side of the family. Possibly it was in my Irish genes from some previous generation. A good excuse for shifting the blame.

I desperately needed to boost my income. The most obvious way was to start a garage business that would include MOT testing and second hand car sales. Was there a big enough market? According to research, car ownership was set to rise dramatically in future years, with some analysts even predicting that many households would boast two cars within twenty years. This was a common occurrence in America, but would it happen here? It was widely accepted that most of our current trends and fashions, such as televisions and refrigerators, had originated in the States. Even during my short time on the road I'd noticed an increase in traffic, but two cars in the family? No, that would never happen. The factory job had only been intended as a temporary stopgap measure, but for how long?

Road haulage was another possible avenue. I considered the pros and cons of tipper trucks. With the recently introduced drink/driving laws starting to bite, mini-buses also appeared a feasible proposition. Pubs and clubs were forming darts, dominoes and snooker leagues, which required transport for away fixtures in neighbouring towns and villages.

My eventual destiny was decided by a game of football on a snowy winter's day in the heart of Weardale. The factory football team was short of players, and even though I had two left feet I was gratefully accepted as a defender. The game was at Wearhead. Although only twenty miles from Crook, it was 1,100ft above sea level. Snowflakes and the bleak, barren landscape greeting us at the ground. Wearhead always boasted a good football team, and true to form they trounced us 7-0. In upper Weardale the long, cold winters seemed to drag on forever, with regular tots of whisky needed to keep the blood circulating. This was in total contrast to Hall's Creek in northwest Oz, where bush hats, beer and the grace of God were the ingredients needed to keep cool.

On heading back home, a 16-seater mini-bus with a large FOR SALE notice caught my eye. It was parked at Corbett's transport depot in the small community of Frosterley. The bus was seven years old, priced £250. This was an ideal workhorse for me to earn a few quid. The immediate problem was breaking the news to Ann, especially when she greeted me with her come-to-bed eyes. We had been saving for a holiday, and I didn't think she'd be too amused exchanging a fortnight in Jersey for a caravan in the Lake District. Surprisingly she was all in agreement. A mini-bus covered in snow, parked all alone in a one-horse dales town, was my grand entrance into the business world.

And so I assumed the title of bus proprietor, the youngest coach operator in the northern traffic area. On many occasions my working day extended to sixteen hours, as I beat a continuous path to the grindstone for more pennies. The pay-outs were endless, with a telephone the latest necessity to grace the hallway furniture. Decades of uncertainty had dominated my parent's lives, when poverty and unemployment were part and parcel of the working classes. Their thinking would never change, with the thought of investing money without any concrete guarantees totally out of the question.

We would usually take Lynda to see my folks once a week, while Ann's parents saw Lynda on a daily basis. I always detected a cool response from Mother towards her. She didn't lavish love on anyone. Rather than mellowing with age, her temperament was as rigid as ever. Unfortunately, my genetic make-up was similar to Mother's. Although I aspired to think and do otherwise, I was not for spoiling Lynda or Ann with affection. To say I was incapable of expressing love openly would possibly be a true representation, even though deep down inside I had the same feelings as anyone else. Mother constantly reminded me of consolidating my marriage vows and educating Lynda in the ways of the church. I failed miserably, but still held the belief that all children should share the Lord's word. Leo was still a regular churchgoer, as was my sister, so I wonder where I went astray? Many of my school friends had also fallen by the wayside. The Salvation Army had a band, so maybe the church needed a facelift to attract the modern generation.

A letter bearing an Australian stamp landed on the doormat. At last, some news from Ray, after a year of hearing nothing. It bore good news but not what I'd been expecting. During the time I worked for Utah at Dampier a pay rise was negotiated, with them enclosing a cheque for 112 dollars (£47), backdated to the time I commenced working for them. They needn't have sent anything, I wasn't to know about any pay negotiations. What a grand gesture, proving what a fine upstanding organisation they were.

Bob Dowson, landlord of the Mill House pub, had a smile from ear to ear as I walked to the bar. The look on his face told it all, as I gazed at the newly installed pump on the bar top advertising Harp Lager. Was there a demand for lager? It was for a trial period only to test the market, with hopes for its survival not high. The new drink was being termed "cat's piss," suitable for woman only, or that "Yankee shit" seen on the films. It brought back lots of memories, and although it was nowhere near the potency of Swan, it still had the same effect if you drank enough.

Besides the new drink, the Crown pub near the town centre was undergoing a facelift. Landlord Peter Mackay was a cantankerous bastard, full of his own self-importance. He thought more of his Great Dane dog than he did of his wife, Mary, whose full time occupation seemed to be that of floor-scrubber cum skivvy. He catered strictly for the male, no-nonsense type, preferably over thirty, who would enjoy the drink and play dominoes without so much as a raised voice. The town's prominent citizens and businessmen frequently graced the bar, along with Sir William Chaytor from nearby Witton Castle. Darts throwers and music makers gave it a wide berth, with the younger generation not encouraged in the least - not that he'd refuse point-blank to serve them. Their presence would be ignored, much the same as the "black fellas" in Oz.

What happened with Peter's thinking nobody knew for sure, but a jukebox, one-armed bandit, darts board and snooker table suddenly blended in with the pub's décor. It was an amazing transformation, attracting clientele of all descriptions, coinciding with his previous regulars rapidly departing for pastures new. It's possible that Peter, a staunch left-footer, had guidance from above, but whatever it was he seemed to relish his new-found surroundings. It was always accepted that the younger ones drank more, so maybe it was a question of economics. Jukeboxes were still slow to gain a foothold in the pubs. The surprise addition of the Crown joined those of the King's, Queen's and Royal Oak, who for many years had carried the banner as the only rockin' houses in town.

Demand for coach hire was such, that the purchase of a larger coach was very much at the forefront of things. It would also allow me to finish work at the factory and concentrate full-time on the business. A long-established bus company from Manchester, A Mayne & Son, was selling some six-year old 41-seater coaches for £1,250 each. It was near West Gorton, so I decided to kill two birds with one stone by calling on Ray. Hopefully, with a bit of good fortune, he'd have flown the nest. Even though it was close to Easter, crossing the desolate snow-covered moors between Huddersfield and Ashton-under-Lyne was not the most inviting. However, everything went according to plan, and by late afternoon I was the proud owner of 9085 ND. Once again I was in debt, with £300 deposit and the balance on hire purchase. I was paying as much for a bus as a house!

I was told it would be very busy on the roads until well after six, causing me to rethink my strategy on visiting Gorton. I wasn't keen on driving an unfamiliar size vehicle in the thick of traffic. Another consideration was the weather, not wanting to cross the moors in the dark. Anyhow, what sort of a reunion would it be without toasting it in his local bar? Ideally, it would be better to come by train and spend the night, rather than just talk for two hours. Once again, so near yet so far away. It was only after buying the coach that I realised the problems associated with running a business, especially drivers. Some part-timers were a constant pain in the arse, either through drink, gambling or domestic problems. On top of which, they knew they had you by the balls, and would try to screw you as much as they could for a few extra shekels.

History was again in the making on July 21st, with Neil Armstrong claiming his place in the hall of fame as the first man on the moon. Only fifteen years earlier, I'd been glued to the cinema screen watching Flash Gordon and Creatures from Outer Space. Now it appeared as though reality had overtaken fantasy. Rolf Harris sounded the end of the swinging sixties with his No.1 hit "Two Little Boys," an unusual song with a catchy tune. I was pleased that an Aussie from Perth should herald the end of the decade. Welcome to the seventies, an era which for me would have as much adventure and heartache as its predecessor. Pure magic!

Ann passed her mini-bus test with flying colours, later upgrading to another addition, UTD 934D, a twin-steer 53-seater. It was the first time the examiner had encountered a woman bus driver, but his methods of examination were just as strict if not more so. Ann's handling of such a large vehicle, accompanied by her good looks, drew lots of admiring glances. The schoolboys she chauffeured even used her as their role model. Quite for what I wasn't sure, but I could guess.

I started a regular Saturday night service to

Sunderland's Locarno ballroom, the town for once having the edge on its Newcastle neighbour. We had the odd problem with parents concerned about the welfare of their daughters. For girls wanting to shack up with someone they'd met, I was made the scapegoat. They would relay a message home, informing their parents that the bus had left early, and that some kind old lady had let them stay at her house for the night. Either that or they'd been allowed to bunk down in the local police station. Next day the parents would vent their anger on me, having been awake all night fearing the worst. I could have told them the truth but there was no point. Anyhow, I had no intention of spoiling their daughters' fun. They were only doing what I enjoyed doing.

By now the relics of the area's earlier wealth had all but disappeared, with only disused colliery buildings serving as a reminder of the days when coal was the main artery of existence. Once the bulldozers moved in, it took little more than two years to mould the unsightly spoil heaps back into the landscape. For Crook, the town that was once the heart of 26 pits, the dream was over, never to return, along with the thousands of men and their hard-working skills. The Central snooker hall, for so long the hub of activity of the town's social scene, was being turned into a bingo establishment. Gone also were the "pitch and toss" sessions at Dovefold quarries, the majority of gamblers preferring the more relaxed surroundings of the bookmakers.

Gas was being projected as the fuel of the future, with the country assured of vast underground reserves of gas in the North Sea. In 1960, the eminent professors and geologists of the day had predicted that many of the world's oilfields would dry up by the year 2000. Future engine designs centred on the gas turbine engine, widely forecasted to power both car and commercial applications by the end of the century. As yet there were no signs of gas replacing petrol or diesel.

On the engineering front, we began to see a gradual transition in the road haulage and passenger transport sector, due mainly to the introduction of vehicles from the Swedish motor giants of Volvo and Scania. First impressions were that they were well ahead of the times, coupled with engineering excellence. Many cabs were still being manufactured in fibreglass, whereas the Swedish all-steel types incorporated many structural safety features as well as highly efficient heating systems, de-luxe upholstery and laminated glass. The main talking points were the quiet, turbocharged, highly-powerful seven, eight, ten and eleven-litre engines, easy operation syncromesh gearboxes, and power steering. At last, vehicles that catered for the needs of operator and driver alike.

Before the Swedish invasion, Leyland, Scammell, Albion, AEC, Foden, ERF, Guy and Atkinson, had been the backbone of Britain's heavy haulage since Adam was a lad. The British way of thinking tended to be "if it's big it's strong, and if it's noisy it's powerful." The Swedes proved otherwise. Volvo boasted that their engines would do at least 500,000 miles without any major problems, working hard day in, day out. Buses would be expected to double that, due to their lighter overall weight. There would even be celebrations among the garage staff when a British vehicle clocked 100,000 miles without a problem, let alone a million!

I mentioned Volvo and Scania to the Gardner diesel engine representative at the 1970 commercial motor

show. He laughed at the suggestion that the Swedes
would have a major impact in the UK, calling them one-
horse wonders. Also adding that turbo-charging was an
unnatural progression in engine design, and would cause
premature failure of components. He, like many others,
would have to eat their words in years to come, with
modern technology rapidly overtaking our lives. The
Swedes' fast growing sales were backed up with a
reputation for reliability, and to us workshop men they
were a generation apart from anything else on offer. It was
much the same as the Merseysound had been – a breath
of fresh air.

The same could be said about the cars and
motorbikes that were suddenly appearing on the high
street. Volvo and Saab supplied quality cars, while the
Japanese created a market share for the working classes,
with the likes of Toyota, Datsun and Mazda. Many were
supplied with radios, tinted glass and sunroofs as
standard, plus a host of optional extras. Once again the
main talking point was reliability, for which the Japanese
were also renowned. Honda's quality motor-cycles also
proved the point, providing fierce competition to long-
standing firms such as Triumph and BSA. Ex-Japanese
POWs were not so welcoming. They fiercely opposed any
products being marketed from the land of the rising sun,
treating it as a sign of government "betrayal."

Ann finally made her maiden flight on our first
venture onto the European mainland, Benidorm on
Spain's Costa Blanca. For her it was a bit of a culture
shock, especially the smells, the primitive conditions and
the armed police. Heading through the back streets of
Alicante didn't exactly paint an enticing picture either,
but at least the hotel lived up to its spotless brochure

presentation, which was a huge relief. It was the first time I'd been in 80F degrees since Oz, besides being surrounded by golden sands and crystal-clear waters. I'd been practising the Spanish language, with many of the words and numbers similar to Italian. I had a fascination for the Latin dialects, loving the way they rolled off the tongue, compared with German or Slavonic. It probably dated back to my childhood days, trying to imitate the American/Italian gangsters. My attempts didn't hit the dizzy heights I'd hoped for, but at least I could order food, drink and count pesetas, which were the main things. The only way to be conversant with the language was to live in the country for at least a year. That would have to go on hold until I received a telegram from Littlewoods pools.

In 1971, George Harrison's debut single "My Sweet Lord" stayed at No.1 for five weeks, even though it was scant consolation for the loss of the "Fab Four." On the fashion front we were suddenly being introduced to a whole new dress sense, with flared trousers, brightly coloured "kipper" ties and large breast-pocket handkerchiefs. Added to these were the tinted glasses and mandarin-type moustache, which were the trademark features of TV icon Jason King.

On February 15th the long awaited D-Day currency change arrived. The new money was easier to count, except for the elderly, who were opposed to change whatever the nature. We now joining the rest of Europe, using units of tens, hundreds and thousands, which would make the counting of pesetas, drachma and dinars much simpler on holiday. The timing of the changeover was five years, all but a day, after the Australians.

We had a major decision to make about whether to increase the family, a matter I left entirely up to Ann. We could well afford it, but she was against having any more children, so I went along with her decision. Maybe she saw me as not being suited to the maternal role. Whatever the reason it was quietly swept under the carpet, so I agreed to get the "snip." Two months later and £33 poorer, I was blessed with the privilege of being one of the early private guinea-pigs at Bishop Auckland hospital. At the ripe old age of 27 I was on the scrapheap insofar as increasing the world's population was concerned. I would have to rely on Leo to carry on the family name, hopefully after he was married.

Next on the agenda was a new home, something with more space and a garden. A small private estate was being developed on the outskirts of town, offering three-bedroom semis with garages for £3,050. Could we afford to step up? I would have to find the extra money for the additional mortgage repayments, which would rise from £15 to £28 a month. I couldn't work any more hours, with only the Beatles managing to achieve the impossible "Eight Days A Week."

Tony Christie was entertaining us all with his deep rich voice, which I felt would give Tom Jones and Engelbert a run for their money. I was convinced he was from the other side of the pond, due to his songs "Las Vegas" and "Maria" having that American flavour. Imagine my surprise to discover he was a Yorkshireman.

The old cliché of the customer always being right didn't always ring true. Often your patience would be tested to the limit, especially late at night when inebriated punters demanded door-to-door service. With trucks it was different. The cargo not demanding to call at the fish and chip shop after a boozy night out, or cause mayhem in Uttoxeter after a football match in Bristol. Christmas festivities were also a time when most people's inhibitions would run riot, with women usually the worst. Alcohol never distinguished between rich or poor, male or female, doctor, banker, civil servant, council official or the common factory worker. The well-groomed polite couples sporting expensive clothes, earlier conveyed to the Ramside Hall Hotel at Durham, were totally unrecognisable five hours later.

Most surprisingly the Locarno ballroom was never a source of festive problems, with the New Year celebrations a rather muted affair. The bus would only be half full on the journey home, the majority having holed in somewhere to party the night away. It was also the final chance for any last minute liaisons. It wasn't unknown for standing pricks to be performing in any position offered by a bus seat.

The past year had seen many changes. Not only a new home and change of currency, but also by a marked increase in the number of foreign vehicles. A former Beatle had got to No. 1, whilst the singer of American lyrics from Conisbrough was trying to find his way to Amarillo.

Running a coach business was a seven day a week job. I had little contact with Lynda, who was usually in bed by the time I returned home. Dad must have noticed this, warning me of the consequences.

"One day she'll be a young woman, and you'll suddenly wonder where all the years have gone." He was only too aware of my ambitions of trying to gain a foothold on the ladder of success, but it was a question of finding the right balance.

Finally we decided on an addition to the family, a golden Labrador pup, perfect company for Lynda. We named him Lloyd, after Lloyd Triestino, the owner of the Galileo ship that brought me back from Oz. Lloyd's kennel was kept in the garage, from where he could access the garden through an open door. He was never comfortable indoors for more than an hour, even in the depths of winter, preferring instead his own snug home inside the garage.

There was a noticeable increase in daytime trade, mainly due to young ladies taking their clothes off. Workingmen's clubs, keen to appease the demands of customers, billed these striptease artists as "exotic dancers." It created the impression to churchgoers that it was some form of oriental entertaining act, with the Lord's day set- aside for more things than prayer. Entertainers they were, but from the shores of north-east England, rather than Thailand.

The city also beckoned, with Newcastle's Stoll picture house providing even more delights with uncensored films. Patrons could now view the hardcore version of "What the Butler Saw." The seedier element would always carry a raincoat, come hail, rain or shine, besides occupying the front rows of seats. Once the film started getting steamy, they would proceed to fondle "john thomas" under the gabardine camouflage, thus earning the title "the raincoat men."

One day, after delivering punters to the Stoll, I proceeded to the nearby Bigg Market to buy a half-price coat in a gent's outfitters sale. Unfortunately the shop was closed for the midday break, so I just hung around for waiting for it to open.

"Have yer got a cigarette?" was the startling call from behind.

I quickly turned, finding myself face to face with a

bottle blonde in her late thirties. Judging by the strong smell of drink and her unsteady condition, she must have come from the nearby Half Moon pub.

"I'm sorry, but I don't smoke" was the only reply I could think of, hoping that at any moment the sign inside the shop would change from closed to open.

"Are yer gonna buy me a drink?"

"I'm afraid I don't drink." At that point she came close to my face.

"Do yer fuck?" she shouted, for everyone in close proximity to enjoy the benefit.

"Oh yes, but not for money."

She then proceeded to curse me into hell, accusing me of not knowing my father, and hoping I succumbed to galloping cock rot.

The seventies saw a boom in pubs and after-hours entertainment, with nightclubs being very much in demand. One popular venue was the Northumberland Arms, commonly known as "The Jungle", close to the river Tyne ferry landing at North Shields. The drink was good, the ladies even better. Newcastle's Bier Kellar was another. Its decor resembled a Bavarian drinking hall, along with busty waitresses in traditional German dress. It also introduced the females to steins of bier, and as the night wore on, dancing on the tables and anything else that appealed would be encouraged. Many a striptease was performed in public, the stage quite often being in front of the bus headlights.

My life had taken a totally different turn since my return from Oz. Reluctantly accepting that holidays would have to satisfy my passion for travel. From time to time I immersed myself in books and maps, momentarily escaping into a mystic world. In the real world I must admit to having been guilty of mixing business with pleasure, sowing my seeds on numerous occasions. I can't begin to offer any explanation as to my philandering. One would have thought that having a desirable wife who catered for my every need would have been more than enough, but apparently not. The appeal of a cloak-and-dagger liaison must have given me that extra high I'd been craving for. It never ceases to amaze me insofar as the lust stakes are concerned. A man can work twenty-four hours a day, or be on his death bed preparing to meet the good Lord above, but he'd always find the time and the energy to taste the forbidden fruit!

In May 1973 I heard that the elderly proprietors of Stephenson Bros, a long established bus company near Bishop Auckland, were retiring. Was I interested in taking over the remainder of their business and renting their premises? This included three coaches, special school contracts and an abundance of drivers. Though outdated, the garage facilities were spacious enough to house six vehicles under cover. The twenty-minute drive from the house would make my day even longer, but I saw it as a step in the right direction. Ann agreed with my thinking of expansion, expansion, expansion, as long as we were going to be rewarded for all the effort. It would mean that overnight we were moving up to six vehicles, the words "hire purchase" having a more than familiar ring.

What intrigued me about the garage was its height, which had been extended at some time by an extra four feet. Willie, the oldest brother, satisfied my curiosity. After the Second World War, passenger demand was such that extra capacity double deck buses were needed. In order to house the latest acquisitions, the height of the garage had to be increased. The task was planned for a

Sunday in mid-summer. Considering he was a devout chapel man, I was rather surprised he chose the Lord's day, but it was the only day when there was a surplus of labour in the village. He'd already had thirty steel extensions made; all that was required was the roof to be lifted by four feet. The most obvious solution would have been to hire a crane, but like all penny-pinchers the price must have frightened him.

Willie let it be known, that he would pay £1 to any man willing to work on the Sunday morning, starting at seven. The only stipulation was that no one must smell of alcohol. About forty males of all description turned up, eager to earn a week's drinking money for a few hours' labour. Willie dispersed his new recruits to all areas around the edge of the roof. Inside the garage, preparations had been under way for days. Makeshift scaffolding had been erected, and large lifting jacks, "borrowed" from the railway and colliery workshops, were in position. The object of the exercise was to jack up the roof a few inches at a time, inserting chocks as packing, until it was high enough to install the extensions.

The sole purpose of hiring the men was to try and limit the roof's sideways movement with ropes and crowbars. Willie had picked midsummer to try and avoid any problems with the wind. The garage was in an exposed position, 500 feet above sea level, and a fierce wind could whip up within minutes. People from the surrounding villages flocked to the scene, more interested in whether Willie would lose his roof, causing a bottleneck on the A68. The crowds were disappointed. Nothing went wrong, with no reports of fingers missing or bodies trapped. Churches and chapels reported a marked drop in attendances, while publicans complained about the previous night's poor trading.

On August 25th Dad finally hung up his trowel, looking forward to a well-earned rest. He was born on May 8th, but had to work the extra three months due to his mother's delay in registering his birth. When I asked him if he was ready to retire, he replied he'd had enough. His body was tired and worn out due to the long hours worked in years past. It was the first time I looked upon him as old, because I knew he was being honest. A heart attack five years earlier had left its mark.

In October the country was rocked by an oil crisis, due to Egypt and Syria being involved in armed conflict with the Israelis. The government classed the situation as so serious that they issued all coach companies with fuel ration coupons. Everything I had depended on regular monthly income, but if there were a dip in the finances I would be struggling, especially with winter looming. Being self-employed definitely wasn't worth the hassle, but it wasn't possible to get out, having too many commitments for the next three years. By the time I'd familiarised myself with the recently introduced VAT and the acquisition of Stephensons, we were hit by a fuel crisis. What do they mean about light at the end of the tunnel?

Swedish trucks were beginning to be a familiar sight on our roads, while the coach companies were gradually warming to the new imports. One local firm that definitely amazed me was Weardale Motor Services, a long established outfit, whose association with the Leyland badge seemed part of their heritage. It was something of a pleasant surprise to witness their latest acquisitions of Volvo coaches making their way up and down the Wear Valley. The Volvo's exhaust note, similar to the whispering jets, was most pleasing on the ear, compared to the Leyland's high decibel output. Dalespeople were usually the last to adapt to change, the only foreign invaders being on two legs, to admire the scenery. I would have liked one of the new breeds of engineering, but for the time being I would have to content myself with British second-hand cast-offs.

It didn't matter to the passengers what type of coach they travelled on, as long as it was clean, warm in the winter and not an antique. The main piece of the jigsaw was the driver. If he wasn't pleasant and obliging then you risked a sharp tongue on the end of the phone next day. Full-time drivers were no problem, and even though I now had an excess of good part-timers, I'd had a few nightmares along the way. The worst ones were those who never had a penny. I'd help them out by paying in advance, even settling their electric bills, HP, rent, or repairs to their cars. Despite all the help it was never appreciated, making me sometimes wonder if I was really cut out to be a boss.

Giving people in authority "recognition" for awarding you a contract, or helping to secure it, sometimes meant crossing their palms with silver. This form of bribery was an accepted practice with certain individuals. Sometimes these officials got too greedy. I knew of one such person who, once a month, would call at the garage of one of his "favoured" transport companies monthly for his envelope of pound notes. In addition, his car would be checked over, washed and filled with petrol. After a few months his visits became more frequent, his "back-hander" payments also moving to a higher level. He got the nick-name Oliver Twist, due to his constant requests for more. Then his wife complained to the owner of the transport company that her husband was frequenting nightclubs with a "dolly bird" in tow. After a year they parted company, the contract, the official and his wife being more hassle than they were worth.

A three-year-old 53-seater coach acquired in the summer of '76 had a remote Beatles connection. Coming from the same operator, Fox of Hayes, who had previously had one of its coaches used in the filming of the Fab Four's legendary "Magical Mystery Tour." Our coach was in the same original livery of blue and yellow, but unfortunately that's where the similarity ended, with definitely no magic involved with GNM 220N. Within two months of its purchase it sustained extensive damage, returning from Blackpool in the early hours. Luckily there were no passengers aboard and the driver was unhurt, but the coach was out of service for five months.

Lynda had a liking for music, having tried the recorder and violin at school, so when she expressed an interest in learning the organ we were naturally all in favour. The keyboards were becoming the latest sought-after sound among all generations, aided by the popular wizardry of Klaus Wunderlich. After an absence of twelve years, I was back again in Williams's music shop in Darlington. I little knew what I was bringing into my life.

Chapter Seven

Seeds of Lust

I can't remember who was the "first-foot" for 1977, but whoever it was must have committed some foul and wicked deed. That was the year everything came off the rails. Tradition holds that everything happens in threes, so three good kicks in the balls were forecast. The year started on a high. On New Year's Day my sister Anne gave birth to a boy, Ian, a brother for Marie. She'd waited nine years for the first, now she had two in three years. After that, things went downhill.

In May I lost the special school contract I'd inherited from Stephensons. Instead of being renewed automatically, it went to tender. My price was beaten and two of my buses were no longer needed.

August 16th – another bombshell. Elvis Presley, the king of rock'n'roll was dead. The world's greatest icon of modern music had passed on to greater heights at just 42 years of age. In the fifties, sixties and seventies, Elvis had been an inspiration to us all with his variation of sounds, films and hip-swinging ways.

Yet worse still was to come. After a full day tour of the Lake District I arrived home around ten. Lloyd greeted me as usual at the garden gate, but strangely the house was in darkness. On the kitchen table was a piece of paper. There were just two lines of writing.

"Kevin. I am leaving because I don't love you anymore. My solicitor will be contacting you about a divorce and the

sale of the house, Ann."

I was absolutely dumbfounded. Not knowing what to do, I kept staring at the words, hoping they would change. Uncannily, it was just like years earlier, but on the other side of the world, when I read the news that Ann was pregnant. The feeling is difficult to explain. Once again I was rocked back on my heels, followed by a numbness that seemed as though everything was moving in slow motion.

Ann and I had just had a mini-weekend in London. She'd been on about it for months, but as the time neared she seemed less enthusiastic by the day. She'd been having regular tantrums about nothing in particular, and the last weeks had been particularly stormy, but I was at a loss as to what was disturbing her. We enjoyed the sights of London, but the tensions between us seemed to be getting worse. Ann was somehow troubled in a way I'd never seen her before, with a self-assured, domineering attitude that simply just wasn't part of her nature. Days later came this final hammer blow. It stunned me for a long, long time, and totally re-shaped my life – but gave me an unexpected return to the fields of adventure.

But where was Ann? Phonecalls galore brought no positive news. Fortunately, our daughter Lynda was staying with her grandparents for a few days during the school holidays. I honestly had no idea what to say to a ten-year-old girl, let alone look after her needs. Despite all the upheaval, I still had to be up and running at six. First and foremost I had to make a living, no matter what pain I was suffering. It was a long, long night, as I desperately begged the phone to ring. I sat in the darkness of the lounge, chain-smoking, until the rising sun signalled the start of another day. By the third day I'd exhausted all lines of enquiry, with everyone by now well aware of the latest gossip. Finally Ann surfaced with the new man in her life.

This was the news I'd been secretly dreading. I'd been kidding myself that this sort of thing couldn't happen to me. Having tasted the forbidden fruit on several occasions, it seemed my past indiscretions were returning to haunt me with a vengeance. Ann's recent erratic behaviour was now self-explanatory. My initial reaction was to seek revenge, to harm the bloke involved, with the thought of being charged with criminal behaviour furthest from my mind. Although he lived out of the area, I tried to confront him on several occasions, but our paths never seemed to cross.

I'd found solace in drink on previous occasions, only this time the torment was far worse. At least alcohol drowned the pains of sorrow, if only for a few hours. I'd been hit below the belt a few times over the years, but this latest hit had definitely brought me to my knees. It was difficult breaking the news to my parents. At 68 years of age, it was a scandal they could do without. Privately I was racked with guilt, knowing that I was responsible for a large chunk of the misery that everyone close to me was suffering. Surprisingly, Mother's wrath wasn't directed at me but at Ann. Possibly she held a small part of my welfare close to her heart after all?

My relationship with Lynda was sadly never to be the same again. News gradually filtered through that I was being branded a wife-beater, alcoholic and womaniser, on top of being labelled an evil bastard. The tongues were wagging yet again, from people whose predictions of ten years earlier had finally materialised. The marriage that had defied all the odds had failed to survive.

Ann's solicitors seemed determined to strip me of everything down to the clothes I stood in. They seemed to be of the opinion that having a university degree entitled them to rob you lawfully and not give a fuck about the hardship it caused. Maybe I took the wrong path in life. I should have spent a few more years in education, before seeking work in the legal profession and changing my name to "Dick Turpin." If I wanted to continue in business I would have to pay my wife a substantial weekly income, so that she and her fancy man could enjoy a few of life's luxuries. As far as she was concerned, it was a case of I don't want you but I want your money, and I'll screw you for every fuckin' penny.

On returning home one day, the sound associated with the closing of the front door just didn't seem right, more like an echo. The hallway seemed normal enough, but a further inspection revealed the house was bereft of furnishings, apart from carpets, tv, bed, cooker, kitchen table and two pedestal chairs. Even the lounge and dining room light-clusters had been removed, leaving the bare wires hanging from the ceiling. I'd already changed the locks, keen not to have people wandering in and out at will, but entry was gained through an upstairs window I'd left ajar. I don't know why and can't explain, but I had a good laugh at the turn of events, which were petty, childish and totally unnecessary. Arrangements had already been made with the solicitors as to the disposal of the furnishings, but Ann was making sure she got her pound of flesh in advance. The neighbours must have been licking their lips, anticipating a backlash, but I had to disappoint them on that score. My life went on as if nothing had happened.

I gave my social activities a wide berth, keeping a low

profile, my confidence being at an all-time low. One week before Christmas, I made an exception to the rule by visiting the local club. Next thing I was aware of was being drenched by one of Ann's uncles, who'd walked up behind me and poured a pint of beer over my head. It was pointless retaliating, he was over sixty, and would have been fed with plenty of bullshit to fuel his actions. There was also the advice from the so-called experts on how to run your life. The by now familiar quotes of "I'd never get married again," "if she'll do it once she'll do it again," kept ringing in my ears, all from people who were still married. How could they be qualified to give advice? What the hell did they know – fuck all. It was much the same story regarding cooking. Anyone can rustle up bacon and eggs, I was told. Too right, but not twenty-one times a week.

Christmas was the only time I would have expected the empty surroundings to affect me badly, but for some reason it didn't. Normally the house would be covered in decorations, but instead everything was plain and peaceful, with no visible signs of festivities. One sore point was the lack of cards, letters and phone calls. In the previous eight years I'd helped well over a dozen drivers attain their bus driving licenses, at no cost to themselves. All had eventually moved on to other firms, who offered new coaches and better hire work. Most would have been aware of my situation through the grapevine, yet not one ever contacted me to enquire about my welfare. I didn't want sympathy, just an acknowledgement that I still existed on the planet.

On New Year's Eve I took a party to Durham for their annual Hogmanay get-together. By the time I got finished it was nearly three. Before entering the house I invited Lloyd to join me. The kitchen mirror was the only place I could view myself, so after a short dialogue with my shining glass image I raised a glass of whisky to my lips and toasted in the New Year. My only wish was lots of happiness for Lynda and Lloyd.

I sat on the lounge carpet, my back against the wall, with only the glow of the gas fire to light the room. I couldn't help but think of how the stardust romance, with all its earlier problems, had ended with two lines scribbled on a piece of paper. I was alone and unhappy at the middle of the crossroads. For the first time in my life, I didn't know what to do or which way to go. When the booze-fuelled reality finally took hold it was one of tears. Much the same as in Australia, I'd get over it. I had to. Drink's not a problem when talking to one's self, it's when you're tired of your own company that it has finally taken control. Next thing I was aware of was Lloyd whining.

I was now faced with the stark choice of carrying on trading as normal or selling up. I had no intention of working seven days a week so that Ann and her lover could enjoy further comforts, so the choice was simple. I decided to finish in October, at the end of the Blackpool illuminations. To keep my mind occupied during the long summer nights, I started a kit car project. The "Magenta" fibreglass sports car was based on the mechanics of the MG 1300. There was a lot of unforeseen work, especially in the refurbishment of rusty components, in what could only be classed as a labour of love. On a brighter note, I was enjoying female company from time to time. At least it indicated that at last I was getting back to a state of normality, besides helping me to abstain from the extreme rigours of the right hand.

One of the trade magazines mentioned that Leyland

buses were considering marketing their range of vehicles in the United States, with Raleigh in North Carolina as the hub of operations. UK workshop personnel were required for the initial launch. It sounded interesting, especially with a city called Durham only 30 miles to the west. America was another place I'd visited on paper, but with the government operating strict criteria for would-be migrants, it was difficult to obtain a work permit. If all else failed I'd consider marrying an American citizen, once I was divorced.

I had to get away from the area, especially the house. Everything I'd done in recent years had been family orientated, so it was time to sling my hook and move to pastures new. The only two problems that stood between me and my gateway to the outside world were my daughter and the dog, the latter being the more difficult. Wherever I went I could always return once or twice a year to see Lynda. With Lloyd it was different. Once we parted it would be forever.

Sunday afternoons always belonged to Lynda. We'd head for Newcastle or Sunderland, dining in Wimpy bars or Chinese restaurants. Next it was the pictures. I would usually fall asleep, until a dig in the ribs was the signal that my snoring was getting out of control. "Grease" and "Superman" are most memorable, while an extra favourite of Lynda's was the rather unusual choice of "Heaven can Wait." I never thought for one moment it would appeal to her, but what did I know about the tastes a twelve-year-old?

Whatever my future ventures entailed I wanted to be well prepared, with an HGV Class 1 driving licence my top priority. The main differences between an articulated vehicle and a coach were the length, reversing procedures and the extra weight, besides bending in the middle. After a few lessons I was raring to go, only to fail miserably within minutes of leaving the Darlington test centre. On entering the first roundabout I failed to notice a pedal cyclist until the last second, depositing the examiner in the footwell, after applying the brakes with full vigour. I apologised and begged for mercy but he insisted we carry on. I accepted the inevitable, so for the next hour it was more like a driving lesson. Two weeks later I took another test and was allotted the same examiner. This time I hit the kerb with the trailer wheels whilst negotiating the bridge at Croft, immediately voicing my concern. For the rest of the test the examiner sent me around every tight corner in Darlington. The truck had no power steering, and beads of sweat were running down my face. After a barrage of questions, I was granted my licence.

The more I thought about the Carolina position the less I warmed to it, while Australia seemed more appealing than ever. I had ideas for starting a garage, offering the latest in electronic engine tuning and re-conditioning of all major components. Being in the workshop was something I enjoyed, compared with the chauffeuring activities I'd been performing of late.

I thought about going into partnership with Ray, who was an excellent machine-shop technician. At least we would be on a totally different footing, not having to work in the bush for a quick dollar. It had been more than eleven years since our last meeting. His letter was still lying in my bedroom drawer, unanswered. Ray had probably forgotten all about me by now. I often wondered if "Coventry Johnny" ever lent him the fare to get back to Perth. Perhaps Ray was still in Manchester, possibly married with kids.

Times had changed. Travelling to Australia by ship was no longer an option. With modern high-speed aircraft, flying hours had also been significantly reduced. Once the business and house were sold I'd look for him. If Ray was back in Australia I could track him down, thanks to the modern computer systems that many government departments now possessed.

My final day in business was one of relief. Being tied to a job that no longer held any joy was just one of the battles I'd had to endure. The house was being sold for a staggering £18,000. Ann would be happy. She was now back working at the hairdressers where she first started. The divorce would be finalised within a year, so everything appeared to be on track for us both to be legally single once again.

My parents were naturally uneasy, but I detected a sense of satisfaction on Mother's face when I mentioned going back to Australia. The embarrassment of my divorce would be short-lived once I was out of sight. The next piece of news caught me totally unprepared. While I was making enquires about my flight, I was faced with the blow that returning to Oz wasn't quite as straightforward as it seemed. I'd been under the misconception that as long as you paid your own fare there wasn't a problem. Maybe there wasn't if you were touring or on an educational visit, but to start a new life there required going through the vetting procedure all over again.

The immigration office in Newcastle was now part of the recently built Swan House building near the Tyne Bridge. Its name was not even remotely connected with the Perth river or the grog. A chap from Brisbane told me point-blank that my previous visit to their country counted for nothing. I was being classed as a new applicant. I'd been expecting to go within days of leaving the house, now it looked increasingly likely to be months. One of my biggest drawbacks was not being divorced. I never enlightened him as to my previous problems, just showing him my Canberra-issued passport. It seemed too crazy to believe that the same woman was involved, not only in my return from the land of opportunity but indirectly in my future travels there. I mentioned taking £10,000 to start a garage business. After further form-filling I was given an unofficial nod of acceptance.

If I'd wanted to roam Australia at will, doing cash-in-hand casual work along the way, I'd have gone for a month's holiday and disappeared into the bush. Those notions were in the past. The thought of building up a successful business was very much at the forefront of things. All of a sudden the American job seemed much more appealing. It's just a pity I never followed it up.

On vacating the house I wanted to move as far away as possible. The south coast beckoned. I could take a temporary job as a heavy goods driver, visiting Lynda and my folks on my travels up north. My faithful dog Lloyd was my biggest concern. I'd even considered putting him to sleep, but the more I thought about it, the more I began to accept that any reasonable existence must surely be better than none at all. By good fortune I found a local family whose children were eagerly awaiting Lloyd's arrival, so in that respect I was happy.

On New Year's Eve I kept everything low key, with parties the furthest from my mind. Lloyd came in for his usual visit, with me toasting his future like never before amid a sea of tears. The road ahead would take an unexpected turn in the coming weeks, furthering my adventures, and introducing me to some of the places of my childhood dreams. As we headed towards February the house was finally signed over, leaving only Lloyd to break my heart. He'd stood up to things much better than I'd imagined, with no whimpering or crying at night, even though I was a poor substitute for the female touch. With two days to go it wasn't difficult to figure out that we only had a few more walks together, before heading in different directions.

Even though Dad was reticent in giving his opinions, I got the feeling he was disappointed in me, thinking I'd under-achieved. Both he and Mother would have hoped that their rebellious son would have by now settled down to a more composed lifestyle. I'd spurned chance after chance, even the offer of a garage partnership with my former employer, brushing them all aside to do my own thing. After gaining my technician's qualifications at twenty-one, I could have furthered myself in college lecturing in automobile engineering, or took up some local government position. The idea of parking the car in the same place day after day, whilst strutting the same old jargon until retirement age didn't appeal to me in the slightest. I classed those jobs, positions, professions, or whatever you cared to call them, "dead man's boots." Promotion was achieved, not through dedicated hard work, but rather through someone retiring or running out of breath, besides having to grease a few arses along the way. It's just as well the college tutors didn't have a similar attitude, or else none of us would have succeeded.

What I didn't want in the foreseeable future was repetition in any shape or form, like the past eleven years. Maybe I'd have a different outlook as I got older, but the way things stood I was restless and needed a new challenge. Mother blamed my neglect of the Lord among other less virtuous actions for things not working out, and no-one could blame her for sticking to what she believed in. Our relationship was much the same as it had been throughout the years, but I'd grown accustomed to the fact that no one is perfect.

Chapter Eight

The Fiery Welshman

The day I finally left the marital home, by far the most difficult and heart-wrenching task was to take Lloyd to his new abode, along with his kennel. I'd had it tailor-made, using hardwood for the floor and sides to minimise the risk of splinters, so it was a rather heavy bulky lump to manoeuvre. I was just about to lift it into the van when another pair of hands helped me complete the operation with ease. The helpful hands belonged to the new owner of the detached house across the way. He'd been exercising his dog before tying it to the nearby lamppost to assist me.

"Someone was saying you're moving out today?"

"Yes, I'm going down country for a change of scenery."

"Any place in particular?"

"Not really. Bournemouth or Southampton, just depends who wants a driver."

"What kind of driving do you do?"

"Anything from minibuses to trucks, but I was looking to get some class 1 driving experience."

"That's interesting, I'm looking for a class 1 driver with a current passport for an immediate start."

"Well, I've got a passport, because I intend going to Australia at some future date. My reversing of trailers isn't the best, and why is a passport necessary?"

"Don't worry about the reversing, that comes with

practice," he said, reminding me that ninety-nine percent of accidents happened going forward. "The reason I asked about a passport is that I run trucks to the Middle East. One driver has suddenly finished without warning. The job would entail starting tonight and you'd be away for about a month. Are you interested?"

Was I interested? Of course I was interested, but I couldn't begin to imagine the reality of being a continental truck driver, let alone going to the Middle East. After composing myself for a little over two seconds I gave the only reply I could.

"If it's alright with you, then it's alright by me. So, where am I going?"

"Baghdad!"

My new boss extended his hand. "I'm Taffy, Taffy Davies," His growling bull terrier was straining at the leash, desperate to meet the barking labrador behind the garden gate. I had Lloyd to thank for the chance-of-a-lifetime meeting. Baghdad – I was shell-shocked. I could mention the word fate yet again, but that excuse was far beyond my comprehension.

Lloyd jumped in the passenger side of the van for our final get-together, his new owners eagerly awaiting his arrival. Poor Lloyd. His only crime was being a victim of circumstances, in which his adoptive parents could not see eye to eye. Next stop was the Welshman's house, for a crash course in Middle East operations. I'd have to notify Lynda of my sudden change of plans, but my parents would take it all in their stride. So Lady Luck had returned to whisk me away on further adventures. As usual, I was getting thrown in at the deep end!

Farewell to Lynda's Sunday afternoon treats. Farewell to my faithful friend Lloyd. Farewell to the marriage blessed in Heaven.

Lewis Samuel Davies was forty-five. He'd been in road haulage since his mid-twenties, first as a driver, most notably with Dents of Spennymoor, then with his own trucks. Prior to that he'd been a regular soldier. Originally from Pontypridd in South Wales, he still retained the accent of the valleys, which naturally earned him the name Taffy. He was short and squat, but that certainly never handicapped him. Taffy was more than a match for most men.

In the early seventies the oil-producing Middle Eastern countries were rapidly expanding their infrastructure. They needed all types of goods, ranging from medical equipment and machinery to military hardware. Manufacturing firms in the UK had what the Arab countries required, so it was just a question of transportation. The cheapest method was by ship, but this took up to three months. Although road haulage was much more expensive, the journey only took between ten and twenty days. It was the price to pay for door-to-door service, with the oil-rich countries spending seemingly endless.

For British hauliers, the lure of trucking to Iraq, Iran and Saudi Arabia for mega-money far outweighed travelling from Leeds to Glasgow on a foggy November day. Many owner-drivers went into the operation without realising the pitfalls. The main areas of concern were vehicle reliability and finance, or lack of it. Some remortgaged their homes and possessions to raise the deposit for a truck and trailer, only to end up getting their fingers burnt. For many of the larger outfits who could afford to buy the latest equipment, the dream did come true.

Taffy was keen to try his hand at anything that would generate extra income. He was fully aware of the problems encountered en-route, thanks to his overseas experience in the army. Taffy's preferred workhorse was a Gardner-powered Atkinson (Atky). Reliability was without question in the UK, but operating in extreme conditions, on deeply rutted tracks or sand, or in temperatures over the ton, was another matter.

The sixties pioneer of Middle Eastern haulage was London-based Astran International. Their first overland adventures on the silk trade routes were undertaken using home-grown vehicles. These eventually gave way to Swedish Scanias and Volvos, which were stamping their authority throughout Europe and Asia, adding to the likes of MAN, Fiat, Mercedes and Daf. Bulgarian transport was state-owned, with a predominantly Mercedes fleet. Even though the country was just above the poverty line, they ran the most expensive trucks, with the route from Afghanistan to the UK regarded as the ultimate test. Thereafter Taffy formed a long-standing alliance with Stuttgart, his preference being the V8 and V10 powered models.

Taffy dealt exclusively in Middle Eastern operations, concentrating mostly on Iraq and Iran. By limiting his operations to two countries, he knew exactly the duration of each journey and could budget accordingly. By the mid-seventies he was running a dozen trucks, but being the true traditionalist he also had three Atkys in the fleet, two powered by Cummins. Among the many vehicles travelling abroad, the DAVIES name emblazoned across the front of each truck was always to be seen, whether in Belgrade, Istanbul, Baghdad or Tehran. However, the job wasn't without its problems. These long and challenging journeys tested the best of trucks and exposed many human frailties.

The unrest in Iran during the latter part of 1978 made Taffy ponder over future operations there. As the Islamic people awaited the return of their spiritual leader, Ayatollah Khomeini, law and order were the main areas of concern. One driver was stranded at the Iran/Turkish border for weeks, and had to rely on the International Red Cross for his survival. With one lucrative lifeline severed and a large income-tax bill looming, Taffy decided to concentrate solely on Iraq. He kept two Mercs and a Volvo, and sold the surplus rigs.

Trucking to the Middle East was the dream of most drivers. The jobs were never advertised. It was something of a closed shop for the elite, something I had no right to be a part of. I just happened to be in the right place at the right time. I had the credentials but not the experience. Even though Taffy's depot was only a mile from Stephenson's garage, we'd never met. His rigs certainly couldn't be missed, especially the GB and TIR logos, in addition to the bold lettered advertising.

At Taffy's house I was given an hour-long crash course in basic procedures and relevant paperwork. At the end of the briefing I signed for the receipt of £2,000 in various currencies and travellers cheques. Later that night, Taffy introduced me to a Mercedes truck and trailer at his West Auckland depot, and within minutes I was on the open road under a frosty moonlight sky. My only concern on joining the motorway near Darlington was to familiarise myself with the empty twelve-ton rig for the next 260 miles. Waterskills' factory in Commercial Road, London, was my destination. I was getting a chance to drive the best in trucks, so I guess you could say I was starting at the top.

Everyone in transport either knew or had heard of Taffy Davies, the fiery-tempered, cigar-smoking Welshman. Taffy was a typical Jekyll and Hyde character, heartily laughing one moment, then full of hell the next. Most of it was hot wind caused by pure frustration. Sending drivers away for weeks on end was a continuous twenty-four hour, seven-days a week nightmare. What made it worse was that he was a hands-on man, living the job day and night, even at home. If you were a day early returning from a trip Taffy would accuse you of flogging the motor, or if you were a day late you'd been on the piss. I've witnessed Taffy's impatience and temper on numerous occasions, with one incident at a filling station near Mosul in the north of Iraq coming to mind. Some locals were filling two 45-gallon drums on the back of a pick-up. Behind them, Taffy was constantly sounding his horn, revving his engine and gradually easing forward, trying to intimidate them. They would only be a few minutes but Taffy couldn't wait, classing his need for fuel greater than theirs.

His foot must have somehow slipped off the clutch, because the truck suddenly lurched forward and hit the back of the pick-up, upending the Arabs and covering them in diesel. The air was well and truly hot. So, after a thousand apologies from a now smiling Taffy, plus gifts of cigarettes and whisky, we continued on our way – minus diesel.

One day in the Londra camp on the outskirts of Istanbul, we were checking a damaged tyre when two drivers parked nearby sauntered across. The first thing they asked was why we worked for a "fuckin' bastard" such as Davies, unaware they were talking to the man in person. My response was that the pay was good and that I didn't have much contact with the boss. At that point Taffy chipped in, trying to keep his accent under wraps.

"Do you know him?" he asked, probably intending to enlighten them as to how nice he was by offering a beer.

"Oh yes," they replied adamantly, "we've met him before, but he'd be the last person on earth we'd work for."

Taffy kept up the charade for the rest of the night. He wasn't bothered in the slightest if they unearthed his identity. He loved dealing with bullshiters.

Once in Istanbul I got a telex detailing my loading arrangements and proposing I do a u-turn at Ostend and head back east. Things turned out better than expected, with Taffy bringing the Basra-bound trailer to Golling services in Austria and exchanging it for the one I'd loaded at Villach in southern Austria. Wife Jill and some friends accompanied Taffy in a luxury camper. They intended to have a few days' holiday on the journey home. Taffy's favourite holiday spot was Benidorm in Spain. His "party piece" was to tear a 1,000-peseta note in half, giving the hotel waiter one half, and promising him the other half if he was fed and watered promptly throughout his stay.

The medieval port of Tartous in Syria bordered the eastern perimeter of the Mediterranean, but in winter the weather could be cold and wet. A café in the town catered for all our requirements, with a full chicken, chips and bread served in a basket for the unbeatable price of a pound. The spits roasting the birds worked non-stop, preparing dozens for the table at any given time. Besides food and drink they also sold the latest counterfeit music tapes and clothes. I was interested in a Seiko calculator/alarm watch, which were new on the market and housed the latest technology. They carried a price tag of £120 in the shops and £85 on the ferries, but after much bartering I managed to secure one for £50, also acquiring two petite Seiko ladies watches for Mother and Lynda.

One cold winter's afternoon, Taffy, after having his fill, decided to have some shut-eye in the truck while waiting for the ferry to load. He set the engine running to enjoy the benefit of the heaters. Two hours later he was in a flap, almost to the point of hysteria. Someone had cut the truck's fuel line, resulting in the engine stopping. The fumes being emitted from the exhaust must obviously have annoyed the likely culprit, a Hungarian. The ferry had already commenced loading. It was impossible to execute an immediate repair, and Taffy thought he might be left on the dockside. In the end, amid much shouting and facial colouring, I towed him onto the ferry before repairing the pipe in the hold. Taffy was frantically puffing on his "King Edward" until the turbo roared once again.

The totally bad bugger Taffy was made out to be, was not the one I personally witnessed lending drivers from other firms a few quid to get home. Nor the man who paid for repairs to a London firm's truck and never recovered the debt. Nor the man who paid for an owner-driver's diesel and return journey expenses for ten days. It's easy to forget about the good points, help rendered and favours given without expecting anything in return.

Early one morning near Damascus, we came across an English truck that had collided with the rear of a large broken-down van left by the roadside. Sadly it had resulted in the driver being decapitated, due to his load of steel structures crushing the cab. The body had been removed but the scene of carnage sent shivers down my spine. Taffy noted all the details, and stopped at the nearest town to phone the Leicester firm. They seemed more interested in the damage to the rig rather than the young driver. The owner then asked Taffy if he'd phone the driver's parents and break the news, seeing that he had first-hand knowledge of the situation. I thought it was a rather cowardly request, but Taffy readily took on this difficult task.

Throughout the Middle East, the biggest scourge of night driving, besides potholes and debris, were broken down vehicles without lights or markers. This made them difficult to recognise until the last second. Added to that were vehicles with one or two wrongly aligned, blinding headlamps, or some with none at all.

A few years later, a driver working for local firm Stirk International met with an untimely death in Turkey. Ray Williams was travelling at night near Ankara, when he was involved in a fatal accident with a farm vehicle that was travelling on the highway without lights. After all the formalities were completed, it was three weeks before his body was flown home in a lead-lined casket. He was buried in his native Bowes, a village on the A66 trans-Pennine route. Snowploughs worked non-stop to make sure the funeral cortège travelled unhindered. Thirty-one year old Ray, a married father of two, was the victim of travelling during the hours of darkness, in a country where the law always sided with its own.

As a final note I must commend Taffy for the maintenance standards of his vehicles. He left no stone unturned with regard to safety and reliability. Even though he usually bought the trucks new, nearly two-thirds of the 90,000 miles they averaged each year was in third world conditions. It was essential they were kept in peak condition. In Taffy's employ, my breakdowns were restricted mainly to punctures and changing bulbs.

Taffy died in 2002. The fiery Welshman had a huge impact on many of us in one way or another, and I will always be grateful for that.

Chapter Nine

Destination Baghdad

DAY 1

My Mercedes 1632 truck, powered by a V10 320-horsepower engine, was just over a year old. It had a synchromesh, eight-speed range-change gearbox, with high and low ratios controlled by the flick of a switch. The cab comforts included a radio-cassette and dashboard-mounted cooling fan. Davies trucks weren't decked out with grids over the windows, built-in kitchens or air-conditioning. They were strictly top-quality vehicles, with two foglamps and air horns for extras. In the compartments under the bottom bunk were a variety of engine spares, including fan belts, hoses, fuel filters and light bulbs, besides emergency warning triangles and wheel chocks. Mercedes literature and vehicle handbooks were in the glove compartment, along with tachograph cards and a European map book. The tachograph was an instrument I'd read about, with the trade unions fiercely opposing its planned introduction in 1981, classing it as "the spy in the cab." The truck's two fuel tanks had a capacity of 700 litres (154 gallons).

The 12-metre (40 feet) trailer was of the TILT design, meaning its framework from the floor upwards could be partly or totally dismantled for forklift or crane access. A large tarpaulin (sheet) covered the whole structure, giving the appearance of a box-type trailer. A steel security cord passed through eyelets in the sheet, and around the complete trailer, with the two ends being joined at the rear by means of a customs seal. If the sheet was damaged, it had to be repaired using a special hot-weld apparatus to ensure it was tamper-proof.

Four 66-gallon fuel tanks containing red diesel were fitted to either side of the trailer. Two storage boxes were next to the tanks. One housed my toolbox, engine oil and water. The other contained airlines, ropes, a shovel and two sets of snow chains – snow chains? A heavy-duty tow-bar was secured to the trailer chassis, along with a spare suspension spring and two spare wheel carriers. At the rear of the trailer were airline connections and a towing hitch. If a truck became incapacitated, it was not only possible to tow it, but also to supply it with air to operate its brakes.

I knew the layout of the capital reasonably well from my coaching days. Buses could virtually travel anywhere, whereas there were strict limits for heavy commercials, with ignorance of the law not an excuse for incurring a fine. The entrance to Waterskills was only inches wider than the trailer. Reversing into it across the main A13 London to Tilbury road was no easy task, being busier than a motorway at eight in the morning. Not helped by the heavy rain, the tooting of horns, and the gesturing of lips, arms and fingers. After four attempts I managed to manoeuvre through the narrow doorway, much to my relief and that of the queues of buses, trucks and cars, who'd been witnessing my first reversing lesson in the real world.

My cargo was twenty irrigation pipes, thirty feet long and eighteen inches in diameter, along with several large boxes of valves and fittings, all bound for Iraq. On leaving

Waterskills twenty tons heavier, I was pulled along by traffic heading into the city. Eventually, after missing several turnings, being overweight for bridges and fighting no-entry signs, I arrived at the offices of Davies Turner Ltd (not connected to Taffy) in Queenstown Road, Battersea, close to Chelsea Bridge. They were a long-established international import/export company, arranging everything for firms wanting to export their wares to any part of the globe. The paperwork also included a document called a "carnet," which detailed the goods I was carrying in accordance with TIR regulations.

The "Transports Internationaux Routiers" (TIR) agreement, covers the international transport of goods from supplier to consignee, with the least possible inconvenience to hauliers and Customs alike. Many countries are party to the agreement, so goods sealed by Customs at Dover can travel unhindered to their destination. This eliminates the need for the goods to be inspected, either visually or manually, at border controls in the countries transited. It worked smoothly on paper, with documentation much easier and delays reduced, but what about in practice?

The carnet contained up to 20 pages of vouchers, with two vouchers needed for each country transited on entry and exit. Travelling to Iraq could entail passing through eight countries. At your destination the carnet was given the final stamp of approval. It was then returned to the International Freight Office in Newcastle, as proof that the goods had been delivered in accordance with the TIR agreement.

Then I was off on the A2, later linking up with the cigar-smoking Taffy at the M2 Farthing Corner/Medway services. He was also going to Iraq with a cargo of new-type aluminium scaffolding, his workhorse being a Volvo F88. Taffy climbed into the back of my trailer to access the security of the irrigation equipment, before double-checking my documents and currency.

Essential items:

- Passport (Iraq visa to be obtained in Belgrade).
- Travel Permits.
- TIR completed Carnet.
- Spare blank Carnet.
- Carnet-de-passage document (triptyque) for truck identification.
- GV60 document for trailer identification.
- CMR consignment note and manifest.
- International motor insurance certificate (green card).
- Vehicle registration documents.
- Sealink ferry / road / rail / return ticket.
- Driving licence.

Currency:

- £500 in deutschmarks.
- £400 in American dollars.
- £300 in Turkish lira.
- £100 in Austrian schillings.
- £100 in Yugoslav dinar.
- £ 20 in Greek drachma.
- £600 in sterling travellers cheques.

I was still up in the clouds trying to digest all the latest happenings. We were booked on the midnight ferry from Dover to Ostend. Dropping down the steep hill towards the docks reminded me of my last visit to the port eleven years earlier, when the white cliffs were welcoming me home. Now I was heading in the opposite direction, desperate to leave the past behind, but still with a thirst for adventure. I'd had seventy miles to familiarise myself with a loaded truck. Once we'd crossed the Channel I was to embark on a 3,200-mile journey, driving a right hand drive vehicle on the "wrong" side of the road.

The first bit of advice I was given was to leave the cab interior light on before leaving the truck, making it easier to monitor thieves. In the Customs office the carnet and other documents were checked and stamped, along with a community transit form (T form), declaring I would be carrying tanks of red diesel (cherry) across the EEC. The customs official then fitted a seal to each of the caps on the four tanks. Next the trailer was sealed, securing the contents. The seals consisted of a fine strand of wire passed through a small round piece of lead. It was then crushed with special pliers, leaving the official customs insignia embedded in it.

Within the EEC countries it was illegal to use red diesel in road vehicles, simply because no tax had been paid on it. In the UK its use was strictly limited to off-road vehicles and equipment. Red diesel is exactly the same as the white variant, but dyed red to distinguish it as duty-free fuel. Once out of the EEC you could run on whatever you wanted – whisky if it was cheap enough. With white diesel costing £1.13 a gallon and red being only 35 pence, the savings made on 264 gallons of cherry were all part of the economics.

Next stop were the offices of ferry operator Sealink,

where the stamping of forms continued. Then it was only a question of waiting your turn to board the ferry, with the butterflies churning my stomach even more during another spell of tight manoeuvring. After a quick shower I joined Taffy in the cafeteria. Other drivers were spreading their wings as far as Holland and Germany, us being the only ones for further afield. I'd be able to get some shut-eye during the four-hour crossing, my only brief nap in the past forty hours being at Leicester Forest services.

DAY 2

Next thing I was aware of was being awakened as we approached Ostend. It was four in the morning, so hopefully the roads would be quiet. After collecting our paperwork, we headed for the dingy customs office at top speed, followed by several overweight drivers desperate to be at the front of the queue. Here I saw the advantages of the TIR carnet, the stamp of Belgium customs taking only seconds. Then it was into the unknown, keeping a close distance behind Taffy's trailer lights as we picked up the E5 highway. If we lost each other I had a map book that would get me as far as Istanbul, but quite how I would fare after that I hadn't a clue.

The illuminated Belgian motorway was most impressive, helping me adapt quickly to my new surroundings. On reaching Brussels my cigarette intake had dropped alarmingly, more so by the time we'd passed the home of the famous Standard Liege football club. Flurries of snow greeted us at the German border post of Aachen. It was also my first introduction to the many nationalities of trucks in the parking area. Taffy had his usual large cigar between his lips as we made ourselves busy presenting the necessary documents. A volatile character, Taffy had no patience whatsoever. For him, everything had to be done instantly, besides always wanting to be at the front of the queue. The Customs procedure involved lots of form filling, not helped by the fact that they were all in the language of the fatherland.

The one form that was in English was for the "Declaration of Fuel." It carried the warning that incorrect disclosure implied tax evasion, and that violation of the law would be punished. The maximum white diesel allowed to enter the country was 300 litres (66 gallons), with tax payable on any surplus. Our passports were also photographed. This was standard procedure, due to terrorist activities within Germany's borders, most notably by the Baader-Meinhof gang.

It took two hours to complete the border formalities, after which time we made the short journey to Cologne railway freight terminal. Taffy told me to bring all my paperwork to the rail office. At first I thought he was joking, only later realising that the trucks would be travelling through Germany on a train!

A restricted number of road permits were issued annually by the International Freight Office for travel throughout Europe, those most in demand being for Germany, France and Italy. Once you'd used your quota of German permits, then the only way to transit the country was by the piggy-back rail service. This operated between Cologne in the north and Munich in the south. The seventies had seen a huge increase in freight across Europe, with countries opting for harsher legislation to protect their highways and environment from the avalanche of trucks. I wasn't aware of the cost-effectiveness of the operation, only that it saved nine hours driving.

In late afternoon the train entered the siding with two carriages, followed by a long flat low deck, possibly two hundred yards in length. At the end of the deck was a ramp to drive up. In the snowy conditions, I gradually inched my way up the ramp and onto the deck, before applying the brakes and securing the wheels with chocks. Another point of note was the electric train, a feature nowhere to be seen on UK mainline operations. The carriages were old but warm, with everyone assured of at least a double seat. Kolsch bier and sandwiches provided the supper, as we settled down for the overnight journey.

DAY 3

We arrived in Munich at six to be greeted by a severe frost, with Taffy's Volvo taking some winding over before bursting into life. The unloading process was a much less arduous operation, driving straight onto the platform. I was desperate to get back in the saddle, even though the thought of travelling through Munich didn't exactly whet my appetite. I was constantly playing "catch-up" with the rear of Taffy's trailer, with only the overhead signposts giving any indication that we were heading towards Austria. Before departing Deutschland, customs checked that the seals on our trailer "cherry" tanks were still intact. Taffy's reasonable command of the German language got us through the paperwork at Salzburg, but it still took two hours. Austrian schillings providing the transit tax payment.

I was warned about the penalties imposed for travelling too close to the vehicle in front. Trucks were required by law to keep at least one vehicle length apart, or risk an on-the-spot fine of 100 schillings (£3). Even though we were now out of the EEC, I was further warned that the Austrians were staunch advocates of the tachograph. The scenery of snow-covered hills and mountains was breathtaking. This was the area made famous by the film "The Sound of Music." Dad had brought three prints of Austria back from the war. I would often gaze at them for long periods, with the mountains, rivers and a shrine of the crucifixion on a forest hillside path having a magnetic effect.

A few miles further south we called at Golling services, famous for its ham and eggs, besides the piping-hot showers. Later, we entered the tunnels under the mountain ranges. My only other experiences had been the short crossing under the river Tyne and the Blackwall Tunnel under the Thames, but these were on a much grandeur scale. Next stop was Graz in the south of the country. Despite heavy snowfalls the roads were reasonably clear, but we were now confronted with another hazard – freezing fog. In Wienerstrasse we entered the office of Helmut Haid, a heavy-set, pleasant chap in his forties who spoke good English. He had a long-standing association with the Davies name, being instrumental in arranging return loads from Austria. After the brief introduction we were back in the saddle and back into the darkness. Thirty miles further on we encountered the Yugoslav border at Sentil, signalling the end of the tachograph regulations. After handing over the transit tax in dinars, it was explained that if we'd been carrying only sterling currency, the border banks would have offered a poor exchange rate, (refer to data in chapter twenty).

At the nearby Maribor services I was given my first lesson in fuel economics, after breaking the seal on one of the "cherry" tanks. We'd travelled from the depot to northern Yugoslavia on white diesel. We would now run on red diesel for as long as it lasted. Another addition to the trailer's accessories was a 24-volt pump. This could pump 60 gallons of "cherry" from the trailer tanks to the running tanks within minutes. I was advised to transfer the fuel discreetly out of the public eye. Not that we were doing anything illegal, as we weren't in the EEC, but anyone not familiar with the operation could be excused for thinking it was a case of ill-gotten gains. The mpg depended on what weight you were carrying. My papers put me at thirty-two tons, whereas Taffy was only eighteen tons with his cargo of aluminium scaffolding.

I was then introduced to the portable kitchen. One of Taff's trailer lockers housed a neatly fitted, twin ring stove, the locker lid acting as a table. Taffy was strictly a bacon, eggs and tomatoes man, even though we'd had something similar a few hours earlier. I classed myself as reasonably proficient at cooking, so future expeditions wouldn't pose a problem. Taffy was keen to press on, due to us not having driven through Germany. He suggested we drive the 400 miles to Belgrade before parking up. It was a tall order but he felt confident of the fog clearing, whilst at the same time issuing a strict rule of the road.

"If you feel tired, stop and sleep. The alternative's not even worth thinking about."

It had been twelve hours since leaving the train at Munich, but I was still wide-awake, spurred on by the excitement. As we passed Ljubljana and Zagreb, I chuckled to myself, thinking about bed-wetting Ivan. Dampier was now just a memory, thirteen years having elapsed. By now the fog had abated, only to be replaced by light snow. My last visit to Yugoslavia was in the hot August sunshine – what a disappointment. The speed limit for commercial vehicles was 80 kilometres (50 mph), as it had been since Ostend. The man from the Rhonda was travelling at 100 kph (63 mph), with me having no choice other than to follow him and his trail of discarded cigar butts. The signposts revealed Budapest as being 350km.

At Nova Gradiska, about 90 miles from Zagreb, we came across a challenging situation. A local truck travelling in the opposite direction had somehow ran off the road and embedded itself in the snow-covered earth. We had no choice but to slow down. Another truck partly blocked the road, attempting without much success to free the stricken vehicle. After such a long day we wanted to get to Belgrade, but I saw a different side to Taffy in the following minutes. He could have easily ignored the driver, who meant nothing to him. After all it was snowing, cold and nor far off midnight.

After donning some overalls and work boots I removed my tow-bar, fitting it from my front tow-pin to the towing hitch on the rear of Taffy's trailer. This locked us together as one unit. Our stranded colleague then connected a long steel rope from his vehicle onto the Volvo's front tow-pin. Taffy instructed me to reverse as quickly as possible when he sounded his air horn. Within seconds we had the stranded driver back on terra firma. It was just as well that I only had to reverse about twenty yards in a straight line. The whole operation was concluded in twenty minutes. Taffy accepted the driver's grateful thanks, but refused all offers of payment. Some stretches of the two-lane highway from Zagreb to

Belgrade were a recipe for disaster, so God only knows what the minor roads were like.

No sooner had we got back into the rhythm than a blue flashing light appeared some distance behind. It took the best part of five minutes for the small Seat car with POLICISE splashed across it to stop me. Taffy carried on regardless, disappearing into the darkness, leaving me to face the tender mercies of the local police on my own. Out of the car stepped a colossus of a man. He was dressed in a long, heavy coat with bright buttons and a flat-topped hat, looking more like a cinema usher. We had only one word in common, tachograph, even though they weren't obligatory in Yugoslavia. He clearly didn't have a clue how to read it. After consulting with his colleagues I was accused of speeding and was issued with an-on-the spot fine, the equivalent of two pounds. Asked for English cigarettes, I willingly handed over two packets. Then it was goodbye, au revoir and auf wiedersehen, before continuing down the E94. Once the Seat was out of sight, I had the needle constantly on 100kph. As I headed for the National Hotel on the northern outskirts of Belgrade, it was now 2.30am.

DAY 4

Daybreak revealed a parking area for twenty rigs at the rear of the hotel. The half-dozen present were a mixture of Dutch and Swedish, the one exception being Lancashire owner-driver Geoff Forshaw. Our first task was to call at the Iraq Embassy in Belgrade for my passport visa; so after barely four hours' sleep we took a taxi into the city, only to be told to call back at one. Middle East drivers normally had two current passports, one being issued with a visa for the next trip while the other was being used. British passports, with their rugged hard-backed cover, conveyed the appearance of something special, while other countries favoured a more flexible type.

The snow had stopped, but it was bitterly cold. I was totally unprepared for the Balkan weather, while Taffy had the benefit of a fleece-lined Mercedes jacket. Had I been forewarned, I could have brought some warmer clothing. Instead, I was strutting about in a lightweight polo-neck jumper. I was tempted to buy a heavy coat, but with the mention of Istanbul and Baghdad on everyone's lips I saw it as an unnecessary expense. We breakfasted at a small café at the foot of a long line of steps ascending to the football stadium of Red Star Belgrade, a top European side. The steps seemed to go on forever, as if to heaven, no doubt descending on the other side into the hell of action.

The toilet at the rear of the National Hotel was indeed an eye-opener. It was the hole in the ground type, reserved for tradesmen and pedal-pushers. You had to be careful not to slip, or be in an unsteady condition, when adopting the stand and shit posture. Our target for the rest of the day was the 350 miles to the Bulgarian city of Plovdiv. Hopefully we'd make it before four in the morning, having covered nearly 600 miles the previous day, in what turned out to be a twenty-two hour shift. In countries with no tachograph legislation it encouraged drivers to flout the rules, effectively meaning you could drive as long as you felt able. The overhead signs and traffic lights were a great help when travelling through Austria and Yugoslavia, even on minor roads, making them easier to identify from a distance. Back home, the signs were usually mounted on a pavement near a road junction, more often than not impeded by greenery.

We linked up again with the E5 highway, having left it at Cologne when we boarded the train. It had also followed a scenic route, accompanying the river Danube for most of its journey to Vienna, Bratislava, Budapest and Belgrade. Unfortunately we had to bid the Danube farewell, leaving it to continue its journey through Romania to the Black Sea. I then experienced my first motorway toll road. It was totally alien to its surroundings, with one pound's worth of dinars ensuring I enjoyed a few kilometres of my own private highway. At Nis, 145 miles south of the capital, we headed east towards Bulgaria, still on the E5. There were few hair-raising moments at Sicevacka Klisura gorge. With the wintry conditions, the narrow, debris-strewn road and a succession of short tunnels added to the drama.

At Dimitrovgrad on the Bulgarian border, a transit visa in the form of some brightly coloured stamps was added to my passport in exchange for a few dollars. Then it was on to the duty-free shop. Rothmans and Johnny Walker were popular in the Middle East, so I bought five cartons of cigs and five bottles of firewater for £20. This would do for "baksheesh." The weather was still cold and wintry. The towns we passed through appeared drab and uninviting. To experience snow and ice 600 miles southeast of Austria was indeed a shock.

As we headed into Sofia, Taffy decided to call it a day. We parked up alongside a eating house around ten, having only put 250 miles under our belts due to the late start. We hadn't eaten since Belgrade, apart from some biscuits and black, bitter tasting coffee at the duty-free. Steak, chips, bread and generous side-salad, plus some of the local brew, came to no more than £3 for the two of us, including the tip. Considering we were in a poor country, there were plenty of gold teeth on show among the locals. Was it a sign of beauty or an insurance policy for old age? That night I had my first good sleep for four days.

DAY 5

It was 200 miles to the Turkish frontier at Kapikule. We joined the ring road out of Sofia to avoid the nightmare of low bridges. Instead, being rewarded with cobbled streets, clapped out smokey cars and horses and carts. Taffy was keen to make Istanbul by nightfall, delaying breakfast until the border, whilst warning me about the worsening road conditions. I got the feeling that Turkey wasn't a favourite jaunt of his. At the border there was a queue of around sixty trucks, the majority being Bulgarian, Romanian and Turkish. Just days after leaving home, I was parked alongside drivers from Transylvania, the land of Dracula and vampires. Normally it took eight hours for Customs clearance. That was nothing compared with two, three or even five days delay, when freight was non-stop to Iran. This was due entirely to the Turks' insistence on doing everything according to their rules, with baksheesh a necessity to speed things along.

Taffy gave me a sly wink as he removed a package from behind his seat, before lighting one of his huge cigars. After collecting our paperwork we proceeded on foot to the customs area, with its dirty unmade roads and old run-down buildings. Taff emphasised to one of the clerks that he had something for the "gross chef" (big boss). We were then shown into a sparsely-furnished office. Taffy greeted the heavy-set man behind the desk, puffing on some sort of strong smelling weed. An armed guard and office junior were also present. The package revealed a Polaroid instamatic camera. These were all the rage back home, but the boss man's guard quickly tried to intervene, as if it were some sort of booby trap. He was silenced by a few choice words from the boss, no doubt telling him that Englishmen didn't do that sort of thing. Taking on the air of a military general, the chef then posed beneath a picture of Kemel Ataturk, as the flash lit up the room. Seconds later, there was his portrait. Naturally, Taffy offered the camera as a gift.

The big boss immediately barked out his orders, motioning for us to bring our trucks to the central area. Our preferential treatment caused a mini-riot among the other drivers, who weren't in such a privileged position as Taffy. Even after all the hype the TIR agreement held no water with the Turks whatsoever. After breaking the trailer seals to inspect the goods at close quarters, the workers also wanted a few cigs for their part of the action. Thanks to Taffy's friendly persuasion, we were on the move in less than three hours. We were only 150 miles from magical Istanbul, the gateway to Asia.

It was raining and definitely colder than London, shattering my illusions of bygone Sultans basking in everlasting sunshine. Our final resting-place for the day was the Londra camp at Bakirkoy, on the western perimeter of the city, four miles from the Bosporus. It was a well-presented complex, offering secure parking, camping areas, fuel, restaurant, telex service and a bustling mini-market for truckers and tourists alike. Many English drivers preferred the Harem Hotel on the Asian side of the city, but it was all down to individual choice. The showers were antiquated but most welcome. Even though we were in kebab country, I would keep to the basic chicken and chips for the present time, not wanting to risk any irregular bowel movements. Five days into the journey I was relaxing in the only city to span two continents. The skyline was awash with mosques and minarets. There, the legendary Orient Express terminated its journey from Paris.

I'd always held the belief that Yugoslavia, Bulgaria and Turkey enjoyed a similar climate to that of Australia, never once thinking that they suffered from the same winter extremes as beset northern European countries. But there were further shocks in store.

DAY 6

Dawn was breaking as we departed the Londra camp, having already topped up with "cherry." Within minutes we were crossing the bridge straddling the Bosporus waterway, linking Europe and Asia Minor. Open for only six years, its design was similar to that of the Severn Bridge connecting England and south Wales. Cleveland Bridge and Engineering from Darlington had built both. The twinkling early-morning lights gave the city an enchanting appearance, as the ferries plied their trade in the merging waters of the Marmara and Black Seas. At last my prayers were being answered, with the rising sun looking like it was preparing for business.

Soon we were subjected to a military stop and search. The young soldier clumsily moving around the cab with a rifle on his shoulder needed constant prompting to ensure that it didn't protrude the headlining. He found the cigs and whisky, which weren't illegal, stuffing two packets inside his uniform, followed by a handshake and smile. Travelling to the coastal town of Izmit you were never far away from the shoreline of the Marmara Sea, but the picturesque surroundings would have to stay in my memory for quite a while as we headed inland.

The area between Istanbul and Bolu was commonly referred to as "earthquake alley." The twists and turns involved climbing the 2,400 feet up Bolu was not for the faint-hearted. The biggest hazards were the poor quality of the road surface and the amount of traffic, even though it was the main highway to the capital, Ankara. The climb in itself was one of the worst stretches of the entire journey. The scene of many fatal accidents, it was termed "death canyon." On reaching the summit we prepared for breakfast, even though snowflakes had replaced the sunshine. The wintry conditions dictated that I immediately don some overalls and a cap. Taffy said that once you'd ascended Bolu you were in a totally different world. People living in Istanbul, the Agean or the Mediterranean coastal fringes, were totally unaware of the climatic rigours of the central and eastern areas. Who'd ever have thought of snow and freezing temperatures being even remotely associated with the land of eastern promise? Within half an hour we were on the move, with the ancient caravan oasis of Aksaray our target for the day. It was some 260 miles away, but at least the road was clear.

Overtaking with right-hand drive vehicles in foreign countries was a dangerous practice, but something you had to get used to. Lots of different systems had been pioneered. Some even tried angled forward-facing mirrors, but there were reports of difficulties in gauging the distance of oncoming traffic, especially at dawn, dusk or in bright sunlight. One of the advantages of right-handers was being able to keep close to the gutter, down to the last few inches. When preparing to overtake you would move to the right, to the very edge of the road if necessary, allowing you to see past the vehicle in front in order monitor the approaching traffic:

Step 1 – Pull slightly to the right.
Step 2 – Check forward vision.
Step 3 – Glance in rear view mirrors.
Step 4 – If all clear, pull out and overtake. As simple as that!

Around two o' clock, Taffy sustained a double puncture on the Volvo's rear wheels, his colourful expressions forcing even the sheep to run for cover. Two punctures at any one time was just sheer bad luck. Even though the tyres were practically new, they didn't prevent three nails from penetrating, two in one wheel. We were near Kazan, not far from Ankara. Fortunately, Taffy wasn't loaded to the maximum weight, there being only one truck spare wheel. After fitting the spare wheel alongside one of the punctures as a temporary stop-gap measure, we limped along for a few miles to a restaurant on the outskirts of the capital, close to a small airport. Taffy immediately made arrangements for repairs. He then introduced me as a first-timer to Bill Forman of Kenilworth, the proud owner-driver of a new left-hand drive Volvo F12.

"Welcome to arse-bandit country, Kevin, make sure you keep your nose clean," he said. "If you have an accident in Turkey, you're imprisoned until the other victims are adequately compensated, whether it's your

fault or not. In their eyes, if you hadn't been in the
country it would never have happened."

It was made all too clear to me, that should you be
the recipient of rough justice and sent to prison, then the
staff and inmates would fuck the arse off you. The
recently-released film "Midnight Express," with its
graphic portrayal of the brutal Turkish penal system,
especially the bastinado treatment, immediately sprang to
mind. Although Taffy was laughing, he was able to cite a
few instances, including that of a driver who'd been
involved in a minor incident and was banged up for five
years. He lost everything, including his back-end.
Welcome to Turkey!

The garage man set about repairing the punctures,
assisted by his young son. His wife and other children sat
on the back of his pick-up truck. They huddled around a
small stove and kettle, witnessing us westerners at close
hand, not an everyday occurrence in Ankara. The cost of
the puncture repairs was 1,000 Turkish lira, a little over
five pounds. Taffy paid him the equivalent in US dollars,
along with a few packets of Rothmans. The son, no more
than ten, was smoking, evidently normal in Turkey. By
now it was five and nearly dark. After a few beers we hit
the sack, using the dash-mounted hand throttles to run
our engines at 1,000revs for a few minutes to power the
heaters. The last thing on my mind when I took the job
was keeping warm, more a question of keeping cool.

DAY 7

Next morning there was a severe frost. The Volvo was
reluctant to fire up, its pre-heat system having little effect.
Taffy located a tin of "laughing gas" (Easy Start), spraying

some of the ether-smelling aerosol into the air intake. The starter was operated and the engine burst into life. From an engineering point of view, I was disappointed at the two-year old F88's refusal to start under its own steam.

Ankara didn't lift my spirits. In the outlying areas, the houses were dingy and dismal, much the same as the weather. The road skirting the city crossed some railway lines. There was a group of black-faced men milling around, as though they'd just come out of a coal mine. It had been a long time since I'd seen miners, with the clouds of smoke and heaps of coal reminiscent of Crook in the fifties. Besides being the seat of government, Ankara was also classed as the dividing point, the last farewell for many drivers. Freight bound for Iran and Afghanistan continued east along the E23, while trucks for Iraq, Kuwait, Syria, Saudi Arabia, Bahrain, Qatar and the United Arab Emirates headed south on the E5.

Two hours into the journey we ran alongside a huge salt lake, Tuz Gol, which looked like an endless skating rink, before stopping for breakfast at Aksaray, our previous day's target. Although the sun appeared periodically, it was getting colder by the minute. Overalls, cap and workboots were now part of my normal outdoor attire. I couldn't understand why we were entering yet again into arctic conditions, having expected it to get warmer. Apparently, rain, hail, fog, snow, thunderstorms, sunshine and sub-zero temperatures were common in central Turkey during the winter months. Taffy assured me it would definitely get warmer in a couple of days. Even if he'd told me about the conditions before we left the UK, I would have thought he was taking the piss. In my first experience of Turkish shopping, I found pointing of fingers and a few coins enough to purchase a crispy-coated loaf of ekmek bread.

The towns and communities we passed didn't appear at their best in the wintry conditions. Many houses were built with a grey coloured stone or blockwork, much the same as Ankara. Since leaving Istanbul there was a marked difference in dress, with the Turkish baggy trousers a common sight among all ages. Nearing Pozanti, the high peaks of the Taurus mountain range created an intimidating atmosphere, giving the appearance of a huge white wall of snow. The snow-chains in the side locker didn't seem so much of a joke anymore. On approaching the Tarsus road that crossed the range, it was obvious that clearance gangs had already been hard at work. Large volumes of snow were heaped up at the roadside. This was not only the main artery to the south of the country, but also to Syria and Iraq.

The climb seemed endless as we wound our way towards the heavens. There was snow, pine trees and greenery in abundance, similar to the English Lake district. As we neared the summit, everything was shrouded in mist. At the top the road narrowed, with barely enough room for vehicles to pass. Small pockets of traders hugged the roadside, bartering goods from their shantytown surroundings. A café displayed its offerings in the open, the temperature much too cold for the meat to be troubled by flies. Then it was the long descent to Adana, the road zigzagging for thousands of feet. This was another "death valley" scenario, as we passed the occasional remnants of dismembered vehicles that had taken the wrong path. The Merc's brilliant exhaust brake ensured sparing use of the foot-brake, thereby eliminating the risk of brake fade and increasing our chances of getting to the bottom in one piece. Fortunately the road was one way, allowing us more room to manoeuvre on the tight bends, even though our speed was restricted to around 20mph.

Gradually the snowy surroundings disappeared into the background. The further we descended, the warmer it got. The engine temperature appeared normal, but over the next few minutes I was frantically checking everything, even tapping the water gauge with a finger to make sure the needle was free. Suddenly, like an aircraft coming out of cloud, everything was crystal clear. With the Mediterranean in the distance and the sun shining brightly overhead, the sudden transformation left me dumbfounded. At the end of our descent we turned left for Adana, while just to the right was the town of Tarsus. It was not only famous as the home of St Paul, but was also reputedly where Cleopatra and Mark Anthony first met. Mother would indeed be pleased that her wayward son was passing through the Saint's birthplace.

At Incirlik, on the outskirts of Adana, we pulled onto a garage forecourt. It offered free parking, fuel and cold showers. According to the wall-mounted weather clock the temperature was in the sixties (18C). Taffy took it all in his stride, saying that in a few months I would be cursing the sun to hell. I dressed for the occasion, even stripping down to a T-shirt, or was it a false dawn? We were now in cotton-growing country with its Mediterranean-type climate. Adana was also my first fuel stop (300litres), with the diesel carried (both white and red) having taken me nearly across Asia Minor since leaving the depot. The Turkish price of 55 pence per gallon was half that of the UK, but still double the cost of "cherry."

Nearby was a gift shop selling onyx of all

descriptions, with a good selection of tables, vases, wine-sets, chess sets etc, in varying colours. The owner's business card introduced him as Groovy Hasan, a rather cool-sounding name. His phone number (17) indicated that at least he was the seventeenth wealthiest person in Incirlik. Somewhat off the beaten track, Groovy's best customers were the military personnel from the nearby American airforce base.

On leaving Groovy's we continued east for an hour, before losing the E5 for the final time. The E5 had been with us for most of the way since Ostend, but was now turning south to Antakya and onwards into Syria. This was where all the traffic turned south, other than that bound for Iraq and Kuwait. The return journey to Dubai took up to two months. The Med also disappeared from view, signalling the end of our European connections, as we headed east on the E24. High on a hill was a stone ruin, a relic of a Crusader fortress, built at a time of constant conflict in the Holy Land. The terrain gradually started rising again, combined with a slight drop in temperature, but as yet no cab heaters were required between the spells of sunshine and showers. Olive and lemon groves, along with fields full of crops littered the countryside. With 440 gruelling miles in thirteen hours behind us, our resting-place for the night was the TIR compound at Gaziantep, an important industrial and agricultural centre. It was dark with just a slight chill in the air, but at least the freezing temperatures of the past days had receded, allowing the overalls and workboots to be returned to the bottom bunk.

Saxophone Joe, a lad in his thirties, was the compound supervisor. His eyes lit up when he saw us, and he was soon asking for "good English cigarette." Joe, more dark-skinned than the average Turk, was blessed with a permanent smile under his London bus-driver's cap. According to Bill, Joe's name was an abridged version of something unpronounceable. The other trucks were mainly eastern European, the majority being dual-crewed. As soon as Joe parked us in line we helped ourselves to some Efos beer from the tatty fridge in his small cramped cabin, while he busied himself with our meal orders. There was an abundance of chickens, sheep and goats, so it seemed white meat and kebabs were to be my regular diet. For the next two hours we ate, drank, joked and smoked in Joe's makeshift cafe before hitting the sack.

There were TIR compounds in most Turkish cities and towns, dotted along the main highways to Iraq and Iran, usually away from the congested central areas. Garages, restaurants, hotels and even one-man bands operated the pounds, which provided secure parking, but not always washing facilities. Any mechanical problems could be quickly addressed by informing the owner, who was familiar with all the local trades. It was essential for foreign vehicles transiting the country to use these protected enclaves for overnight parking, safe in the knowledge that for a small fee you had the satisfaction of knowing you would wake up next morning. When travelling alone, the most important thing was to get to a compound before nightfall. If you had a breakdown, you had no choice but to sleep where you were, hoping that thieves targeting money and fuel would give you a wide berth. We saw the remains of an English furniture van delivering to Istanbul that had parked in a lay-by for the night. During the early hours, a substance had been sprayed through the roof air vents, rendering the driver and mate unconscious. When they finally awoke, not only were their belongings and money missing, but also the goods they'd been transporting.

DAY 8

We awoke to a slight chill in the air, but nothing like that experienced in Ankara, and the F88 fired up first time. The Iraq border was only 330 miles away. Was it possible for the temperature to rise so dramatically in such a short space of time? Surely they didn't have frosty mornings in Baghdad? It was just breaking light as we approached Birecik, fifty miles further on. The road rose steeply through a cut in the hillside, restricting our speed to crawling pace. Bands of young boys were positioned on the hill at various points, putting two fingers to their mouths and mimicking the actions of a smoker. I'd been instructed to throw some loose cigarettes out of the window as we crawled our way up the cut, or risk possible damage to the cab. I duly obliged the junior Al Capones by dropping two at regular intervals, probably twenty in all. This was my second experience of young boys smoking in as many days, with some no more than six years old. Birecik was our final refuelling stop in Turkey. We bought only enough to get into Iraq, due to the colossal difference in price between the two countries.

Since leaving Adana, the amount of cars on the road had gradually diminished to the point of being a rarity. It was the same for trucks heading west, none for miles then five in five minutes. We continued winding our way through the masses of lemon groves. A brand new French Pinguely telescopic boom machine was lying upside-down at the side of the road. It had parted company with its transporter on the way to Iraq, and would remain there until there was nothing left to pillage. Its only companion was a shepherd resting his weary legs, puffing away on a cig while his flock grazed nearby.

At one point the road seemed to rise forever, as if to the gods. You could see for possibly twenty or thirty miles across into Syria, with the fields below looking like a patchwork quilt. The only frightening aspect of the two-lane highway was the absence of crash barriers. One slip and you would be shaking hands with the devil. Although the majority of the highway was of asphalt construction, it was deeply rutted in places, especially on inclines where slow moving, overweight vehicles ground into the surface. Another constant scourge was potholes. Hitting one at ten miles an hour was enough to cause your teeth to rattle and temporarily jolt you out of the seat, accompanied by contents falling from the overhead shelves. After Urfa the road was particularly bad. It ran alongside a military institution. Judging by the lookout towers and armed guards, there was no chance of a quick getaway.

My main concern was the security of the irrigation pipes, stacked on top of one another. I'd checked them at the border when the Turks inspected the cargo, but since then the road had been one of bumps, twists and turns. Turkish customs had re-sealed the trailer at Kapicule so it wasn't possible to check them. Many of the places we passed seemed to have houses built into the hillsides, as if hewed out of stone, making them appear from a distance like large dolls' houses.

Breakfast at Viransehir was one of eggs, beans and bread. The bacon was long gone. This was a Kurdish stronghold, whose people were fighting for their recognised homeland. The people in the southeast seemed to endure a harsher lifestyle compared with those from the capital or Istanbul, besides being miles apart in their attitude and outlook. In contrast to the previous twenty-four hours, the landscape was wild and barren in places, more so the further east we travelled. At Nusaybin, we ran alongside the Istanbul/Baghdad railway, close to the Syrian border. Finally we turned onto the E20 at Cizre and passed through the border town of Silopi, before arriving at the Habur/Zacho frontier. Although the sun was shining it was bitterly cold, the snow-covered mountain scenery more reminiscent of the Swiss Alps.

Iraqi Customs insisted on inspecting our cargoes, which at least gave me the opportunity to check the security of the pipes. Transit taxes were levied on the value of goods, along with a commission paid to agents for translating documents into Arabic. Although the atmosphere seemed somewhat more relaxed, there was a noticeable military presence, due to sporadic clashes with the Kurdish freedom fighters from the mountainous border region. After a two-hour delay, we finally entered Iraq. Relief was etched on the faces of Taffy and Bil, now that the previous three days were history. They said that Iraq was the safest place of the entire journey, with the rig and your personal welfare at no risk whatsoever. To say I was disappointed with the events of the past days would be putting it mildly, the biggest shock being the temperatures. Added to that was the Welshman, who never seemed at peace with himself never mind others. The thrill of living life on the edge far outweighed anything he could throw at me.

The road from the border was a continuous downward spiral, similar to that of Tarsus. The undulating, deeply-rutted surfaces required extreme caution. Our descent coincided once again with an increase in temperature. Days before, we'd left the snows of Central Turkey for a Mediterranean-type climate, now we were leaving behind the snow covered peaks of Kurdistan for a land of palm trees and sand. Many of the flat-topped houses were of light or sandy coloured brick and blockwork, appearing much more homely than the Turkish retreats.

As we passed through the small townships, the kids gave us a warm welcome. They waved their hands in the air as if we were people of importance, a blast on the air horns encouraging them even more. It was getting warmer, possibly around seventy, (21C), with the prospect of a mild suntan most encouraging. Another striking difference was the dress. The women wore traditional long flowing black robes. A close-fitting type of cape, similar to nun's clothing, covered the hair and the sides of the face. The men were also dressed in robes, mainly white, accompanied by a loose fitting chequered headscarf in colours of black/red/white, although some of the younger males were dressed in western clothing. It was indeed a pleasant surprise coming face to face with Arabian traditional dress, although the films didn't prepare me for the reality.

At Iraq's most northerly city, Mosul, we parked up in an unmanned area, with the security of the TIR compounds no longer needed in the relaxed atmosphere. Nearby were five Turkish Tonka drivers on their way to Baghdad with bagged cement. They posed for a fleet photo, alongside their colourful and well-kept Ford Cargo trucks.

We dined at a cheap hotel, my preference being a shish kebab, while Taffy and Bill stuck to European diets.

There was plenty on offer, with one skewer being replaced by another until I'd had my fill. Everything was going along fine, until the none-too-friendly hotel manager suddenly decided to spoil our bit of fun and close the bar at nine. It was there that we met up with Keith, a driver with Hertfordshire-based Funstons. After a freak accident in Turkey, he was experiencing problems with his left-hand drive Volvo F89. A stone had damaged the radiator, causing the engine to overheat. A garage in Urfa repaired the radiator but not the engine, so Keith had to limp for the next 480 miles to Mosul on five cylinders, which speaks highly of the Volvo's mechanics. A local garage was fitting a new piston kit. Keith's situation highlighted the need to carry extra money for emergencies.

DAY 9

On the 280-mile drive to Baghdad, the Tigris River shadowed us on one side of the road. The Istanbul-Baghdad railway was on the other. Its course had been similar to that of the road since Tarsus, apart from a brief excursion into Syria. It was evident that the luxury of asphalt was strictly reserved for the main highway. This resulted in a noticeable amount of dust and sand in the pedestrian areas, hence my initial impressions of Tikrit and Sumarra being one of untidiness. Everyone enjoyed the luxury of television, judging by the number of aerials dotted around the rooftops. To a westerner, twentieth-century TV and traditional Arab dress looked a mismatch. The most pleasing aspects were the winter colours of mother nature, which along with the sun represented a typical English summer day.

By late afternoon we were parked up on a quiet

service road next to the IBN Fernas Hotel, close to the Baghdad International Airport Highway. My first visit to Baghdad, on my way to Australia, had been a tearful affair. Now I was back, but I can't say I felt exhilarated, more a feeling of a job well done. Ten days before I didn't even know Taffy Davies, now I was 3,537 miles from home, witnessing a donkey laden with wood being hurried along with the help of a stick. For the entire journey my eyes had been transfixed on the trailer in front, with number VBR 70R firmly imprinted in my mind. At least my new-found role and total change of scenery had helped put Lynda and Lloyd to the back of my mind.

With the Customs warehouses already closed for the day, Taffy was keen to familiarise me with some of the landmarks. After a quick sponge-down and change of clothes we took a taxi for the six-mile ride into the city. Placards at regular intervals on the airport highway advertised a planned programme of education by the recently-elected President, Saddam Hussein. The taxi driver was full of hope. A bigger airport was being built, just one example of a series of similar projects involving schools, hospitals and hotels.

THE MASSES PLEDGE THE PATERNAL LEADER PRESIDENT SADDAM HUSSEIN TO ACHIEVE THE CAMPAIGN AGAINST ILLITERACY WITHIN SPECIFIED TIME.

THE MASSES SHALL ADHERE TO THE DECISION OF THE POLITICAL LEADERSHIP TO ERADICATE ILLITERACY.

Our first call was the British club on the south-eastern side of the city. It was close to the Baghdad Cabaret, an upmarket area of hotels and diplomatic missions. The Arab doorman welcomed Taffy like a long lost brother. Bill and I were told to sign the book as engineering workers, which in a way was technically correct. The powers that-be tended to frown upon drivers as being the bottom of the barrel. The club was a spacious building within its own walled grounds. It housed a bar and dining area on the ground floor with guest rooms upstairs, and a swimming pool in the large rear garden. On the bar wall, a small bronze plaque depicted a Hurricane fighter plane. Words written underneath expressed thanks to the people of Iraq, on behalf of His Majesty's Government, for their contribution towards buying an aircraft to help the WW2 war effort. Fifty miles to the west of the city near Lake Habbaniya there'd been an air force base, with the British club one of the many legacies of the era.

Taffy was engaged in the latest gossip with people who were either in the employ of the government, or the many engineering and construction schemes. To help them with a few home comforts he would bring them certain items of food, this time being tins upon tins of pork sausages. The pig held no standing with the followers of Islam, being classed as a lazy and unclean animal. It would eat anything, whereas sheep, goats, chickens and beasts feed naturally off the land.

Later we visited the Anbar Hotel, formally the Opera, in nearby Ukba Bin, Nafi Square. Its heyday had long passed along with the military, resulting in its rather neglected appearance, but at least the meals were cheap and plentiful. Even though the night was cool I was comfortable in a short-sleeved shirt, so at least I wouldn't have to sleep in overalls or awake to a frost. Palm trees and telegraph poles were in abundance, the latter being overburdened with masses of wires. Baghdad appeared to have more taxis than private cars, with the orange and white cabs occupying every available inch of road. Unlike the truckers, who opted for Europe's best, the car owners preferred the products from the Far East. Our taxi driver spoke highly of his Toyota.

At seven next morning, under a clear blue sky, we reported to the Abu-Ghraib customs to register our cargoes. The Eastern Europeans were well represented, especially the Romanians and Bulgarians, along with their gold teeth, the smell of garlic and strong tobacco. Taffy had to report to the trade fair, where the new-type scaffolding was to be exhibited, while Bill was sent south to Hillah with his machinery. I was told to wait for a mobile crane, which would accompany me to discharge my water equipment. What surprised me was the lack of official dress within the Customs, with no distinction between the forklift driver and the manager. The reception area was little more than an old table and chair covered in dust. Directing operations was Mr Ali, a baby faced youth who looked no more than fifteen. Opposite the customs entrance a red Leyland Atlantean double-decker bus was picking up passengers. Nearby, outside a makeshift café, three women dressed in black from head to toe were loading a farm trailer with wood from a demolished building. Half an hour later the tractor pulled away with the women sitting on top of the timber. Were they labourers?

It was midday before the crane arrived, its young

operator grinning from ear to ear, probably expecting a few Rothmans. Also present to oversee the operation were three government agents, who I had to accommodate in the cab. The boss man was in traditional dress, whereas his understudies were more westernised, with one adopting the pose of Wyatt Earp, complete with Cuban-heeled boots and square tin belt buckle. Two sat on the bottom bunk, the other on the passenger seat. Naturally they all smoked, but my camera was definitely not for baksheesh.

"Wyatt" spoke reasonable English, so I asked him about the women loading wood. He explained that the tractor driver would be a farmer, the three women being his wives. They loaded the trailer while their husband socialised in the teahouse – lucky man. I was directed twenty miles north of the city, before leaving the main highway and travelling down a dirt track to a pumping station. This was to be the final destination for Waterskills' equipment, a journey that had started in the east-end of London only ten days earlier.

Almost immediately we were joined by five boys, whose ages ranged from seven to twelve. The pumping station serving as their playground. In the trailer locker containing my toolbox was a sack of nearly-new children's clothes I used for hand wipes or polishing. The boys took their pick, even finding a suit for the youngest, so at least the man with the funny accent had made them happy. The extra hands of the agents came in very useful for unloading. We were all mighty relieved at having a full compliment of fingers at the finish, due to the crane's jerking movement.

By the time I arrived back at Abu-Ghraib it was well past the two o'clock finishing time, too late to get my papers cleared. Unless all documents were stamped and signed it wasn't possible to get out of the country, and neither Davies Turner or Taffy would get paid. When I caught up with Taffy at the hotel park, he was stamped up, re-fuelled and ready to go, having unloaded his scaffolding at the trade fair almost immediately. He'd already contacted the Davies Turner representative in Baghdad about the possibility of a return load but had drawn a blank, before phoning home and informing his office he was ready to leave.

Chapter Ten

Return Trip

Taffy offered to stay until I was ready to leave, but there was no point. I'd got there and discharged my cargo, so returning was no problem. The Volvo then sprang into life, along with a cigar and he was gone. Also disappearing out of sight was the mobile café that had satisfied my thirst and hunger for the past days. My first priority was 1,300 litres of diesel from a station near the Baghdad Fair. The two lads manning the pumps greeted me with everything but kisses. After discharging 200 litres they held up their hands, signalling "no more", followed by the words "sex book, Rothmans, Johnny Walker." At all times I was politely addressed as "Mr," but it was clear from the outset that they knew all about the outside world.

I'd already been forewarned about the 200-litre limit, but I had no intention of hawking around the city for 200 litres at a time. We agreed on a carton of cigarettes or a bottle of whisky each time the truck tanks were replenished. They steadfastly refused to fill any tanks on the trailer, possibly for fear of retribution from the authorities. After locating a secluded parking area I pumped the diesel from the truck tanks to the trailer tanks, the reverse procedure of the outward journey, with two further visits to the station ensuring I departed the capital with full tanks all round. Since entering Iraq 350 gallons had cost me £28, with baksheesh accounting for another £6. That would take some believing back home.

Next morning I was stamped up and heading towards the border well before eight. I called at a roadside café, which was little better then a hovel, intending to try some tea (chay). It was served hot, black and sweet, but I backed down at the last minute in case it was unsavoury, settling instead for two bottles of pepsi. Heading north on highway one, I called in for further 100-litre top-ups, ensuring I entered Turkey with tanks full to the brim.

Just before the Zacho border post I was subjected to a military roadside check, with a barrier straddling the road alongside a small hut. The two soldiers were only interested in the amount of fuel I was taking out of the country, classing the diesel in the trailer tanks as a marketable commodity in Turkey. Turks and Arabs had long been enjoying handsome profits smuggling diesel across the border, some carrying in excess of 500 gallons daily. This finally forced the Iraqi government to take drastic measures by taxing excess fuel. After a short discussion with myself, I was faced with the choice of either paying nearly forty pence a gallon tax on 250 gallons, or offering a bribe. It was pointless dumping it, because I'd have to buy more at Turkish prices.

Nearby a Turk had pulled off the road and was draining diesel from a tank mounted inside his truck body. He'd tried to disguise it by covering it with goods, but the eagle-eyed guards were one step ahead. Once he'd drained the fuel, his tank would also be removed and dumped in the customs area as a stark reminder. I was left with two cartons of cigarettes and three bottles of whisky, having given a bottle to the water company agents. If there was no alternative, then 72 Iraqi dinar (£97) it would have to be, but I'd try to save the boss a few quid.

I had nothing to lose by offering a bribe, other than being shot, shackled or shagged! One glance at the goods on offer was enough to convince even the most loyal members of Saddam Hussein's armed forces, that it was only right and proper to accept gifts off an English gentleman. Inside the frontier post the evidence of diesel smuggling was there for all to see, with tanks of all descriptions lying abandoned on the ground. At least I had a genuine reason for carrying the extra fuel, which the Iraqi authorities were well aware of. It was simply to get home.

I imagined the average Turk to be law-abiding and honourable, with the chances of being held up at gunpoint for money extremely remote. As to him wanting your diesel, I couldn't be sure. The poor bastards whose fuel had been confiscated, would know that the foreign hauliers had plenty on board, besides being aware of the baksheesh payments. I guess it all depended on how desperate they were, especially in the Kurdish-controlled areas. There was a history of bad blood between the Kurds and the army and police. Taffy had insisted that under no circumstances should I drive alone during the dark hours in Turkey, so I stayed put at the border until first light. There was little on offer in the fly-ridden shop, apart from some unfamiliar looking cake and a bottle of 7up, but they went down the same as everything else. Soon I was in the land of nod.

Gaziantep would have to be my destination for the day. Incerlik (Adana) would have been an ideal target, but I was fearful of losing the light, with darkness descending around four. Three hours later I stopped at a rainy Kiziltepe for breakfast, ordering a cheese omelette (om-el-let) and a bottle of cola, added to which was a plate of salad and bread. Since crossing the channel, I'd noticed side salads as an integral part of the main meal, right through the Balkans, Turkey and Iraq. The few meals I'd had en-route were tasty and well-presented concoctions, despite primitive facilities in southern Turkey. The local chay drinkers were curious about the new arrival, whose steering wheel was in the wrong place. I cannot speak too highly of their friendliness, besides being offered the best table in the house next to a pot-bellied stove. When it was time to depart the grins got wider and wider, the elders sporting a fine variety of yellow and black teeth.

Two chaps from Lincoln were already parked up at Gaziantep. They were travelling east. The talk in Joe's office-cum-diner eventually got round to the pleasures of the flesh. One jokingly asked Joe what was Turkish for fondling "john thomas," to which he surprisingly remarked "saxophone," causing a huge roar of laughter. I don't know how it was spelt, only how it sounded coming from his lips, whilst thinking that the actions of a trombone would have been a more suitable adjective. Joe now had a new name – saxophone. The only disappointment was the showers, absolute shit holes, cold, dingy and filthy.

Saxophone Joe knocked on the cab door at five. To have any chance of making Ankara before nightfall, I needed an earlier than early start. Five minutes later I was on the move, forsaking the cold shave and teeth for a few hours. Cigarettes substituted for food. As I passed Groovy Hasan's shop heading into Adana, it was basking in sunshine. At least I knew what to expect once I'd crossed Tarsus, with the overalls and boots already prepared. The greatest asset of all was my all-round vision, instead of being hypnotised by the back of Taffy's trailer. The road ascending the mountain range was straighter than its downward counterpart, as the sun's rays gradually gave way to the cab's red heater control. The eating house at Pozanti was missing from the TIR calendar, but my belly was rumbling big time, desperate for nourishment. Over the past days I'd realised that to be a successful ambassador in the field you had to posses more than driving skills. A greeting and a pleasant disposition were the essential ingredients of the pioneering spirit. If you were moody or withdrawn, the job wasn't for you.

Two middle-aged Turks, rather bemused as to my overall-clad appearance, were keen to sing the praises of their early sixties Leyland truck. It appeared to have stood the test of time, with the owner keen to prove the point by revving the balls off the engine. Tamam (tah-mahm) was a Turkish word often used in our conversation, meaning okay/good, which I would later adopt, along with counting to ten.

It was obvious within a few miles of leaving Pozanti that Aksaray would be a more realistic overnight target, with a mixture of fog and sleet dictating proceedings. Reaching Ankara would have been a welcome bonus, but there were only two light hours remaining to cover 140 miles, an impossible task. Naturally it was easier travelling empty, especially on hill climbs, descents and acceleration, but racing against the clock in wintry conditions was tempting fate. It was a bitterly cold night, causing me to wake several times, but I was reluctant to run the engine to power the heaters due to recent arrivals parked alongside.

On arrival at Istanbul it was still raining, but two coats warmer than Ankara. A telex at the Londra camp advised me of a return load from Austria. My fuel reserves were better than expected, having returned over 10 mpg, albeit travelling slower and twenty tons lighter. Next morning I made a final diesel top-up at the border town of Edirne, along with some bread, cheese and tomatoes. Even though I was empty, Turkish clearance to enter Bulgaria was still a two-hour affair. Bulgaria hadn't changed, it was still covered in snow. At the duty-free shop, I bought brandy and cigarettes for Dad, chocolates and holy relics for Mother. The sun did appear over the following days, but generally speaking it was a mixture of snow, rain, fog and hailstorms, with the overnight Austrian temperatures in minus double figures. My return load, from Fuchs Engineering in Graz, was a wire-drawing machine destined for a factory in Northampton. What a stroke of luck, just off the M1 on the way home.

At Salzburg, a border freight agency, Schenkers, prepared the necessary transit document (T form) to accompany the cargo. It cost 170 Austrian schillings (about £5.50). Any minor discrepancy resulted in delays, so until I was more familiar with the procedure I would use the agents. On the German side the Customs officials sympathised with my plight of being a first-timer, helping me with the forms, and not even bothering to check my fuel. Driving on the autobahn was light years away from the rigours of the east. My next stop was the freight terminal in Munich, if I could find it. Most railway stations built in the days of steam were usually in or near city centres. On this assumption I would head for the centre (zentrum) and the railway station (hauptbahnhof), with sign language and nodding of heads eventually leading me to the terminal. It was easier being lost with a large truck than a car, mainly because you could take your time looking for signs or landmarks, or change lanes to suit. Nobody locked horns with you as long as you didn't do anything drastic, with people just accepting that you were another lost "wanker."

This time I was much better prepared for the "piggy-back" train. The loading was not half as daunting as in Cologne. Even though I'd been travelling alone over the past days, the atmosphere had been much more relaxed, without the border pranks and tantrums of King Edward Taffy to contend with. At Dover the goods I was carrying had to be cleared by the relevant agencies before entry was permitted. I was just thankful that I wasn't waiting to enter Turkey, or else the two-hour delay might have stretched to ten.

I was then greeted with the cold early morning air and a road sign displaying "Links fahren" (drive on the left), which felt strange for a few miles. I'd been away for 21 days and covered 7,100 miles. I felt elation, pride, relief, on top of the world. On arriving at the depot I was greeted by Taffy, who was more interested in how much diesel I had left than anything else. There were no congratulations or mutterings of "well done." Instead I was ordered to uncouple the trailer, don a wet suit and steam-clean the truck underneath, before it was dispatched to a nearby garage to be serviced.

An hour later I entered the office for another very important lesson: no receipt no pay. Receipts for every transaction had to be produced, so if I'd lost the one for crossing the Bosporus then I wouldn't be paid, even though it was impossible to by-pass. I'd already mislaid a Turkish diesel and parking receipt, so I was £25 down before I even started. Taffy wasn't interested when I asked for an extra ten pounds to compensate for the whisky and cigarettes that I'd given to the soldiers at Zacho to escape the tax. He knew all about the situation, having gone through the border earlier. Even though I'd saved him £87, that didn't alter his stance of no-receipt-no-pay, which I found rather strange.

Taffy's argument was that drivers in the past had tried to fiddle expenses so everyone was treated alike, with his accountant requiring all receipts for tax purposes. I had used just over £200 of the firm's money to fund my three weeks on the road, taking into account presents and personal items purchased, but was still highly satisfied with my nett wage. My first journey had definitely been an eye-opener, but the fun, excitement and drama was just about to begin. I wanted to be well prepared for my next excursion east, but before that I would contact Lynda, enjoy a few beers and maybe strike lucky with the fairer sex.

The majority of the next day was spent stocking up on food and equipment. Bishop Auckland's new supermarket, Hintons, offered a huge choice. My shopping list comprised of: pot noodles, packs of bacon, eggs, sugar, salt, instant packet soups, beans, marmalade, cooking oil, coffee, tea bags, biscuits, butter, cartons of orange, grapefruit and apple juices, powdered milk, tinned sausages, tomatoes, Irish Stew, corned beef, creamed rice, pears, peas, large bag of potatoes.

Equipment:

Twin ring gas cooking stove and two bottles of butane.
Small camping gaz stove for emergencies
Two esky-type picnic boxes
Two fold away chairs
Two clean five gallon water drums

Two heavy duty ex-army blankets
Folder or attaché case for paperwork
Kettle – two saucepans – frying pan
Quick drying shampoo for the cab's upholstery, pine disinfectant and flora fragrance

Many people held the belief that Middle East drivers were constantly basking in sunshine, besides enjoying the temptations of exotic locations. It was much the same with the meals, with the Middle East trucker never for once being depicted as an out and out self-caterer.

What I did appreciate was having someone at home, namely Mother, to keep my wardrobe washed and ironed. No doubt there'd be something I'd forgotten, but at least I was independent, not having to rely solely on others. One of the eskys would go in a trailer box, filled with bacon, butter and cartons of orange and apple juice, with the winter elements keeping them cool. Another rule Taffy insisted on was no cooking in the cab, being classed by the insurers as a potential fire risk. With a few minor adjustments, the trailer locker was converted into a kitchen. I didn't know how long I'd be doing the job, but wanted to be aware of everything around me. This prompted me to order some road maps of Turkey and the Middle East

Within two days I was back in the saddle, my next running mate being Gorden (with an e) Crisp, a seasoned campaigner. The things we had in common were age, marital status and offspring, besides enjoying man's three vices. Our relationship got off to the worst possible start. Taffy had promised the next vacancy to Gorden's mate, but instead gave it to me. Naturally, Gorden deeply resented me from day one. Whether Taffy felt that

Gorden and his mate might arrange the job to suit themselves I don't know, but I had to carry the label of an unwelcome guest at the party. His mind was put slightly at ease when I revealed my Australian plans. If I'd had to travel with Taffy on a permanent basis I would have finished after a few trips. Surely Gorden couldn't be any worse.

We left in identical trucks. At DT's Battersea warehouse there were trucks from all over Europe coming and going non-stop. An Irishman from Killarney provided the entertainment on his harmonica, sipping whisky between tunes. Half of the bottle's contents had already disappeared when I casually mentioned about drink-driving, but he was not the slightest bit concerned.

"The English Police don't bother us boys, if we make a mistake on the road they just refer to us as fuckin' thick Irish bastards!"

My payload was workshop machinery and an assortment of car and van windscreens. This time we were driving through Germany, so a West German road permit was added to the contents of my newly-acquired attaché case. After Yugoslavia we would continue south into Greece, before boarding a ferry across the Mediterranean to Syria. The tensions between the Kurds and the military in eastern Turkey were escalating. Taffy not at all keen to have any more trucks stranded in a war zone.

At Aachen we declared 350litres, even though our tanks were showing nearer to 400. The authorities were concerned only that the red diesel tanks were adequately sealed. Driving through Germany was an absolute pleasure. It was a chance to admire the wintry landscape, even though foggy conditions dictated proceedings for part of the way. It reminded me very much of A1 scenic route, and in parts you could be forgiven for thinking you were driving in Scotland. There were stark differences between the German autobahn network and English motorways, most noticeably the lay-bys, which were equipped with toilets, seating and recreational facilities. The service areas were similar to those throughout mainland Europe, providing fuel, restaurants and accommodation, but with one addition, alcohol. The UK motorway services appeared to be strictly money orientated, whereas the German facilities seemed to create a much more homely atmosphere.

Under EEC regulations, the permitted daily driving time for heavy goods vehicles was eight hours, which could be increased to nine twice a week. It wasn't possible to drive through Germany legally in nine hours, with the distance from Aachen to Salzburg being over 500 miles. Gorden was adamant that you couldn't fool the Germans by fiddling the tachograph. After all, they invented it. Police BMWs and speed traps were very much in evidence, especially for commercial vehicles on long downward gradients. Speed limits were strictly enforced by automatic cameras.

Our first break near Frankfurt Main Airport coincided with visiting a sex shop, the onus being on cheap books for baksheesh. I'd visited these establishments before but this one had everything imaginable, from flavoured french letters to torture chambers. Gorden suggested a mixture of sex books, saying that the philosophy of many men in Turkey and the Middle East; seemed to favour the boy for pleasure and the woman for babies. In western society, boys, girls, men and woman enjoyed a more liberal level of socialising than those in Islamic countries, where cultures and religion tended to be the dominant factors. I bought 17 deutchmarks (£4) worth of books, each containing a few pages of immoral acts between males. Just for good measure I also purchased a few conventional books that would help rock me to sleep.

After leaving the E5 highway to continue its journey eastwards we headed south, with Wiesbaden 30 miles to the west. Wiesbaden, a city of 160,000 inhabitants, is internationally renowned as a health resort due to its rock-salt springs. That was according to the unusual six feet long by ten inches wide map that dad had brought back from the war, covering the path of the Rhine from Cologne to Wiesbaden. Besides the many colourful illustrations of the towns and cities hugging its banks it also detailed a wealth of information, from the celebrated wine-growing town of Bacharach, to the heights of Drachenfels and its ten-minute cog-wheel railway journey. The scroll-type map was kept in an old shoebox on top of Mother's wardrobe, next to a large brown envelope containing Dad's platoon photograph, pictures of Bailey bridges across the Rhine and his army paybook. There was also a small hardback publication entitled "French for Travellers and Troops." During my younger days the contents would get an occasional airing at my insistence, the map being all I was interested in, besides wanting to know the French word for bicycle.

The expiry of our legal nine-hour driving time coincided with parking up at Heidelberg, south of Mannheim, having travelled 400 miles since Ostend. It gave me the opportunity to don the chef's hat for the first time and try out the kitchen, with Gorden ordering his usual eggs, chips and beans. I wasn't enjoying the healthiest of diets, but hopefully the daily abuse of the frying pan would only cause temporary calorific disharmony. We were keen to be on the move just as soon as our eleven hours' compulsory resting time had expired. My sleeping arrangements were now much better, thanks to the extra blankets. At four next morning we were back in the saddle, leaving the boundaries of the Rhine at Karlsruhe and heading southeast on the E11 towards Stuttgart and Munich. On arrival at the Freilassing Customs, we were required not only to produce our paperwork but also two days' tachogragh cards. Any speeding violations recorded with the automatic cameras throughout the journey would have already been noted, resulting in an on-the-spot fine.

Once in Austria our first job was to replenish the running tanks at Golling services, having travelled 1,143 miles since leaving the depot. The large 16-litre engines returned over 7mpg, helped enormously by the European speed limit and the unladen journey to London. After showering, the mouth-watering ham, eggs, bread rolls and coffee for a bargain price of thirty Austrian schillings (£1) proved to be irresistible. In Graz we parked for the night near the offices of Helmut Haid, with Gorden suggesting we have a look at the ladies. Even though it was nine and we'd covered over 450 miles, the latter part illegally, the sight of a fair maiden would surely banish the cobwebs from my eyelids. Helmut was still working at his desk when we entered the office, with the by now traditional handshakes all round, plus the latest gossip, before moving further along the strasse for a brief overture to heaven. After sampling a glass or two of excellent bier, the madame of the establishment introduced us to some stunning females, certainly causing an acceleration of the heartbeat. Later we retired to the rear quarters, engaging with the frauleins in further adrenaline pumping activities, using the rest of Taffy's baksheesh money to pay for the pleasure.

In daylight, the drop in standards on either side of the Austrian/Yugoslav border was alarming. The quality of the road surface, coupled to the general untidiness, made it difficult to believe that Ljubljana and Graz were only 120 miles apart. We'd just left a country of impeccable charm, which could only be described as the last bastion of northern European culture. At least the weather had improved, even though there was still a chill in the air. Road conditions in Yugoslavia dictated that there would be many fatalities, signified by crosses, wreaths and flowers placed at regular intervals along the highway. Much of it was two-lane, old and worn, with a constant bump, bump, bump, when travelling across the undulating surfaces. Apparently accidents were at their peak during the holiday season, many involving Turks returning home after working in the German car factories, besides local drivers favouring a regular tipple.

At the National Hotel in Belgrade we joined other British and Swedish drivers to exchange banter. The bar manager, a friend of Gorden, was always on the lookout to top up his income and was keen to buy any drink acquired from the duty free in Bulgaria. Seemingly, a few quid profit, plus a few beers, was the reward for a gallon bottle of Scotch whisky.

Our objective was the Greek port of Volos, a distance of 550 miles, a new experience for us both. The ferry wasn't departing for another sixty hours, allowing me plenty of time to enjoy the sights, targeting the northern Greek port of Thessaloniki (Salonica) as our resting-place for the night. There were a few hair-raising moments between Skopje and the Greek border, when the snow briefly returned with a vengeance on the high windswept terrain. At the border we were charged the princely sum of 600drachma (£7) road tax, which was peanuts compared with the £224 to transit Turkey. Possibly the imminent admission of the country into the European Community had some bearing on the low tariff. Close to midnight we parked up, with visions of snow chains long gone.

We awoke to the delights of the bright March sunshine before heading south along the coastal highway. The last of the bacon and eggs provided the morning meal between Katerini and Larisa. We had Mount Olympus and the clear blue waters of the Aegean for company, a perfect combination. I was warned that the roads in Greece could be as lethal as a skating rink in wet conditions. This was confirmed by the small shrines dotted along the roadside, with photographs of the deceased alongside Jesus or the Madonna.

Volos was a popular weekend retreat and holiday destination for the Greeks, with the boats and yachts moored alongside the promenade giving the place a picture-postcard look. The ferry looked more like a cruise ship than a workhorse, making the voyage appear much more attractive than the trek through Turkey. A chap on the prom, whose only workbench was a wooden crate, was repairing and refilling lighters, even plastic ones. Back home they were thrown away when empty, with no means of filling them. The Greek had other ideas. He promptly drilled a small hole in the base, fitted a valve and filled the lighter with fuel, whilst also renewing the flint. The operation was completed in less than a minute for the equivalent of 10 pence. While sunning ourselves outside a café we met up with an Iraq bound Falcongate owner-driver (subbie), with the Glaswegian suggesting we order a large pizza between the three of us. It was my first. When it arrived on a large round tray, it measured two feet in diameter and an inch thick, with the ham, cheese and tomato flavour absolutely luscious.

The ferry had three loading levels plus the deck. The flights of stairs from the hold seemed endless, making the channel ferries seem tiny by comparison. Large steel containers were stored on the deck, as were the refrigerated trailers, coupled to electrical power points. Tankers containing inflammable liquids were also kept in the open, ensuring that in the event of a mishap the offending cargo could be dumped overboard. The "Challenger" vessel was only recently off the stocks. Its owners, the Nordoe Line, were based in the Swedish port of Malmo. It seemed the Scandinavians, who were already staking their claim in the transport, music and strong lager sector, were also attempting to be masters of the oceans. We were the only Brits among the ferry's full compliment of 175 truckers, with Swedes, Dutch and Germans in the majority. All the deluxe double bunk cabins had en-suite shower and private bath, besides being fully air-conditioned and heated to cover all climates. There was also a small cinema, shop, telex and radiotelephone facilities for the latest information. The restaurant and bar areas were decked out to a luxurious standard.

We would all be living the life of Riley for the best part of three days. Our chartered course would take us down through the Aegean, past the Cyclades and Rhodes, before joining the Mediterranean. We'd then head east, passing Cyprus, before finally docking in the Syrian port of Tartous, 120 miles north of Beirut. One thing definitely lacking was a gym, or a small indoor swimming pool to keep the mind and body occupied. I would imagine in the summer months that the trip would have been most enjoyable, but the weather was a mixture of wind and rain, the rough seas limiting our wanderings on deck. An abundance of drink and boredom was a recipe for disaster, leaving the majority of drivers pissed off after a couple of days. I would keep myself occupied in the bottom loading deck, cleaning the truck or reading, with the drone of the ship's engines for company. I also had a "Teach Yourself German" cassette which I would play for hours on end, but found the phrase book more helpful. According to hearsay, anyone with a Scots accent is best equipped to speak the German language, so I guess a Geordie dialect is second best.

By the third day we were all pleased to see Syria, with the weather warmer but raining heavily. Further transit stamps were added to my passport, with Gorden having lost count of the number he'd filled in during his six years of globetrotting. As best we could ascertain the Iraq border was about 270 miles, with us keen to get some miles under our belts, even though it was dark before all the formalities were completed. Between Tartous and the oil refining town of Homs the road conditions were appalling, the worst I'd ever seen, with ruts and stones all over the place. It was like driving along a riverbed. Despite all that it was busier than a motorway, with Arab truckers nose to tail in every direction. The majority displayed only one headlamp and some none at all, relying solely on others for guidance.

On skirting the northern boundary of Lebanon we suddenly embarked on a large collection of market stalls, selling everything from needle and thread to "happy-backy." Each stall had at least two high-powered gas lamps, giving the place the appearance of a mini sunset-strip. Amazingly, the road travelled through the middle of the market. This reduced the flow of traffic to walking pace, convenient for traders to barter their goods. I'd bought a few items on the ferry, seeing that we were missing out on the Bulgarian duty-free shop. With four cartons of Marlborough for £5, this place put them all to shame. All the leading brands of cigarettes, drinks, watches and leather goods were in abundance, while the "Lebanese gold" would be of more interest to the Dutch chauffeurs. Even though the police were in attendance, it was quite obvious they were being paid to look the other way.

By midnight it had taken four hours to travel 60 miles, but the road from Homs to Damascus was very quiet indeed. Sometimes lights would appear in the distance, indicating some activity or township, but on arrival the streets would be a deserted with not a soul in sight, just masses of fluorescent lights. I guess it was understandable at such a late hour, with many resting in their beds, preparing to be up and about at sunrise. Shortly before Damascus we turned onto the desert road towards Iraq. Although the surface was asphalt our eyes were constantly peeled for potholes, large stones or abandoned vehicles, with Gorden and Jock taking turns to lead the way. At least we had the benefit of a sealed road, however bad, whereas trucks heading south to Saudi and the UAE had the added problem of having to run part of the journey on sand. At Sad'Biyar we parked up for the night, even though we fell short of our target. With no CB radios, we had no way of communicating with each other, so when Jock pulled off the road and doused his lights we knew he'd had enough. Conditions had taken their toll on the eyes and mind, making it unsafe to continue. The golden rule is to stop at the first signs of elephants crossing the road.

The Syria/Iraq frontier post left a lot to be desired. It was a group of ancient buildings in the middle of nowhere serviced by two dirt tracks, one east, one west. The surroundings certainly didn't reflect the mood of the office staff, who were their usual courteous selves. The Arab drivers were keen to inspect the German-manufactured vehicles with the steering wheel on the wrong side. The Middle East also favoured Stuttgart engineering, with nearly all the minibuses and trucks carrying the Mercedes emblem.

It wasn't until we stopped for a pepsi at the bus depot in Rutba that I noticed my "Long Vehicle" signs were missing, with the thief having either removed them when we were sleeping, or at the border. No doubt he'd be the envy of his trucker mates when they were displayed on his vehicle, increasing his status no end. Rutba was little more than an oasis in the desert, a halfway house for travellers from Baghdad, Damascus and Jordan. The bus depot, which resembled a military establishment, was buzzing with passengers, mainly women. Maybe it was an important day in the Islamic calendar? They were all dressed in long robes, with some having black tattoos on their fingers, hands and face, an odd mixture of dots, dashes and lines, which I was told signified beauty and fertility.

For the next 180 miles the asphalt strip ran through the desert, with only mountains of sand and camels for company. Later we passed by Ramadi, Lake Habbaniya and Falluja. Jock and I then entered the sand-covered Haswa customs park twenty miles to the west of the capital, while Gorden was faced with a further 300-mile drive south to the Gulf port of Basra with welding supplies.

Another Liverpool-based Falcongate rig was in attendance, its Brummy driver a stocky bundle of dynamite. Peter Stockdale was in his late twenties, chasing the big bucks to invest in a hairdressing business along with his future bride. He'd travelled overland in the company of two Swedes, with nothing drastic to report in eastern Turkey apart from distant gunfire. He was heavily tattooed, which attracted some strange looks from the locals. Funnily enough tattoos were possibly the only vice I never succumbed to, for once listening to Dad. On hearing of my Australian ambitions Peter immediately christened me "bluey," an expression used to describe a bushman's swag.

Next morning I unloaded part of my cargo in the customs warehouse, the remainder being printing machinery for Ramadan Street at Al Mansur, close to the city fair and racetrack. It was also conveniently situated near the filling station, with some of Frankfurt's sex books assuring the tanks were replenished with diesel, accompanied by non-stop giggles. For the final top-up I had Jock and Peter as passengers, en-route to the British club. The tattooed man laughingly accused me of causing gridlock at the filling station, especially when the two boys beat a hasty retreat to the rear of the building after filling the tanks. To do what? Feast their greedy eyes and/or play pocket billiards!

According to the locals, the name Yerjanick S Babaian was Armenian. He was the Davies Turner representative in Baghdad. Should any emergency occur, either through damaged or missing goods, or to arrange return cargoes, he was the man to contact. I'd already phoned on arrival, he indicating there might be something t take back to the UK for a haulage fee of £2,000. In the event I didn't get loaded for two days, with Gorden going on ahead. The goods weighed only three tons. It was Embassy equipment and personal effects, but it was well worth waiting two days for the 10% commission. This also proved the benefits of carrying a spare TIR carnet.

Travelling back towards Syria the true enormity of the desert in daylight was awesome, with only the occasional vehicle to break the deadly silence. It was here that I joined up with some camels for a photo shoot, even though my camera was bought for taking shots in Oz, not the kingdom of Ali Baba. Arabia's most famous son was mightily revered for his deeds. One of the traffic islands in Saadoun Street, Baghdad, was especially dedicated to Ali and his forty thieves. It was covered in greenery, and sported an array of trees, shrubs and flowers. The thieves were represented by different size urns, which spouted water in the winter months. Baghdad had experienced many turbulent times since the days of Ali, both at the hands of the Mongols and Turks, besides the European powers.

At the border I was allowed through without so much as a query as to how much fuel I was carrying. Maybe the British government had granted Iraq a diplomatic favour, causing them to have a temporary brain blockage. LSD would be happy. As luck would have it, my delay in Baghdad was compensated by the fact that I caught the ferry with only hours to spare. Gorden was pulling out his afro hairstyle in frustration, having been at the port for more than 48 hours. He was pulling it out even more when he received a telex on board, instructing him to load furniture near Sarajevo in Yugoslavia, extending his journey time to 24 days. My first priority on disembarking in Volos was an urgent repair to the trailer. As with most ports Volos catered for all types of repairs, marine or otherwise. A dockside workshop immediately welded a suspension bracket that had detached itself from the chassis, leaving me just a few dollars poorer.

My first trips had been different from one another, mainly through using the German train and the Greek ferry. With further allocations of road permits, and my reluctance to idle away on boredom cruises, those luxuries would be few and far between in the months ahead.

Chapter Eleven

Rigs, Revenue & Rules

Three trucks predominant in operations throughout mainland Europe and the Middle East, were Mercedes, Volvo and Scania, the Swedes being great advocates of turbo-charged power. They were classed as the best, both in comfort and reliability. My regular workhorse was a Mercedes, my experience on Volvos limited to three excursions. The Scanias were another fine example of precision engineering, and I ran alongside some for many thousands of miles.

Mercedes 1632 (15.9 Litre 320 HP Engine)

- Instant engine starting, even in the coldest of conditions.
- Excellent exhaust brake.
- Good quality interior trim.
- Cab easily lifted by a hydraulic jacking system.
- Semi walk-thru cab, due to the low mounted V engine.
- Possible to get dressed in a crouched upright posture.
- Noisy engine.

Volvo F88. (Turbocharged 9.6 litre 290 HP Engine)

- Everybody's dream to own or drive one.
- Quiet engine.

- High driving position, good all round vision.
- Cab to tilt manually, problem if facing uphill.
- Starting problems in excessive minus temperatures.
- Poor exhaust brake
- Not a walk-thru cab, with dressing restricted to the horizontal position.

Being right hand drive, the Volvo F88s were naturally expected to operate on the home front, where winter temperatures rarely dipped below –10C. It was when the engines were subjected to arctic conditions that the starting problems occurred. The engine designers never anticipated that the low-compression 290 turbo engine would be plying its trade abroad. In the cold winter areas of eastern Turkey overnight temperatures could plummet to –30C. Once on the open road they were flying machines, much faster than the Mercs and quite capable of 70mph. The most obvious choice would have been Volvo's left-hand drive F89, with its proven 12-litre engine, used extensively by many European companies but only a handful of British.

One would have thought that firms engaged exclusively in Middle East operations would have used "left-hookers" as a matter of course. Apparently it was all a question of economics concerning the vehicles resale values, and whether the traffic heading east would continue to flourish. Volvo did supply a hydraulic tilt cab mechanism as an optional extra, although they would be quick to point out that their vehicles didn't break down going uphill. Both them and the Mercs were well insulated, but neither was warm for sleeping in extreme sub-zero temperatures. Keeping the engine running all night to power the heaters was the only alternative, with five gallons of diesel a worthwhile price to pay for the central heating atmosphere.

Apart from the occasional sighting en-route of the Ford Transcontinental and Seddon Atkinson, the home market was poorly represented. The days when British engineering was the envy of the world were gone. The Mercedes hadn't as yet caught the imagination of many British hauliers, who shuddered at the thought of the fuel consumption on the V8 and V10 engines. Surprisingly they were economical. Another advantage was the servicing and spares facilities in all major cities en-route, besides being a pleasure to drive. It was as simple as a transit van.

In 1973 Leyland unveiled its latest gem to combat the foreign onslaught that was seriously threatening the existence of British truck manufacturing. After years of promises we finally had a truck to beat them all. This was the Leyland Marathon, powered by an AEC 280 horsepower turbo-charged engine. With the names Leyland and AEC noted for their reliability, it was just what the hauliers had been waiting for. The new truck was paraded at every show possible. It won a host of accolades, and was splashed on the front cover of every transport journal in the land. Some were adapted for Middle East operations, with sleeper cab, air-conditioning and fitted kitchen just a few of the extras. The name Marathon was perfect but could it last the pace? Unfortunately, the mechanics of the truck never quite lived up to the cosmetics, and it was tagged as unreliable.

In my teens, the "British is Best" slogan made us all proud of the fact that we were a nation the rest of the world envied. Among other things, we claimed to have the best footballers and brew the strongest beers, besides being the best lovers. The truck manufacturers were probably content with what they supplied for the home market and Commonwealth countries. Never in a million years would they have envisaged the impact of the foreign invaders, who quite literally gave them a good kick up the arse. Nothing would have made drivers prouder, than to be displaying a British logo on the front radiator grill when driving abroad. It's just a pity that the motor industry couldn't provide a truck of near total reliability, backed by a Eurasian network of service centres.

Even though the truck had a twin sleeper cab, it just wasn't practicable for two drivers to travel and sleep together in a confined space for over 7,000 miles. They were designed to be dual-crewed, so many Bulgarian, Romanian and Budapest-based Hungarocamion drivers took advantage of the situation in non-EEC countries. There, you could work and rest in the vehicle for twenty-four hours a day, seven days a week. Even if we had two drivers, little time would be saved on a trip of twenty-one days, and certainly not enough to justify another wage

The payment for each trip was £900, whether it took 18, 21, 25 days or even longer. Even though we were only in the UK for a few days each month, we were paid a basic wage of £72 a week, from which income tax and national insurance was deducted. Previously the wives of the married men had been sent an agreed wage each week, with Taffy keen to safeguard the finances of the families. Demurrage (compensation) was paid at the rate of £10 per day for delays incurred at your destination. Usually the time off between trips was 2-4 days, but as I had no commitments it could be hours, not days.

The expenses for the round trip (excluding ferry and

rail charges) normally bordered around £1,100, leaving you with a £300 float plus traveller's cheques. It was always advisable to separate your personal money from the firms. This gave you some indication as to how much you were spending, with the biggest and most expensive mistake being to eat out regularly. The food bought for each trip cost around £30, and catered for most of my requirements. Only everyday items such as bread and fresh milk were to pay for en-route, along with eggs and perishables when required. If at all possible you'd spend most nights in relaxed surroundings, but even a meal and a few beers could burn a hole in a fiver, depending on the location. Some would stop in Turkey or Greece for the midday meal, enjoying a reasonable spread for less than £2, which was all well and good until you totalled up the finances at the end of the trip.

The only way to save a lot of money was to be teetotal, cook all your own meals and live like a hermit, but none of the people I ever encountered fitted that description. The £900 could easy dwindle to £600, or even a lot less, especially if your receipts weren't in order or you didn't like cooking. At night, where there were no facilities, or in the desert, then you did your own thing if tiredness hadn't overtaken you. Taffy would play cards, usually the game of patience, another startling choice for a hothead. I'd noticed drivers of different nationalities carrying leather wallets with multiple compartments for the various currencies, besides purses and pouches. I wasn't keen on the idea of having so much money in one place, preferring to play the game of hide and seek.

Unless there was a do or die emergency, the office at home was never contacted, other than to say that you were unloaded. Most of the hotels en-route had telex facilities, while the bars and roadhouses catered for international phone calls. It was pointless phoning Taffy from Istanbul, telling him you'd broken a spring or windscreen, or had a minor accident. He was 2,000 miles away, what could he do? You had money and had to exercise your own judgement rightly or wrongly as to the situation. If by chance you'd been robbed or lost the bulk of your money, then you had no alternative but to call the office. Taffy mentioned that he'd had to pay out £6,000 to Mercedes in Graz for a new V10 engine to be fitted to a two-year old vehicle. He wasn't too happy about it twelve months on, nor with the driver who'd caused the damage. In another incident, a driver crossing the Yugoslav/Austrian border inadvertently collided with the rear of another truck, damaging the Atky's (Atkinson) radiator. The local mechanics fitting the replacement were amazed how quietly the Gardners eight-cylinder engine sounded, the old timers referring to them as being as quiet as a "paraffin clock."

Vehicle road tax was another corridor of opportunity seized on by the chancellor. One would have thought that English-registered trucks, returning to the UK for only a few days every trip, would be granted special road tax privileges, but no such luck. Unfortunately the government reserved all the favours for the foreign hauliers coming into the country, with charity definitely not beginning at home. Even though our 60mph speed limit for trucks was the highest in Europe, the foreigners' were allowed to flout the law in every way possible. The UK roads were classed as their favourite playground. There was nothing on motorway signs relating to speed restrictions, or from banning HGVs from using the outside lane. If they happened to be apprehended by police patrols, their inability to speak the language was usually enough to spare them any penalties.

Visual safety checks were carried out daily, either when stopping for a break or a leak. The main areas of concern were the tightness of wheels and overheating of trailer hub bearings. If the wheels had been removed and re-fitted, it was essential to re-check the nuts at least twice over the next twenty-four hours. Hub bearing failure in Turkey would entail travelling cautiously to the nearest repair depot. If the damage was severe, repairs would have to be carried out at the roadside, with possibly a mechanic having to travel distances of up to 200 miles.

One of the most essential considerations was always to relate to the rev counter when descending hilly terrain in the lower gears. The steep descents in Austria and Turkey were testing times on the vehicle's braking systems, with nothing in the UK to remotely compare. Once the correct gear had been selected, the exhaust brake was applied to control the truck's speed. It was crucial that the rev counter wasn't allowed to go into the red. If by some misjudgement or bout of fatigue you allowed the engine to over-rev, then a high pitched deafening buzzer would sound its disapproval.

Due to constant re-fuelling it was inevitable that particles of dust would eventually block the two micro-fine filters, with the fuel obtained in Iraq not considered to be the purest. Before any malfunction occurred on the return journey I would change the filters, usually between Mardin and Urfa, not wanting to experience a loss of power climbing Tarsus. Some drivers never bothered, completing the journey trouble free, with others changing them after experiencing problems. I'm not quite sure how much oil the Merc or Volvo used on a return journey to

Baghdad. I would imagine about one pint every 1200-1800 miles. The engine coolant contained an all year round 50% antifreeze mixture, which acted not only as protection against the arctic conditions, but also as an inhibitor, keeping the waterways rust free.

We carried two sets of snow chains, one for the truck's driven wheels, the other for the rear trailer wheels. They had a combined weight of around two-hundredweight. Few countries have the luxury of 24-hr snow clearing. The trailer chains not only helped with braking, but also minimised the risk of jack-knifing. Once fitted, it was essential to check them regularly for tightness, even though your speed was limited to 30mph. Otherwise you risked damage to mudguards or even the back of the cab if they became detached. If there was sleet or snow at ground level, it was inevitable that the higher you climbed the more there would be. One of the worst scenarios was winding your way up a mountain pass only to find that the white stuff had preceded you, with the rig gradually sliding backwards, even with the brakes applied. Another was opening the locker only to find someone had nicked the snow chains. There was a thriving market in the buying and selling of snow chains among the north European truckers. Especially in the summer, or when someone was due to terminate his employment.

In the late seventies Taffy was delivering goods to his beloved homeland, via Austria and Tehran. On the A5 at Betwys-y-coed snow was falling heavily, causing traffic to come to a halt. Taffy fitted his snow chains, enabling him to travel unhindered and also help another truck in difficulties. When Taffy explained that he'd been using them ten days earlier in Turkey, the bystanders quite clearly didn't believe him. Snow in the land of Sultans – never. As well as Turkey, the hills above Damascus and the mountainous areas of Iraq and Iran were subject to heavy snowfalls.

I was possibly the only long distance driver who wasn't familiar with the art of tying a trucker's hitch. I could drive, my reversing was getting better, but my knowledge of knots was strictly limited to the reef knot, sheepshank and clove hitch from my scouting days. Barry Bradshaw, a jockey for McRae's of Darlington, gave me some private tuition outside the British Club in Baghdad, before I eventually mastered the technique. There was no animosity whatsoever from the other drivers knowing I was a new kid on the block, only that I was a lucky bastard to get the job in the first place.

By now I had more European and Middle East maps for reference. In mainland Europe, a road sign displaying a yellow diamond signified that you were travelling on a main highway, even if it didn't appear so. At least you felt safe in the knowledge that you wouldn't encounter narrow or impassable roads, or weight restrictions. Sometimes the road didn't correspond with what was recorded on the map, especially when distinguishing the differences between asphalt, stabilised gravel or earth surfaces. On crossing the Channel after Easter the sun painted a totally different picture, even though it was possible for parts of the Balkans to experience freak weather from time to time. The time zones were also different due to the clocks going forward, with Graz still one hour ahead, Istanbul two and Baghdad three.

On leaving Ostend shorts and T-shirts tended to be my main attire, while my choice of footwear was heavy shoes. Others, especially the Scandinavians and Dutch, preferred clogs. One problem I did have at home was buying shorts, even trying the boy scouts shop. I would willingly have settled for a pair of boy's shorts with a man's arse, but even that drew a blank. The gent's outfitters weren't expecting grown men to revert to their childhood dress, no matter how hot it was. Even holidaymakers going to Spain preferred to bare their legs in the company of strangers, but definitely not at home. Shorts weren't part of the British culture, whereas Australia, the Americas and mainland Europe had regular seasons of sun. I eventually bought a pair in Munich. I would always arrive back in England dressed in jeans, not shorts, due to Gordens' earlier experience. Returning from Iran, he proceeded to deliver his cargo to Wolverhampton dressed in shorts, only to be greeted with wolf whistles and shouts of "Geordie puff-boy."

Chapter Twelve

Iraq, Kingdom of Ali Baba

Besides supplying three-quarters of the world's dates and much of its oil, Iraq was the home of one of the earliest civilisations and in legend the location of the Garden of Eden. The Hanging Gardens of Babylon was one of the seven wonders of the ancient world. Mesopotamia and Persia became Iraq and Iran. Possibly the names rhymed better with oil. While Turkey has a wide range of climate, its neighbour Iraq is totally the opposite, due to most of the country being less than 500ft above sea level. The west is mainly desert, while much of the south is fertile. The Bedouins of generations past exchanged a tent in the desert for the marshlands of the south. The marsh Arabs eke out a living by fishing or harvesting the reeds. Iraq is totally dependent on its two rivers, the Euphrates and Tigris, not only for residential and industrial demands, but also for the fertility of the land.

The source of the Euphrates lies in eastern Turkey, well over a mile above sea level, passing close to the ancient shrine of Babylon and the holy city of Karbala on its way south of Baghdad, At 1,780 miles, the Euphrates just pips the Danube (1,770miles). The 1,150-mile long Tigris also rises in eastern Turkey, passing Mosul on its way to Baghdad. The Tigris meanders through the city, providing cool relief for many of the residents during the hot summer months, when temperatures can reach in excess of 120F (50C). After passing through the marshlands of the south, these two great rivers join forces in the Shatt-el-Arab waterway at the head of the Persian Gulf.

In my childhood fantasies, Baghdad was a place of marble palaces, temples, endless sunshine, scented gardens, magic carpets and happiness ever after, with Ali Baba and the forty thieves taking on the mantle of Robin Hood and his merry men. I found the reality much more mundane, but the city and its people still oozed charm. Many of the minor streets are narrow and squalid, besides being dark at night, but they present no danger. The sun drenched pictures made no allowances for sanitation, general untidiness and cockroaches. Baghdad's bazaars are not as spacious, nor as much on a grand scale as those in Istanbul, but I always found friendly faces there to welcome me. The capital was made up of cities, around eleven in all. They were recognised as large towns rather than the traditional type of English Cathedral City. Baghdad University City was a prime example.

In the West we used to think that the Arabs lived in the dark ages, partly due to the way they dressed. The only difference I noticed between them and us was the level of illiteracy, which Saddam had pledged to overcome, but in all other respects they stood man for man alongside everyone else. Baghdad had a wide range of facilities on offer, especially for the young, in terms of education and social activities:

- Seventeen public parks, stadiums and swimming pools.
- Fourteen sports and social clubs, plus horse racing track.

- Seventeen universities and high school institutes.
- Eleven youth hostels/centres.
- Nine cinemas.
- Seven nightclubs.
- Thirty-three mosques.
- Twelve churches.
- Twenty-seven historical shrines and monuments.
- Eighteen government hospitals.
- Nine private hospitals.
- Seventeen hotels.
- Forty-eight diplomatic embassies.
- Thirty-three ministry and official administration headquarters.
- Seven centres associated with tourism.
- Twenty-three travel agencies.

The city centre was lively. In the hustle and bustle of Rashid Street and old Baghdad, you could barter for virtually anything. Saadoun Street, the most famous of them all, boasted hotels, restaurants, cinemas, travel agencies, souvenir shops and nightclubs. Every club had its bevy of glamorous dancers and hostesses, mostly from the Philippines and other far-eastern countries, no doubt with Buddha's approval.

People of means, from businessmen to top government officials, even the President himself, tended to reside in Waziriya, Baghdad's most affluent area on the north-eastern bank of the Tigris. Here were the high-class shopping malls, the private schools, science and law colleges, art institutions, sporting clubs and the British Bank. The poorer classes mainly lived on the eastern outskirts near the army canal, in places such as Thawra City and New Baghdad. Military camps were much in evidence on the main highways, although many recruits went home for the night.

Despite being the capital of one of the world's leading oil producers, Baghdad had only fourteen filling stations, which possibly explained why they were always busy. Fuel being so cheap (about 8 pence a gallon) it was ordered by the tankful, large dispensing nozzles filling the average car in seconds. As self-service was too slow, forecourt attendants worked non-stop, their leather cash bags overflowing with dinars. Although the ground was awash with petrol and diesel, that never stopped people smoking! My regular fill-up points were on the western perimeter of the capital, at Jordan Street and Damascus Street, near the Zoo and the Trade Fair.

Illiteracy was widespread. The Iraqi Customs would write the delivery address of the goods in English, but my Geordie pronunciation couldn't always be understood by the man in the street. I say man, simply because, due to their cultural beliefs, the women wouldn't speak to you. On later trips I asked the customs officials to write the delivery addresses in Arabic. It was only then that I realised the seriousness of the problem. Few Iraqi men were capable of reading, but most wouldn't admit it. As soon as they tried to read the print upside down it was time to ask someone else. Their knowledge of the English language extended to yes, no and Oxford, with nearly all claiming to have a brother, cousin or relative studying there. It's just a pity none of them were in Iraq at the time I required directions.

Followers of Islam uphold the strict traditions of their faith. The daily readings from the Koran reminded me of my younger days, visiting church twice every Sunday. It is the world's fastest growing religion, with at least 900 million followers. Muslims are forbidden to drink alcohol. The call to prayer that blasted out from the minaret's loudspeakers made you realise that Jesus Christ wasn't the only almighty God representing the people on earth. To the followers of Islam, Jesus is recognised as a prophet, although not as revered as Muhammad.

The teachings of Allah encourages modesty at all times, forbidding women to expose or display their body or beauty to anyone other than their husbands, or wear see-through garments. Long robes (jilbabs) are the most popular choice. The robes are part of the Arab culture, combating the oppressive heat by allowing the air to circulate more freely around the body. Some women cover their face entirely, leaving only a split for the eyes. Some younger ones prefer only a hijab to cover the head and shoulders

The males also respect the beliefs of the Almighty, being loath to expose bare legs or chests in public places. Their standard dress is an ankle-length cotton robe {dishadasha), with a square-shaped headdress (shimagh). Different countries have their own names for the same type of dress. In Saudi Arabia the garment is a thobe, the headgear a ghutra. A three-quarter length tunic and pyjama type trousers (shalwar kameez) can be worn by either sex in the cooler winter days. Most garments are in traditional earthy colours of blue, olive, grey and tan, besides black and white. Standard footwear is a mixture of thongs, sandals and leather-type socks. I saw plenty of deep cuts, scars and disjointed toes. Even before I arrived in Iraq I was aware of the strict traditions, and so donned a shirt when walking in public places. The Aussies had a similar policy in bars and restaurants, refusing to serve anyone bare-chested. Arab truckers were most fervent in their obedience to Allah. Their strict daily ritual involved kneeling on a prayer-mat at the roadside whilst facing the holy city of Mecca, birthplace of Mohammad. Muslim worshipping was much more resolute than anything I'd ever experienced. After dark, few women and girls are in evidence. Large numbers of men and boys congregate around the tea-houses, in what can only be described as a male dominated atmosphere.

Other than traffic regulations, the law was one of the grey areas I wasn't quite sure about. In Saudi Arabia, having a female passenger in your vehicle other than your wife or family member was classed as a breach of the law. In more serious cases, such as stealing or murder, the guilty parties would be punished in public, with the timetable of events announced on local TV. The repetitive thief would succumb to losing his eating hand, while the murderer or rapist was beheaded. Westerners attending such events would be pushed to the front of the crowd, to witness the executions at close hand.

Hooka pots are a common sight in the chay-drinking (tea) houses throughout the eastern world. Having heard so much about the hooka, I was curious and keen to experience it. Similar in shape to a tall, thin vase, hookas contain water and tobacco in separate chambers. Smoke is inhaled through a long flexible tube and cooled as it passes through the water, producing a gurgling sound. Some use scented water and a sprinkle of "oriental tobacco" to create a more relaxing sensation. It is much the same as smoking a joint, a timeless zone of heaven and laughter, and a much more composed way of enjoying life's offerings rather than alcohol. There are no mood swings or morning-after effects from the pipe of peace.

Occasionally I'd enjoy a puff on a hooka in

downtown Baghdad. The quality of tobacco varied immensely from the Bosporus to the Tigris. While wandering around Istanbul's grand bazaar, I was tempted to buy a richly-decorated hooka that would have looked nice in the corner of Mother's living room. After much thought I abandoned the idea, just in case the temptation proved too much. I didn't want to risk a visit from the local constabulary.

The month of Ramadan, the most important in the Islamic calendar, is devoted to self-sacrifice, charity and prayer. During this time, Muslims will not eat or drink during the hours of daylight. At the end of the month there is a festival atmosphere, with people celebrating their achievements of self-control. During Ramadan I was never aware of anything vastly different in the country, apart from extra activity around the mosques, and the minaret's loudspeakers working non-stop.

The Arabs had a strict policy in relation to Israel. Their visas stated quite clearly, that entry into Iraq would be barred if there was an Israeli visa on your passport. Ford vehicles and Barclays banking facilities were not tolerated in Iraq, being deemed as having connections with Israel. I was advised by border control to carry documentary proof of my faith. In other words to prove I wasn't a Jew. There was a feeling that this was all part of a military strategy. Father Lowrie, by now getting on in years, came to my rescue once again with a copy of my baptismal certificate. He had not realised that trucks travelled such long distances overland, but was greatly impressed by the places mentioned in the holy book. As Mother kept reminding me, I was a lost soul to the Catholic faith. I would jokingly reply that when I died I wanted to be buried, not burnt twice.

Although the thermometer proved otherwise, it never seemed to be as hot in the Middle East as in Australia. The temperatures in Yugoslavia, Bulgaria and central Turkey would creep up into the nineties (34C), but it was Iraq and southeast Turkey that proved to be the most body-sapping. Trying to sleep could be nigh unbearable, with the inside of the cab resembling a sauna. It was difficult to distinguish whether you were breathing in hot air or your own sweat. Your eyes also suffered from the effects of the salt. A few beers combined with the long driving hours helped, even though it was common knowledge that the more you drank the more you perspired. You had to ignore mosquitoes and other insects, because the only way possible to sleep was to leave the windows fully open and enjoy any means of ventilation. The die-hard locals advised me to ignore any strange creatures during the night, which was easier said than done. Gaziantep has its own form of miniature blood-sucking crab. Next morning the pillow would be soaked with sweat, later drying out to reveal a white outline of salt.

Running across the desert roads fully loaded, I would keep my speed at 50mph (80ks) to prevent the tyres overheating in the simmering temperatures, with endless mirages offering lakes of water over the next horizon. Even though tachographs weren't obligatory in the Middle East I would always fit a card, which could later be produced to any unsuspecting lawman in another country. With the onset of summer I decided on a Kojak hairstyle, giving a barber in Saadoun Street the pleasure of shaving my locks. Later Mother expressed her disgust at me looking like a convict.

I was directed to a government establishment in

Karbala, fifty miles south of Baghdad, to deliver laboratory equipment. As with all high-profile institutions in Iraq, a soldier was on guard duty and was keen to inspect the inside of the cab. The experienced old timer wasn't interested in searching for whisky or cigarettes. Instead, he made a beeline for the centre console, my hiding place for pornographic literature, before informing me of the seriousness of the situation.

"Sex book very bad in Iraq mister – kalaboosh," which I understood to mean handcuffs or prison, judging by the way he was crossing his wrists and repeating his threats. For a few moments it looked as though he was going to report me, before unbuttoning the top of his tunic and stuffing the books inside. He then hastily retreated to ground level, before saying goodbye and directing me to the unloading area.

I was not only dumbfounded by his actions, but also annoyed that the greedy bastard had taken all the baksheesh payments, every single book, meaning I would have to disappoint the diesel boys. No doubt "john thomas" would be well looked after by the eventual recipients, but I would have thought a man of his age would have been more interested in whisky or cigarettes.

At the Abu-Ghraib Customs, baby faced Mr Ali, whom I would often refer to as Ali Baba, had a rather unique way of obtaining cigarettes, without even asking for them. He seemed conversant with the basics of most European languages, with his greeting to me always being "tomorrow, tomorrow," even at seven in the morning. "Today, today, Mr Ali, tomorrow never comes," would be my reply, because if you went back the next day it would be the same "tomorrow, tomorrow" routine.

Tomorrow was his indirect way of asking for

cigarettes, knowing full well you'd offer him some sort of bribe to get unloaded quickly. Quite how the less well-off Eastern Block, Balkan and Turkish drivers managed I don't know - possibly with offers of sub-standard cigarettes, drugs, or part of their anatomy. The Romanian drivers were the poorest in Europe, so baksheesh for them would be a problem. Much of their equipment had seen better days, with always something amiss, saddling them with the nickname "F Troop."

I was fortunate on one trip to discharge my complete cargo of machinery in Mosul, ensuring the round trip was completed in eighteen days. It was the height of summer, and having to dismantle part of the trailer for crane access was not the most inviting of tasks. Besides heavy-duty gloves, I also wore safety boots with external steel toecaps, always aware that missing toes and fingers can't be replaced. The government official supervising the unloading extended his hospitality with a kebab and cool drinks, but surprised me by asking how much I wanted for my boots. I explained they weren't for sale, but would get him some within the month from a trader back home on Durham market. They cost him £11, but quite what he wanted them for I never found out.

Desert wind and sand can cause problems at meal times. It's like eating egg-and- tomato sandwiches on a windswept beach at Whitley Bay. Sandstorms are a daunting experience, like being cut off from the rest of civilisation. There's no choice but to park up at the first opportunity. It isn't too bad in the towns, where buildings help to cushion the effects of the wind, but on the open road you are at the full mercy of the elements. Visibility can be down to feet. The driven sand lashes the cab with the sound and fury of hailstones, causing a fine layer of dust to find its way into your cab. A sandstorm can last for ten minutes, two hours or even longer, depending on the time of year. Temperatures plummet as day turns to night. The locals treat sandstorms with disdain, driving around with headlamps blazing and life going on as normal. Dust is an everyday problem in the Middle East. The Iraqis soon show their displeasure if clouds are generated unnecessarily. When pulling off the highway, especially in areas close to cafes and shops, it's advisable to drive slowly and keep dust to a minimum, or face the wrath of shouting or even stone-throwing.

I was assigned to collect an urgent delivery of 360 fire doors from the mid-Wales town of Aberystwyth, for a new hotel in Baghdad. When I arrived in Baghdad, the inside of the trailer was like an oven. The Liverpool foreman hired casual workers to help me unload. Two hours and several visits to the ice-cold water fountain later, the Scouser ushered me into his air-conditioned office for a chicken meal.

Everything went like clockwork. I was stamped-up, filled with diesel and ready to go in no time at all. On the way to the border I was constantly drinking, the heat seeming to affect me more than usual, even though it was well over 100F (40C). That night, and for the following days until reaching Istanbul, I had a severe dose of the trots. I was unable to control my bowels, and was forced to wear a large type of sanitary towel inside my shorts. It was most uncomfortable as I sweated in the high temperatures. I constantly craved for cold drinks, besides wanting to lie on blocks of ice in a quiet darkened room. Two days later and half a stone lighter I started to recover, so that by the time I reached the National Hotel I was ready to eat a horse. It was either the chicken or the water that caused the fever, making me realise just how vulnerable you could be to illness.

Besides being a convenient place to park, the Baghdad Airport Hotel boasted a first-class swimming pool, a reasonably priced menu, and excellent fresh orange juice. The restaurant and bar managers were unpredictable, sometimes closing the facilities at ten instead of midnight, even though we tipped well and gave them a few smokes. Many of the young waiters were from neighbouring Kuwait, studying part-time to better themselves. They were keen on football and were always asking about the English teams, particularly Liverpool. Some older members of staff didn't like the idea of us getting too familiar with the lads, probably thinking we were going shag them first instead of themselves. During the hot summer months, two of a group of drivers would order a room for the benefit of the air-conditioning and shower, the rest sneaking in unnoticed. There you could enjoy a good night's sleep on the floor, or the bed if you were lucky, for a little over a pound. Occasionally you'd wake up during the night shivering, having to alter the air-con setting from cold to cool. Other times we'd book a room at the Anbar Hotel, but the air-conditioning left a lot to be desired. A few drinks were needed to drown out the screeching of the ceiling fans.

I always made a point of phoning home regularly, keeping my folks informed. If I had personal calls of any duration, I would use the PTT (post, telegram and telephone) office in old Baghdad. The surroundings weren't as plush as the hotels but it was much cheaper, besides being more private.

Hot weather, drinking-dens and swimming-pools definitely don't mix, with one afternoon in the British

Club coming to mind. The manager of the Airport Hotel had his head stuck up his arse for some reason or other, so five of us pilled into a taxi and headed downtown to the British Club. Next thing I was aware of was one of the drivers larking about in the pool, complete with shoes and shorts. The powers-that-be were definitely not amused, especially with his language. We were all given a dressing-down, and warned as to our future conduct. The club officials knew we were drivers, and could easily have banned us sine die. The lad in question was a first-timer, celebrating his achievement of having reached Baghdad.

You would have thought that the members of the British Club and the other colonial watering hole, the Embassy Club, would have been pillars of society, but it wasn't always the case. During a friendly competition of darts and snooker, public-school manners gave way to the effects of Satan's brew. This resulted in a massive brawl, causing hundreds of pounds worth of damage to mirrors and furnishings.

We classified watering holes into three categories, good, bad and indifferent. The only bad beer was the beer you couldn't get. Otherwise, it was cold beer, warm beer, strong beer and cat's piss. The drinking dens from Ostend to Baghdad served top quality nectar, whether it was the Munich Hofbrahaus or Gaziantep TIR park. On the rare occasions when all the drivers happened to be back home at the same time, we'd meet up at the Halfway House (Crossways Motel) on the outskirts of Durham.

Returning from the British Club one hot summer's night the road was completely deserted. Suddenly a blue flashing light illuminated the mirror before a police car overtook, causing me to slow and eventually stop. Surely I hadn't been speeding?

"English?"

"Yes."

"Drinking beer?"

"Err – two drinks."

But why were they asking me about drinking? There were no drink-drive laws in Iraq. My driving seemed within reason.

"In Baghdad mister, we drive on the right," both cops laughing and joking at my expense. On exiting the roundabout after the Presidential Palace I'd inadvertently driven up the carriageway on the left. It was a natural reaction, especially with no other traffic on the road. The police took turns sitting in the cab to experience the steering wheel on the right-hand side, before accepting two packets of cigs and heading back towards the city. What nice people, the Iraqi police!

With a right-hand drive rig, it's easy to miscalculate when doing left-hand turns on quiet roads especially when fatigue is a factor. One time during the early hours in Yugoslavia, I must have driven three miles on the left before being confronted by headlamps. I cursed the driver of the oncoming vehicle as having had one too many before I realised my mistake.

The Arab and Turkish truckers were most passionate about a good "honking" horn. It was a status symbol, which would vary from a high-pitched scream to that of a klaxon. This and the waving of arms out of the driver's window were essential for negotiating roundabouts and traffic jams. It was a free-for-all among the many trucks, buses and cars, but miraculously they all emerged unscathed, with right of way not part of their highway code. It was fun being educated in the laws of the land, with my Mercs-adapted "screamer" causing a few hairs to

stand on end back at home. Even though the Arabs ran
the best of European engineering, they would load their
trucks with as much weight as possible, much the same as
the Turks. If the vehicle was designed to carry twenty tons
they would carry thirty, looking upon it more as a bonus
rather than causing extra strain to all the mechanical
components. The amount of rubber on the tyres also left
a lot to be desired. Arab drivers took great pride in the
presentation of their trucks, the highly colourful displays
on the body panels and cab making them look like show
vehicles. MOT regulations were much the same as those
for cars, non-existent.

No-one is immune from mistakes and I hold my
hand up to being one of the many, as was the time I did
450 wasted miles and lost two day's work. I was directed
by Haswa customs to leave part of my cargo of motor
spares in their warehouse and deliver the rest to Rutba,
the last oasis before the Jordan and Syrian borders, some
220 miles away. Bright and early next morning I quickly
unloaded the remaining five crates at Rutba, before
swiftly heading back to Haswa to beat the two-o-clock
deadline. On presenting the documents for clearance I
was informed of an error in the paperwork. The triplicates
had been stamped, but not signed by the manager of the
Rutba depot – what now? Could they phone the manager
to confirm the goods had been delivered, then sign the
papers on his behalf – no. After disconnecting the trailer,
it meant another journey to the desert outpost. Losing
that day costing me dear. Not in terms of having to pay
four extra quid for fuel, but by the enforced break for the
German driving ban. You live and learn.

What I did miss in Turkey and Iraq, were the long
summer days that we enjoyed back home, where daylight

would extend from four in the morning until ten at night. In winter it was totally the opposite, with the UK having the shortest daylight hours. The desert was an eerie experience, watching the big red ball slowly disappearing below the horizon, before everything was plunged into darkness and silence.

Chapter Thirteen

Turkey, Land of Eastern Promise

Besides the maps I'd acquired, I was still short of basic information regarding Turkey and Iraq. In Istanbul I obtained more maps and information pamphlets, written mainly in Turkish, French and German. I also delved into some old encyclopaedias, even if Ankara had replaced Constantinople as the capital in the intervening years.

Turkey is where the world changes completely. The 1,200-mile journey from border to border allows you to witness the gradual transition from western to eastern culture. Parts of it are wild and inhospitable. It is a land that has evaded modern society in many ways, especially the east, with the climate dictating everyone's lifestyle to some degree. Asia Minor spans two-thirds of Turkey, forming the western extremities of the Asian continent. Much of it is an elevated broad plateau, varying in altitude from 1,900 to 4,200ft. The interior experiences huge variations in temperatures, resulting in sandy deserts, fertile valleys, salt and freshwater lakes. The largest salt lake, Tuz Gol, between Ankara and Aksaray, is an incredible 55 miles long, yet almost dry for part of the year. In summer, dust storms blow across the plains, leaving a fine yellow coating on everything and everybody.

The areas bordering the Aegean and Mediterranean enjoy mild winters. In eastern Turkey the long winters from November to April are particularly severe, with overnight temperatures as low as –30C. These eastern border regions adjoining the Soviet Union and Iran are mountainous, with more than twenty snow-capped peaks at altitudes of 10,000 feet and over. The most famous is Mount Ararat at 16,823 feet. According to the Old Testament, this was the resting place for Noah's Ark after the great flood. Instead of looking for a Pasha in his harem, I was more likely to come across mountaineers. Wolves and bears were known to frequent the highlands, so I wouldn't be venturing too far on foot. Many miles transiting Turkey were done so at high altitudes (refer to data in chapter twenty).

Turks are fiercely independent. I found them always willing to work, whatever the day or time. A Turk lives for the present. What has happened in the past is finished and done with. His commitment to Islam is second to none, with minarets signalling the call to prayer even in the remotest of homesteads. Turkish men regard extra hair on their top lips as machismo.

Adana, in the south, has a hot and humid climate, ideal for cotton growing. It is one of the country's most fertile areas, and enjoys a Mediterranean climate for most of the year. "Oriental tobacco" is also grown, which by the sounds of it seemed destined for the hooka pots. The south-eastern region, between Adana and the Iraq border, is far less developed than the western part of the country, due to its geographical position. Some of the houses were built into the hillside, with goats grazing on the roofs. There are a few small oil-producing areas close to the Iraq border, but the bulk is imported from the neighbouring countries of Iraq, Iran and the Soviet Union. Yet Kirkuk, one of Iraq's wealthiest oilfields, is only160 miles from the Turkish border.

In Istanbul most people wear typical European clothing. The traditional dress of baggy trousers (shalvari) and close fitting caps (kufis), are seen much more the further you travel into Asia Minor. It's the same with women's dress, colourful trousers (dimije) and headscarves (samija), although I don't recall any of them wearing the grate-like veils that covered the entire face. There were occasional sightings of fez hats in the bazaars, but the majority have disappeared into the history books, along with the curved-toed shoes.

Shrines of all descriptions dot the landscape in central Turkey. Travelling from the holy city of Konya, down through Aksaray and across to Nevsehir and Kayseri is a cameraman's dream. Not only is the area steeped in religious history, but volcanic eruptions over millions of years have left a lunar-type landscape. Thousands of underground dwellings, churches and caverns have been hollowed out of the resulting lava flow and pyramid-style rocks. Access to the houses is made as difficult as possible to repel any would-be intruders.

Aksaray, one of my regular meal stops and overnight parks, is situated at the crossroads of the ancient silk trade routes. Its history dates back to 8,000 BC. It was a caravan palace (place of rest), for merchants bringing goods and riches from Persia and China, in particular "timbaki," a favourite with the hooka smokers. Aksaray had a rather unusual crooked minaret, which reminded me of the leaning tower of Pisa. In the south and east of the country, the donkey was still favoured by the old timers to carry goods. They would think nothing of travelling for days to the next town to peddle their wares. Even so, donkeys and dogs were particularly badly treated by the Turks.

Travelling with snow chains through eastern Turkey.
Photo supplied by Ferdy of Toprun.

Tyre change – no sign of nearest garage!
© Ian Taylor.

Roll 'em — it's Errol's comeback

By MARTIN SHIPTON

SWASHBUCKLING lorry driver Errol Flynn returns to the North-East from a five-week ordeal tomorrow.

But Mr Flynn's adventurs has been anything but glamorous – he was trapped in a tiny Middle East buffer zone in sub-zero temperatures without fresh food or sanitation.

Errol Flynn lives! Headline 6th February 1979. Reproduced by permission of the Northern Echo, Darlington.

On-board facilities. © Ian Taylor.

London bus in foreign parts. No sign of Cliff Richard!

Italian ship Galileo entering New York Harbour.

Turkish Tonka drivers, Mosul, northern Iraq.

The long descent from Tarsus to Adana, Turkey.

Houses built in a lunar landscape, central Turkey.

Café at the head of Tarsus mountain pass, Turkey. Note the meat hanging in the open – no flies, thanks to the cold!

Turkish Tonka driver. © Ian Taylor.

Ooops! Tonka driver contemplates over-loading at the rear of his truck on Taurus mountain. © Ian Taylor.

Crashed telescopic boom machine parted from its
French truck, southeast Turkey.

Iraq tankstelle (filling station). © Ian Taylor.

Arabs enjoying their hookah pot in the Syrian desert.

A cruel practice of the time. Performing bear at the Harem Hotel, Istanbul. © Ian Taylor.

Groovy Hasan's business card (telephone no. 17); USA air force base badge, Incerlik, Adana, Turkey.

Baghdad Water Company agents, "Wyatt Earp" on right.

Above: Remsi Taz, head waiter of the Harem Hotel, Istanbul, and mentor of countless drivers.
Below: inside the Pudding Shop, Pop the barman, standing second left, "Want-a-Lift" notice-board on right.

Above: a sand-tractor pulls a German Magirus Deutz out of soft sand south of Selwa. *Below:* a convoy of Astran Scanias on a lonely desert track in Iraq.

Below, left: Chris Bedder with a Mol geophysical vehicle. *Right:* a 58-wheeler carrying 400 tons pulled by a mighty Kenworth on the road to Riyadh. Photos on these two pages, supplied by Ferdy of Toprun, first appeared in "Cola Cowboys."

Pudding Shop, Istanbul 1966 (above) and 2006 (below).
Thanks to Namik Colpan and Adem Colpan, of the
Pudding Shop and the Blue House Hotel, Istanbul, for
these pictures.

Crash, eastern Turkey. © Ian Taylor.

3,000 miles from home. An Atkinson Borderer (TBR 737R) back on its wheels after toppling on its side on the slopes of the notorious "Tahir" in eastern Turkey.

Currencies carried by Middle East truckers: German marks,
American Dollars, Austrian schillings, Yugoslav dinars,
Greek drachma, Bulgarian lev, Turkish lira,
Syrian pounds, Iraq dinar.

D-Day (decimal day) in Oz, when pounds, shillings and
pence gave way to dollars and cents (February 14th 1966).

Harem Hotel, Istanbul. © Ian Taylor.

Ali Baba memorial, Sadounn Street, Baghdad,
taken from my cab.

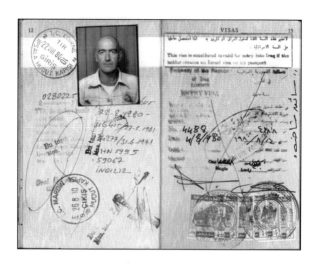

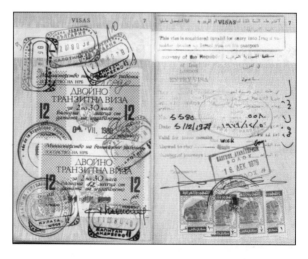

My much-stamped passport!

Davies drivers, Kavala, northern Greece (l-r) Kevin, Taffy, Barry.

Me alongside my beloved Volvo F88.

Upside-down Bulgar. © Ian Taylor.

The lonely desert road.

I was eager to venture into Istanbul, not only to witness the sights, but also to visit the city's famous "Pudding Shop." Luckily I had a good escort, having teamed up at Ankara with Jimmy Richardson, an owner-driver from Glossop. The shop was recognised as the world's most famous meeting-point for travellers moving east or west, whether they be adventurers, students, hippies or drop-outs. Its reputation was further enhanced by the film "Midnight Express." The Bosporus bridge by-passed the city, so this was my first chance to explore part of it at first hand. Rather than go to the Londra camp then hire a cab, we parked at Harem on the Asian side of the city close to the ferry landing. The nearby Harem Hotel was another popular haunt for British truckers. Most of the city's residents used the ferries, a quick and inexpensive way to cross the straits. On entering the Golden Horn waterway you are immediately made aware of the hustle and bustle of this city of seven million people. Even 007 had his moments in, around and under Istanbul, in the film "From Russia with Love."

Besides the smell of spicy foods pedalled by street urchins, water taxis tout business for nearby Eyup, further along the horn. Eyup is a South Yorkshire saying expressing surprise, so possibly it dates from British soldiers being in Istanbul during the Crimean War. The Galata Bridge appeared to have five lanes of traffic, three lanes in one direction, two in the other, to cater for the rush hour. The most striking aspect of the Pudding Shop in Sultanahmet Square, was not its appearance, but its customers. Before entering Jimmy warned me not to divulge we were drivers, besides recommending the goulash, which made a welcome change from kebabs, chicken and chips. The large notice board couldn't be missed, bearing information, photos, notices and pleas for help by way of lifts. Some offered to share expenses, others beds, for destinations from Bangkok to Trafalgar Square.

We got into conversation with some Aussie and Kiwi students who'd travelled overland from India and were heading for London's kangaroo valley. We spun a yarn about assisting surveyors, planning a second road bridge across the Bosporus. There were two Danish cyclists who'd been travelling for over a year and had covered most of Turkey and part of Iran. It sounded a risky adventure, especially when they revealed about being robbed, stabbed and even stoned in the east of the country. Even though I had a spare seat, giving lifts of any distance to either sex was out of the question. You just didn't know if the nice people you'd just met were carrying drugs, with even the tiniest amount enough to have the rig confiscated at the border and you suffering the same fate as William Hayes in "Midnight Express." For the next four hours we wandered around the Horn peninsular, with the Blue Mosque and those of St Sophia and Solomon the Magnificent, breathtaking colourful spectacles.

We even found time to call at the Grand Bazaar (Kapali Carsi), which could easily have had my undivided attention for a full day, or two, or three, with its choice of 4,000 shops. I bought a dagger with an 8in blade, not only to cut bread but also as a precaution against anyone wanting to line their pockets at my expense. I had considered a gun, with all makes and sizes freely available, but I didn't want to end up on the wrong side of the law, especially in Turkey. My virgin rear end was probably the only part of my anatomy that hadn't suffered abuse in one way or another, and I intended to keep it that way.

On heading towards the ferry we got caught in a torrential downpour, with rats the size of cats even running for cover. Now I was familiar with the landscape, I'd venture downtown more often, and could now lay claim in the bars around the world as having been to the great city. I could also bury forever the words repeated by many. "If you've never been to the Pudding Shop, then you've never been to Istanbul."

For many drivers heading east, Istanbul was classed as the end of the easy bit and the start of the hard bit, with tales of atrocities and hostile conditions putting the shits up rookie drivers from day one. Added to that were the military checkpoints, which at times could be hassle, although in most cases were a reassuring sight. Checkpoints could be found anywhere, but were mainly on the outskirts of towns or cities.

On approaching Pozanti in late spring, warning signs gave notice of a weight restriction on the bridge ahead. Heavy rainfall and melting snow from the Taurus mountains resulted in the river flooding and washing away the bridge. It had been replaced with a temporary steel construction, the weight limit set at 30 tons. I was five tons too heavy, but usually bridges could withstand a large margin of error. The temporary bridge had probably been designed to withstand loads of up to 45 tons. Unfortunately for me there was a soldier on guard. The authorities knew their countrymen would overload their trucks to near breaking-point. On checking my papers I was ordered to detour via Konya, an extra 440 miles and at least a day's travelling, something I could ill afford. Six pounds worth of whisky and cigarettes did the trick, much to my relief and the soldier's delight.

The holy city of Konya, at a height of 3,370ft, is believed to be the first place to emerge from the Great Flood. The Apostle Paul was a frequent visitor. German crusaders made camp there on their travels to the Holy Land. Crossing Asia Minor must have been a long and arduous journey for both man and beast, compared with Richard the Lionheart, who had the luxury of travelling by sea.

The two-day, 1,500-mile train journey from Istanbul to Baghdad, provided some remarkable scenery. The railway, called the B-B-B, had originally been the brainwave of the Germans. Berlin was keen to link the Bosporus with Baghdad and beyond to the Persian Gulf. The line ran close to the E5 for fifteen miles from Ulukisla to Pozanti, before negotiating the Taurus Mountains. The building of the 60-mile track from Yenice (Adana) to Ulukisla was considered to be one of the greatest feats of railway engineering, with an almost continuous climb from sea level up to an altitude of 4,585ft. The stretch incorporated 37 tunnels, with a combined length of nine miles.

The Tarsus road pass over the mountains is at a height of 4,000ft. It has to be appreciated that the long descent to sea level couldn't be achieved in a few minutes. The pass, often referred to as the "Cilician Gates," was for centuries the main artery linking Asia Minor with Syria. Alexander the Great marched his victorious army through the Gates on one of his many conquests. St Paul used the route on several of his pilgrimages. It also represented the nearest I would ever get to heaven. Occasionally during the summer months I would stop to eat at the summit. It was much cooler, compared with the oppressive heat on either side of the mountain. The meat was still hanging outside the cafe, only this time slightly darker, due to the covering of flies.

Turkey was a testing journey for the trucks, which had to endure some long and punishing hill-climbs. They never missed a beat in the blazing summer temperatures, even though the engine oil must have been near to boiling point. It was at times like this that I appreciated not only the vehicle's mechanics, but also the designers of such fine specimens. The conditions also tested the mettle of the driver, be it in blistering heat or snow. Spring and autumn were the most comfortable times for travelling.

At Gaziantep, Saxophone Joe gave me an Old Testament history lesson, relating to the 7,000ft Cudi Mountain near the Iraq border. According to many historians it was the final resting-place of the Ark, with Noah's grave is reputed to be in nearby Cizre. So Ararat and Cudi would have to share the honours of claiming the Ark, but it was good for tourism.

Around Easter, a rookie West Country driver was parked at the Londra camp, clad only in shorts and a T-shirt. The rain was lashing down, and the temperature much colder than when he'd left home. He'd also been under the misapprehension that the sun shone forever in that part of the world. For the next two days he wore my overalls until the sun beamed on us at Adana. There was more drama to follow at Kiziltepe TIR park, with the constant cracking of gunfire between the PKK (Kurdish Peoples' Party) and the Turkish militia throughout the dark hours. Next day was even more hair-raising. We slowly made our way down the steep winding road from the border with gunshots ringing in our ears. We would have been easy targets. It was a rough baptism for my Bristol colleague, but the experience didn't dampen his enthusiasm. Either he had balls or was heavily in debt! Periodically we had to travel in convoy, escorted by the army through the Kurdish occupied areas towards the border.

What intrigued me about Turkey and Iraq were the cafes where the local males would meet. They drank chay and smoked all types of pot-pourri while watching television and playing board games, chatting non-stop. The tea was served hot, black and strong from majestic looking teapots into small tulip-shaped glasses around four inches high. A small spoon rattled away inside the glass to dissolve the sugar cubes. The slurping noises were non-stop, the average Turk drinking upwards of twenty glasses a day. Iraq's tea was more pleasing to the palate, having been imported from the former British colonies. The quality of the coffee however was disappointing. To me, it always tasted as though it had an extra ingredient – sand.

One sizzling afternoon I stopped to quench my thirst in Aligor, a small town in south-eastern Turkey. It was much on the same lines as Port Hedland, only without the sea view. Never for one moment did I expect to be offered beer, with the large fridge containing a sizeable array of the Devil's potion. The shop also sold clothes, besides serving as a café and barber's. As soon as the owner realised I was English, he had nothing but praise for our tea, or rather the tea from India and Ceylon. Further explaining in "leetle-Ingiliz" that the tea they were drinking was Turkish, but not of a high quality. I excused myself before going outside to the truck and returning with some teabags, putting three in his elegant-looking pot. He seemed puzzled when I told him to pour hot water on them. Not convinced that tea would emerge from the spout, he was expecting to cut open the bags and pour the contents into the pot. When he tasted the brew I was hailed a saviour. For two boxes of teabags, I enjoyed free drink and food on future visits. I saved the beer for my nightcap.

On the return ferry journey from Syria, I got into conversation with some Swedish and Dutch drivers. They were preparing to join an expedition for an assault on Mt Ararat, in search of the Ark. A reconnaissance plane had reported an outline within a glacier, similar in size to that of a large boat. Recent summers in that part of eastern Turkey had been hotter than usual, with increased melting on Ararat's ice cap adding to the excitement. The American-led expedition involved around eighty people, the drivers paying £2,000 each for the privilege of being gofas. Leo, a Dutch driver in his forties, was helping to compile a book about the adventure. Had I not been pre-occupied with sorting out my own future, my name would definitely have been added to the list.

Young boys were much in evidence at Turkish border posts, helping out in the offices. Some lived on the premises during the week. They were well versed in the arts of smoking, spitting and swearing, whilst also serving the night-time demands of their elders. Returning empty from Iraq into Turkey was a mere formality at Customs. It was just a case of them checking the trailer was empty, stamping a few papers and within half an hour you were on your way. On entering the Habur control a young Turk rushed up to the truck for my paperwork, returning ten minutes later with everything completed. He didn't want any lira, just cigarettes, even though he could not have been more than twelve. I offered him a packet of twenty. He refused, saying he wanted a carton of two hundred. When I refused, he unleashed a tirade of abuse, saying he would make sure that the "fuckin' Ingiliz bastard" would be delayed next time. I swiftly seized my dagger and jumped from the cab. I grabbed hold of this brassy upstart and told him in no uncertain terms, that instead of the big boss feeling his arse he would have a knife stuck up it. The Romanians parked nearby were most amused at the sight of him running away screaming. His greed meant he got nothing.

One morning, after clearing the Kapicule border, I was approached by an English-speaking Turkish student about a lift to Istanbul. Normally carrying passengers was no-go, but I wanted to pick his brains. I stopped shortly after at Edirne for ice, bread, a tomato as big as a cricket ball and a cucumber. I wasn't staying at Istanbul, but was hoping to make Ankara before lights out. We'd travelled only ten miles before being subjected to a police check. They requested my tacho card. Since leaving the border it hadn't been possible to speed, and the tachograph was not obligatory, being just another way of asking for baksheesh. Several high-ranking officers were present, wearing shades and long leather coats, so maybe it was all to impress the men at the top. In Turkey, the law and the army were always on the lookout for easy pickings.

The student tried to intervene, implying that the police actions were wrong. I tried to hush him up, explaining that was the way things were done in the real world. He wouldn't listen, trying to act on my behalf by laying down the law to the police. This clearly irritated the chief. Moments later the passenger door was opened and the student was pulled from the cab to the ground. Three officers kicked hell out of him, showing no mercy. To save the lad a beating, I offered Rothmans and whisky, but to no avail. I was quickly moved on amid the screams and shouts.

Despite the fact that I was a good customer, my relationship with Groovy Hasan came to an abrupt halt in 1980. Ghetto blasters were a big craze among teenagers, and Groovy approached me about the possibility of getting him some from the duty-free shop at Baghdad Airport. The type he required were around £30. He agreed to pay me the equivalent in US dollars, also offering a good discount on onyx goods. I was taking the risk, because I had to produce my passport at the airport, when it was obvious I wasn't travelling by air. The same applied at the Zacho border post, especially if a keen-eyed policeman or soldier searched the cab. Everything went well for months until things turned sour in mid-summer. The blasters were handed over, but Groovy only offered payment in Turkish lira. His excuse was that he didn't have any dollars. As far as I was concerned Turkish currency was useless outside the country, while £60-worth of dollars would buy him near double the value in lira. I also had my own little outlet for a few dollars, mainly with the fairer sex, but I couldn't imagine the pleasures of the flesh being paid for with Turkish lira. I sounded my disgust, but kept calm enough to get a good discount on a chess set for a customer back home. Greed had once again reared its ugly head, causing our relationship to flounder.

On my next trip Groovy rushed out of his store, all smiles. He wanted more ghetto blasters, promising dollars. I said it would be no problem, as long as he paid in advance. That idea didn't appeal to him, confirming once again that all the trust and risks were one-sided. I continued visiting his store, but offered only rock bottom prices. Groovy was making a more than comfortable living from the Yanks.

Shortly afterwards at Incirlik, I encountered a hard-luck story involving a refrigerated rig. A lad in his mid-twenties from Nottingham, bound for Kuwait, had run out of money. He couldn't buy diesel for the truck, or the engine to keep the fridge cool. To make matters worse he'd been on the piss in Istanbul for a few days. The fridge's cargo was chocolate bars and wafers, but the inside would probably be a sea of melted chocolate. He was waiting for money to be transferred to a bank in Adana, but he'd need more than a little help from up above to explain the condition of his cargo once he got to Kuwait. I helped him out with enough fuel to keep him mobile, along with some grub and a few quid, but his actions resulted in losses all round. The insurance company probably coughed up the bulk of the loss.

Driving up Bolu could be hazardous at times, due to the sharp twists, turns and short steep inclines, along with never-ending traffic. One particular day the truck in front, loaded to the hilt, was very slow moving. I made several failed attempts at trying to overtake him, besides having a frustrated bus driver behind me. The bus driver sounded his horn non-stop before finally passing both of us, his rear-seat passengers waving their fists at me. I stayed behind the straggler before pulling into the parking area at the top, only to be confronted by an angry mob of youths with stones in their hands, ready for the kill.

They were from the bus that had earlier overtaken me, with the leader – or mouthpiece – remonstrating about me moving from side-to-side, not allowing the bus to pass. I immediately recognised the problem. Explaining it was a different matter. The bus driver had mistakenly thought that when I pulled slightly to the right to see past the vehicle in front, prior to attempting to go past, that I was in fact giving him the signal to overtake. Quite clearly the driver was inexperienced, besides having landed me with a bloodthirsty mob. It was while I was explaining my right hand drive predicament, that the "mouth" noticed a football magazine with European player of the year Kevin Keegan on the front cover. The instant I pledged it to him, all was forgiven. This misunderstanding was a typical example of how things can easily get out of control. For the Turkish people, bus operations are an essential part of the country's infrastructure. Distances travelled ranged from a few miles to over a thousand.

Even though Turkish football wasn't of the highest standard, they were still passionate about the game, with regular references to my name being the same as their idol. A few years later, England played Turkey for the first time in a world cup qualifier in Istanbul, winning 8-0, with Geordie captain Bryan Robson scoring a hat-trick.

In the late seventies, a Fiat rig loaded with cement was parked at the top of Bolu next to Ted Hannon and Andy Anderson. The local driver was more than interested in acquiring their long vehicle signs, even offering his arse as payment. A short while later, as they descended with care, the Turk flew past them, apparently with brake problems. Minutes later, the scene near the bottom of the hill was unbelievable. The Fiat had hit an oncoming bus, which then overturned, with bodies, arms and legs strewn all over the road. In countries with no MOT regulations in force for either cars or commercial vehicles, such fatalities are inevitable.

There was a choice of two border crossings into

Turkey. The Greek crossing at Ipsala was much quieter and less hassle than Kapicule, but longer. Usually a strip of barren no-mans land separated the high fences between countries, ranging from yards to half a mile. At Ipsala, the dividing barrier between Turkey and Greece is the river Ergene. A few damaged and impounded trucks, buses and cars littered the border areas, with a burnt-out English "Guy Big J" in its final resting place at Kapicule. These were vehicles, which for one reason or another had fallen foul of the authorities, either through improper documentation, transporting illicit cargoes or drugs. Their presence served as a stark reminder of the consequences of dicing with Turkish law.

The weighbridge at Kapicule was a joke. It was nothing more than a legal money-making scam. Many times I was of the opinion that the Turkish scales had different settings, one for poorer Eastern Bloc and Balkan drivers and one for westerners. Sometimes it wasn't possible to check your weight in the UK, especially if you'd loaded at a place where there were no facilities, in which case you had to rely solely on the paperwork for guidance. On top of the cargo was the extra fuel, spare wheels etc, only adding to the weight, so it was advisable to steer well clear of the Canterbury weighbridge during the day if you had any doubts. On entering Germany you were checked to ensure you weren't over their legal limit of 38 tons, so I knew then exactly what gross weight I was running at. The Turkish scales never once coincided with those of the fatherland. They were always above, leaving you no option but to pay more transit tax.

Even though the journeys to Baghdad and Tehran differed by only a hundred miles, the route to Iran was considered to be the tougher on both man and machine.

On leaving Ankara, trucks bound for Baghdad and Saudi headed south, crossing the central part of the country, but at least the terrain was reasonably constant until Tarsus. For drivers travelling east on the E23 to Iran between November and April, it could be a nightmare, with heavy snow and overnight temperatures as low as −30C a common occurrence. For most of the journey you were travelling at high altitudes, with Sivas (4,257ft), Erzincan (3,946), Erzurum (6,386) and Agri (5,370) testing the best. Running on snow chains for two days in conditions such as these was not unusual. Engines and heaters worked non-stop day and night, apart from a few minutes respite to check the oil and water.

Snow was a colossal problem, the word colossal inadequate to describe the drifts of between ten and twenty feet deep that were common to many stretches of the E23. Keeping the main highways clear to Iran and Iraq were given top priority. They were the lifeblood of the country. The Turks excelled in snow clearing. They had teams of men living in huts strategically placed at problem areas, armed with bulldozers, ploughs and shovels. They worked twenty-four hours a day, seven days a week, to keep these vital roads clear.

Taffy copied the tactics adopted by the Turk and Bulgarian hauliers, re-routing the exhaust systems on the trucks and allowing the hot gases to blow onto the fuel tanks. This prevented the diesel gelling, whilst also adding a small amount of petrol (5%) or kerosene (10%). Many first-time truckers were totally unprepared for the conditions. Some were stranded for days or even weeks on end, and had to light fires under the trucks to liquify the fuel or free frozen brakes. There were also the treacherous mountainous passes, with Tahir (8,122ft), between

Erzurum and Agri, the daddy of them all. It alone had broken many hauliers' hearts and pockets, due to mishaps on the steep icy surfaces. Imranli (5,239) Refahiye (5,895) Askale (5,320) and Horasan (5,043) also had their fair share of hazards, including mile upon mile of hairpin bends and corrugated surfaces.

One day, near the notorious Tahir pass, an Atky (Atkinson) destined for Tehran toppled over on its side, shedding its load Lister diesel engines. Fortunately the driver, Alan Bryant, was unhurt after taking evasive action to avoid a head-on collision. Another of Taffy's drivers, Ted Hannon, was following closely behind. He was allotted the task of getting the truck back on its feet. Fortunately it was early April, with only slight snow flurries. If it been in the grip of winter it would have been a totally different story.

The police stressed the need for 24-hour security on the truck. Bandits were all too ready to take advantage of the diesel, wheels and batteries on anything unattended. A nearby villager who possessed a shotgun was appointed a guard for two American dollars a day. The police assured Taffy's drivers that he would honour his commitment, even to the point of shooting his own family. Ted used his truck to scout the nearby towns with the help of a café owner from nearby Eliskirt, eventually located an old German Bussing recovery vehicle at a garage in Erzurum.

Three Bulgarian trucks assisted the recovery, attaching towropes from their vehicles to the Bussing. The Atky was soon back on its wheels, with just a broken side window and minimal bodywork damage. Truck TBR 737R had a lucky escape. The guard got six dollars for his duties, plus an extra four dollars for doing a good job. The joyous family scenes that followed reminded Ted of a football pools winner, with ten dollars buying the Turkish family lots and lots of lira.

The coldest overnight park was the hilltop retreat of Erzurum, being a favourite stop for the Bulgarians (Bulgars or "Bogies"). Besides sporting the odd gold tooth, eating garlic, and fairing well in the weightlifting events at the Olympics, they were never a race which sprang to prominence. What they knew for sure was how to keep cool in the summer and warm in the winter, many doing the Afghanistan to London run. At Erzurum the trucks would form a circle, noses pointing inwards. The heat from the running engines ensured it was reasonably comfortable in the middle of the circle. Drivers could then stretch their legs without the risk of frostbite, taking sips of rakiya, whisky or schnapps to warm the innards.

The Kurds in the mountainous border regions of eastern Turkey endured a harsh existence during the winter months. Falls of snow the height of the rooftops are common. I wondered what they drank to combat the cold - probably home-brewed 60% Raki. Delays at the Barzargan border, waiting to enter Iran, could be many days. The cone-shaped snowcap of Mt Ararat offered little comfort to the Christians from the west.

In summer the landscape looked totally different. Instead of snow you had heat to contend with. The Iraq journey was the worst, with temperatures in Baghdad soaring up to 120F (50C), between May and September. For the Iran drivers it was more tolerable. Erzurum peaked around the high-eighties (32C), Tabriz in the nineties (35C), and Tehran just over the ton (40C). The ideal situation was to transit Iraq in the winter and Iran in the summer.

Mishaps in Turkey were never of a minor nature, due

to a combination of poor quality road surfaces and mechanical faults, or sheer bad luck. Travelling between Mardin and Cizre early one morning I came across a particular nasty accident. Three men pushing a car had been hit from behind by a truck. One had lost the lower part of his leg and was close to death. The injured were being cared for by a passing motorist. My contribution amounted to a first-aid kit, mugs of black sweet tea and hot and cold water. It was over two hours before medical assistance arrived, by which time the elderly man with one and a half legs had expired. Which truck it was I never found out, the driver having hightailed it to the border. The rising sun may have caused the catastrophe.

Chapter Fourteen

Behind the Iron Curtain

The route through Europe was largely dependent on the limited allocation of transit permits. When those for Austria dried up, you were left with an alternative route through communist Eastern Europe, termed "the commi-block." This entailed travelling from Frankfurt across to Nuremberg, before entering Czechoslovakia at the Waidhaus border post. Then it was onward to Hungary, bypassing Austria, before picking up the magical E5 at Budapest for the journey to Belgrade. One of the perks was that everything was cheap, although the hole-in-the-ground "stand-and-shit" facilities were very much the same.

Travelling from the southern Yugo city of Nis to the Bulgarian border could be hazardous in winter, especially the area around the Sicevacka Klisura gorge. Here the road ran through a series of short narrow tunnels that had been formed into the side of steep cliffs, made even more dangerous by fallen debris in the exposed areas. Extra vigilance was required, with any mistake resulting in a sheer drop down the ravine into the Nisava River. Sicevacka Klisura was an area of reverence, home to monks and monasteries. Further on was a restaurant, with an old Dakota aeroplane proudly standing alongside, in totally unfamiliar surroundings. I photographed the plane on the move. Stopping the truck, or even slowing down, could upset your rhythm, even during a 12-hour journey.

New Year's Day 1980 is one I'll never forget. It was a day when tiredness all but sent me to a watery grave. After disembarking the Volos ferry I drove the 200 miles up to the Yugo border in thick fog. The New Year was toasted in with coffee from a plastic cup, as I hung around waiting for the visibility to improve. Belgrade was 350 miles, but I was keen to press on, having been on the high seas for nearly three days. Just before Skopje it started snowing, so there was no chance of making it to Belgrade. Nis was my more realistic target. After a couple of hours the tail-lights of the vehicle in front faded into the distance. With the snow and windscreen wipers, my eyelids grew heavier and heavier. The next thing I remember was riding over rough ground. I was slightly disorientated for a few seconds before bringing the truck to a halt. I'd run off the road! I must have closed my eyes for a split second. In the falling snow everything was silent. The rig was well and truly stuck, but otherwise OK. There was nothing I could do at such an unearthly hour other than go to bed.

When daylight came, I was mightily relieved that there was no one or nothing else involved, and thankful I was running empty. I tried to move, but the wheels just kept churning away in the soft earth under the snow. There was nothing else for it but to hire a recovery vehicle. I was close to the town of Leskovac, 85 miles north of Skopje, and a few miles east of Kosovo. It was a sobering thought, that if I had run into the small lake a mile further on, instead of a field, that would indeed have been the end of the road for both the rig and myself. The local bus company seemed confident of success, but three hours and two broken tow-ropes later they had to admit defeat. One of their administrators was an absolute godsend, endlessly searching for a heavier recovery vehicle, even though our communication was limited to sign language and bits of German.

Leskovac was in the grip of winter, cold and drab. It wasn't on the tourist track, which probably explained the suspicious looks I got. Ordering a coffee was a fascinating experience. The waiter deposited a small, round brass tray on the table containing a cognac, a glass of water and a small cup of strong, thick black coffee. I wasn't quite sure in what rotation you drank them, just assuming that you took a sip of water after the coffee to help neutralise the taste, followed by the brandy. Whether my accent had ordered cognac instead of coffee I don't know, only that it was cheap enough not to worry about.

One morning, just before daybreak, I was suddenly awoken by a tapping noise on the cab outside. Fearing the worst, I quickly dressed in the prostrate position and armed myself with the dagger before gently moving the curtains, just enough to peer outside. Perched on the mirror brackets and pecking away at the ice that had formed in the window channels, were the largest black crows I'd ever seen. It was a relief not having to confront thieves, but initially a shock coming face to face with the huge winged monsters. One day stretched to three, to five, to seven, amid snowfalls and sub-zero temperatures, with nothing positive to report. Despite all this I tried various forms of getting mobile, but with the overnight frosts failing to penetrate the ground underneath the snow it proved futile.

On the ninth day the bus company foreman offered a glimmer of hope. He had heard of three men willing to help. He warned me they were bad people, wanting the equivalent of £250 in dollars for the job, which he thought was extortion. It was extortion of the first degree. I'd already lost nearly £400 in wages, but my main objective was to get back on the road. I didn't want to be stuck there all winter. We met the men at a café on the south side of town. It was clear from the outset that there was a rift between them and my colleague, with voices raised on several occasions. They were like gypsies, shabbily dressed and of scruffy appearance. Each had a small tipper truck loaded with sand. They proposed joining the three trucks with tow-bars, using the same system that Taffy and I had utilised to help one of their stricken countrymen on my first trip. This time here was no room for sentiment, with hard cash being their demands.

They seemed confident enough in their ability to recover me. The highway was now clear of snow, and I couldn't wait to get going. I offered them half payment in dollars with the rest in Deutschmarks, emphasising that they only got paid once I was on the road. It was a deal. The three trucks lined up, locking themselves together, and a large diameter steel rope was attached to my front tow-pin. After lots of shouting and waving it was a huge relief to feel movement once again, with the operation from field to road taking less than a minute. Back at the café it was celebratory cognacs all round as I doled out the booty. They were delighted at being paid over £80 each for an hour's work, more than six weeks' wages. They were happy, I was happy and Taffy would be happy. During my time in the field, scores of drivers of different nationalities had offered to help in one way on another, along with gallons of strong coffee.

On passing Leskovac on future trips, I had fond recollections of the good-hearted bus company foreman who wouldn't accept even the smallest token of thanks. I wrote his name and address in a diary, later to be lost, but at least I have his photo as a memento. Instead of stopping when I felt tired, I'd committed the dreaded sin of falling asleep and was lucky to be alive to tell the tale. Many years later, Kosovo was at the centre of a bitter war. Possibly the busman and the three drivers were from different ethnic backgrounds, that being the reason for their constant arguments.

At the Bulgarian duty-free I topped up with my requirements, besides buying a gallon bottle of whisky for the National Hotel. On arrival, the head barman only offered me the price I'd paid for it, rather than the agreed £18 plus a few free beers. His excuse was that he had more than enough, but there was no way he was getting it on the cheap. After all I didn't want to bugger it up for others, but what the hell was I going to do with a gallon of whisky? There was no option other than to take it home, short of drinking it and rotting away from the shoes upwards. At the time I was carrying three agricultural tractors that had been demonstrating their capabilities to potential customers at the Baghdad trade fair.

In the early hours I presented myself at Freilassing Customs, ready to enter Germany, but after checking my weight and paperwork I was ordered into a large building for an intense examination. I'd been subject to these checks before during daytime, especially with cargoes brought back from the Middle East. I had gambled that they wouldn't be so efficient at three in the morning, but I was wrong. They were looking for drugs, principally heroin and marijuana. To aid their search they had the advantage of the latest X-ray equipment. This could detect anything inside the wheels, fuel tanks and water carriers. The tractors were also scrutinised thoroughly. All the action was relayed to a television monitor, emphasising how easily you could become the victim of unknown circumstances.

During the cab inspection the gallon bottle of whisky came to light, along with 4,000 cigarettes, but the customs chief was not the least bit concerned. Instead, he wrote the details of my excesses on a slip of paper, and stapled it to my passport for presentation at Aachen. He wasn't interested in my illegal cargo, only that I didn't sell it within Germany. English customs weren't as advanced as the men from Deutschland, so after climbing the hill out of Dover I drove a few miles before removing my contraband from a place that will remain secret. The gallon bottle of whisky was sold to my local, the "Travellers Rest" in Crook. The cigarettes sold for £4 a cartoon. I guess you could say that the Krauts were partly responsible for granting me a license to smuggle liquor and tobacco

Another ferry route to Syria was from the Adriatic port of Koper in northern Yugoslavia. It was an unusual time of year for me to be cruising on the high seas, but orders were orders. I arrived at the dock only to miss it by a cat's whisker. I knew on leaving Ostend that the chances of catching the ferry were extremely remote, but to miss it by minutes was most frustrating, especially with two days to wait for the next one. A short while later another rig pulled alongside, with the new left-hand drive English-registered Bedford TM workhorse belonging to owner-driver John Thompson from Northampton.

He was one of a growing number of "subbies" who risked everything to better themselves. Nearly all were financed up to the hilt, with the danger of losing everything if there was a slight dip in profit. Normally they hauled trailers for third parties, who would pay for the ferries and trains and supply all the necessary paperwork, along with some up-front money to cover expenses. Many of these sub-contract drivers preferred groupage (multi-drops) because it generated more money. They would have cargoes for Baghdad, Basra, Nassiriya and Kirkuk, all on the same trailer.

On getting our heads together we decided to hire a car and spend a day in Venice, about 180miles along the coastal highway. Venice, featured in the latest Bond film, "Moonraker," was exactly how I pictured it. After recovering from the shock of paying tourist prices for a snack in St. Mark's Square, we were directed to a cheap watering-hole frequented by the locals. There we drank, sang and danced the night away to the sounds of an accordion, later bedding down on a park bench.

The journey through Bulgaria was a pleasure in the summer months when the countryside was in full bloom. After a late, late breakfast one hot summer's day, I was preparing to have forty winks when I noticed a broken trailer spring. Thanks to some friendly nuts and bolts and much sweat and dirt I was mobile within two hours. Bulgaria was another safe country to drive through, as the police often ignored minor indiscretions. In the rural areas you battled for supremacy with horses and carts, highlighting the time warp between the past and present. Once I was caught by a keen-eyed border clerk at Svilengrad. He noticed my green insurance card had expired by a week. It was my fault entirely, for not having checked my paperwork thoroughly before leaving home. I was ordered to park in the Customs area while waiting for a new card, which could take a week to arrive. Taffy would be pleased. The only consolation was that I hadn't been caught by the Turks.

Eight hours later, around midnight, I decided to take a chance, even though I risked being stopped at gunpoint. Although there'd been a change in personnel the guards would be well aware of my situation. There was not so much as a glance from anyone inside the offices, as I left the floodlit park and gently moved past security. I covered the next 250 miles across Bulgaria in double-quick time. I was expecting to be arrested when I presented myself at the Dimitrovgrad border for clearance to enter Yugo, but surprisingly I was treated in the normal courteous manner.

It was unusual to come across English cars or tourists on the main highways of Yugoslavia, Greece or Bulgaria. Occasionally a red London double-decker bus would make an appearance at the Londra camp, reminding me of the Cliff Richard film "Summer Holiday." Many passengers were students, wanting a peep at the outside world before graduating. Istanbul was the pinnacle of their travels, and they were totally gob-smacked at our escapades. The camp was also famous for its multicoloured t-shirts. The shirts displaying many flags of the world in circular fashion, similar to a dartboard.

One freezing January night, I was parked in a lay-by near the Yugoslav border checking some paperwork when there was a knock on the door. A Romanian, who spoke no English, required a lift to Austria. He was carrying all his worldly goods in a small canvas bag. I motioned to him that no passengers were allowed in the cab, offering him a ride in the empty trailer. He wasn't keen on that idea, but pointed underneath. He seemed willing to risk life and limb whatever the outcome, bedding down near the spare wheels, while I made sure he covered his face as protection against the icy conditions. At Speilfeld, the customs officer shone his torch in the back of the trailer before clearing me to enter Austria. Three miles further on I pulled off the road, waiting for a few minutes before checking my stowaway, only to find that the bird had flown. The poor bugger must have been blue with cold, having endured eight miles of sub-zero temperatures. Either that or he'd fallen off, the price to pay for having no passport.

Travelling from Sofia to the Greek border crossing at Kulata, I was rather surprised to see women re-surfacing the road, a task usually considered too manual for the weaker sex. Judging by their muscles and physique it was difficult to tell otherwise, although I very much doubted if the males would be dressed in skirts and ankle socks. Once in northern Greece, the way of life in towns such as Serrai, Drama, Xanthi and Komotini seemed so relaxing. It was far off the beaten track of tourism, but wherever you stopped you were welcomed by smiling faces. Driving through these picturesque places was an added bonus to the job. The soil was the same reddish-brown colour that I'd experienced in Oz, with the public outdoor swimming pools always a temptation to don the bathers. One afternoon in a Drama taverna, I was tucking into a meal when the shopkeeper, a chap in his sixties, wheeled out an old-fashioned jukebox from behind a curtain, keen to please with some early rock'n'roll sounds. Besides Greek, he spoke only German, learnt during the war years, making you realise the extent of the Nazi occupation.

There was also the beautiful coastal resort of Kavala with its palm tree lined promenade, looking out to the island of Thassos. The town still retained its huge overhead aqueduct, an imposing work of architecture that had served the residents for centuries. St Paul preached there, his first encounter on European soil, also baptising the first woman, Lydia. By all accounts the disciple was well-travelled, considering his conveyances would have been strictly limited to the donkey, horse and ship.

Chapter Fifteen

In Deutschland You Must Obey

Heavy-goods vehicles were prohibited on German highways from midnight Saturday to 10pm on Sunday. If you were leaving the country the ban could be delayed by half an hour. In Austria it was worse, with a 31-hour ban in force from 3pm Saturday until 10pm Sunday. This was primarily to cater for peoples' leisure activities, so that they could enjoy the pleasures of the countryside without being choked by diesel fumes, unsightly cargoes, or congestion. The exception to the rule was perishable goods, so for those driving refrigerated rigs it wasn't a problem. To avoid the bans, it was essential to plan ahead. Some drivers would detour on the return journey, spending a day or two in the Bulgarian Black Sea resort of Burgas. Others preferred Kavala, Istanbul or even Baghdad. The Mediterranean was even inviting in October at Iskenderun near Adana. While enjoying a swim, you could observe the Taurus Mountains, some with their snow-caps on.

During a weekend public holiday, I entered Germany from Austria just after midnight on the Friday. I was desperate to beat the ban, which was due to start at seven on the Saturday morning. Luxembourg, some 460 miles away, was the only realistic means of exiting Deutschland. That morning I took a chance, breaking every rule in the book. Rest periods amounted to a stretch of the legs. At seven-thirty, the limit of my grace period, I was passing

Saarbrucken, still 50 miles from the Remich border post. At eight, with the deadline long gone, I was left with just over 20 miles, when a green and white BMW appeared in the mirror. I wasn't so much bothered about being over the permitted time; it was the tachograph card that was the problem. I'd be better off eating it! As they overtook an officer glanced up at the cab acknowledging my timid hand gesture. I thought they'd be waiting up ahead but they weren't. The German border post was completely free of traffic, as was the Luxembourg control, Formalities were cleared and the barrier raised within minutes. My return cargo was two road rollers for Merthyr Tydfil, South Wales. I could now spend Sunday night having a beer near Pontipridd, the birthplace of both Taffy and Tom Jones, rather than waiting for the ban to end in Germany.

From time to time various forwarding agents would thrust their business cards into your hand, offering return loads. Many were Euro-based with offices in the Middle East, such as Belgium firm Militzer & Munch and M.G. international from Hamburg. Others included Damascus based Sammy Sirissi and Ljubo Lutman of Yugoslavia.

One of my return cargoes was from Wolfsberg in southern Austria, the telex I'd collected from the National Hotel advising of a six-day working cycle at the factory. Early on the Saturday morning I was still in Ljubljana, a hundred miles to the south, but if I got loaded quickly I might still be able to be out of the country before the three o' clock driving ban came into effect. I intended going via Klagenfurt, but noticed a smaller border crossing at Seeberg, which according to the map would save me 20 miles and valuable time. For the final few miles the road was a mixture of twists and turns, rising steeply in places. I was thankful when the Douane-Zoll sign finally came into view. The border was quiet with not another vehicle in sight, bright sunshine only adding to the tranquil surroundings.

Raised eyebrows greeted me on the Austrian side, with the boss man taking a more than passing interest in the trailer fuel tanks, convinced he had a diesel smuggler on his hands. All sorts of things must have been flashing through his mind, the most obvious being, why had I travelled on such an unsuitable road to use a quiet border crossing at nine in the morning? Clearly they hadn't seen a rig decked out for Middle East operations before. Even after presenting the paperwork and loading details, the "gross chef" was not at all convinced, determined to have his moment of glory. We'd always referred to the Austrians as super-Krauts, regarding themselves as elitist Germans, and this chap was no exception. I was carrying around 250 galls (1,136 litres) of diesel, and he insisted that I pay tax on everything over 300 litres! This was all I needed, with the small, quiet border I was hoping to waltz through proving to be as difficult as Turkey. I challenged the 300-litre figure adopted by their neighbours, besides referring to the fact that they weren't even members of the EEC. I needed 800 litres to get home. I also added that I had only enough money left for meals, but the chief wasn't interested. During the entire conflab he adopted a typical upper lip stance of self-importance, even when I jokingly accused him of being worse then Adolf Hitler.

I was then ordered to park in the small courtyard while they decided my fate, hopefully before Monday morning. After making breakfast I busied myself cleaning the cab inside and out. The border control were surprised that I was totally self-sufficient, besides accepting my punishment like a gentleman. After two hours they let me go without paying or doing anything, having proved their powers. The Brit with the Kojak hairstyle would no doubt have been the topic of conversation in the local gasthof later that day. After loading at Wolfsberg I spent an enforced weekend in Graz. It was also subject to a wide range of temperatures, ranging from overnight winter lows of −14C to summer highs of 30C+, much the same as neighbouring northern Yugoslavia. I was surprised to see alcohol vending machines in many Austrian workplaces, apparently a traditional practice.

Austria has some amazing landscapes. It is best appreciated in late spring, when the sun and snow-capped peaks form a striking combination. The alpine scenery south of Salzburg and to the west, differs entirely from the north-eastern areas bordering Vienna. Being right-hand drive definitely had its advantages in mountainous terrain, allowing you to keep in close contact with the edge of the road while negotiating the tight hairpin bends.

One of Taffy's latest acquisitions had only a 300litre (66galls) fuel tank, but within hours of its purchase it was put to work, with us both loading lightweight hi-tech equipment from the same Peterborough factory destined for Samawa, southern Iraq. On the rare occasions we travelled together our relationship could only be described as so-and-so at best, but I was now familiar with the work routine, taking Taffy's mannerisms with a pinch of salt. Delays over paperwork turned our schedule completely upside down, resulting in us getting an afternoon ferry and arriving at a lay-by near Frankfurt during the early hours.

His truck was down to 20 gallons despite having

topped up in Ostend, meaning he would need another 20 as a safety net to get into Austria. After discussing the situation we decided to take a chance and use some cherry. Taffy had plenty of it, so why pay pump prices? His trailer had one underslung "belly tank," mounted between the chassis, containing 250 galls. Fuel was obtained by pressurising the thick-walled tank with an airline. After breaking the customs seal and opening the tap, the red diesel gushed through a plastic pipe into the running tanks. Re-sealing it was no problem. I always carried a few spare plumbs (seals), so a halfpence coin on either side of the lead, crushed by mole grips, would be enough to convince the most sceptical border officials.

Suddenly our quiet surroundings were invaded by the appearance of a green and white police car, whose occupants were keen to stretch their legs and have a smoke. They were parked at least thirty yards away. If they had twigged what we were up to, the rig would be impounded for using illegal fuel. Taffy would be pleased. Normal procedure was to disconnect the airline and allow the tank to de-pressurise before closing the tap. It only needed a minute, but Taffy was in no mood to delay. He swiftly disconnected the airline, jumped in the cab and drove off with fuel spewing out of the filler pipe like a fountain. I waited around for a few minutes, not wanting to arouse suspicion. On the autobahn my headlamps picked up the path of diesel, with probably five gallons emitted from the pipe over the next half-mile. The trail then went cold, but not the smell. Thirty miles further on we finally got the chance to close and re-seal the tap. Taffy had to endure the smell until the Londra camp, using the steam cleaner to get rid of the stinking stuff from the truck chassis and trailer.

As stated earlier, the journey from Aachen to
Freilassing/Salzburg couldn't be legally transited in a day.
Sometimes I'd try to beat the system by interfering with
the tachograph, relying on the usually keen-eyed border
control having an off-day. The tacho had three needles,
plotting a chart of speed, distance and time. By limiting
the upward movement of the speed needle, it was possible
to travel at 100ks, with the needle registering only 80ks
on the card. You could then depart Aachen at midday and
present yourself at the German/Austrian border any time
after midnight. The paperwork would show the previous
days stamp, but not the actual time of the stamp. When
inspecting the tacho cards, their primary concern was
speed, which would appear OK.

What you couldn't alter were the distance or time
needles, which on close inspection would reveal I'd driven
500 miles in one day, an impossible task legally.
Sometimes they didn't even bother asking for the tacho
cards. The best time to pass through the borders was the
quiet early hours, when the night-shift staff were not
always at their best. This would entail a small overtime
charge on the Austrian side, but it was well worth it. Once
I got too confident during the day at Freilassing, with a
chap in a white overall analysing the card before wanting
to inspect the truck. He immediately opened the
tachograph looking for any telltale signs – I'd already
removed the sponge – before summoning me to his office.
I was accused of interfering with the instrument, the
penalty was parking for twenty-four hours at the border.
They kept my carnet and passport as security. You win
some, you lose some.

Even though my Munich experiences were brief, I
still found time to explore the famous city while waiting

for the train to depart. Many magnificent buildings add
to the beauty of the Bavarian surroundings. No wonder
Adolf Hitler chose Munich as a base for the Nazi
movement. The former SS headquarters still displayed its
bullet-damaged exterior. Gorden pointed out the famous
Town Hall glockenspiel clock-tower in St. Mary's Square,
and the skyline legacy of the 1972 Olympic Games.
Needless to say, we visited Munich's world famous
Hofbrauhaus, with its tasty frauleins in traditional dirndls
serving litres of bier. Along with the sounds of the
oompah band, this was as good as it gets. The beer-kellar
craze had all but fizzled out back home, but not before
giving the ladies their first chance to swig liquor from
large glasses. What I did find most appetising in Bavaria
and Austria, were the huge choice of meats and cheeses.

Chapter Sixteen

High Noon Drivers

The Middle East trucker can be described in many ways, from an adventure seeker to someone trying to get out of debt. They are all knights of the road, with many years and miles in the saddle, prepared to lay their heads on the block to better themselves. Many jumped at the chance of driving to dreamland, only for the picture-postcard illusions to be shattered by reality. In the early days Taffy, hired drivers from all over the country with proven pedigrees in Middle Eastern operations, besides having his own band of men who'd worked for him in the UK for many years. These were people you could send abroad, safe in the knowledge that everything was in experienced hands. Other drivers did one or two trips, only to abandon the E5 for the M1, especially if their wives were pulling the strings. For most it was the money and visions of debt-free houses, big cars, brand new furniture and super holidays.

I was divorced and looked at things rather differently. My immediate outlook was to enjoy life while being paid for it. On returning home the married contingent would collect enough wages to sink a ship, whilst I was happy with sinking a rowing boat.

In high temperatures there's nothing worse than being able to smell yourself. The only places of note to freshen up were the ferries, German and Austrian service areas, National Hotel, Londra camp and Incerlik. I always carried five gallons of water, more in the summer months, copying an Aussie shower that I'd used in the bush. After cutting the top off a plastic drum and drilling lots of small holes in the base, I suspended it seven feet from the ground. Two gallons was enough to be presentable, if you were quick.

The cab's upholstery was also subject to regular sprinklings of zoflora-type substances. After all, the cab was my permanent hotel room. A roadside fountain near Plovdiv served not only as a meal stop, but also as a truck wash and bath house. The ice-cold crystal clear water was also suitable for drinking, much the same as at Tarsus.

During the summer months, when delivering south of Baghdad, I'd be tempted to sleep under the stars instead of being confined to a hot cab. I tried it a couple of times until someone mentioned about two Russian drivers who'd done the same, only to be attacked by a pack of wolves or wild dogs near the marshlands. They didn't live to tell the tale. I didn't intend being a meal ticket for any nightime prowlers, so I reverted to my sweatbox. At times you could be excused for thinking you were part of another era, especially when passing historial sites such as Babylon. It was much the same with Tarsus, your imagination helping to fill in between the cracks.

Once the thermometer started rising, it was clear that to make life as comfortable as possible I would have to adopt to the ways of the Turkish and Arab truckers. Nearly all of their vehicles contained properly manufactured iceboxes, whereas I would have to make do and mend. In most towns dotted along the main highways, huge slabs of ice would be stacked up on the pavement, a day's supply costing a few coins or a packet of cigarettes. The vendor would swiftly go to work with an ice pick, transforming part of a slab into small pieces, filling the two eskys about five inches deep. One was kept on the passenger side floor, containing fruit juice, soft drinks and small towels. Once the temperature had topped the ton (40C), I would wrap the towels round my head like a turban, to keep cool. The other was kept in a trailer box, containing anything that was planned for the afternoon meal, along with cucumbers and tomatoes. Tinned corned beef would turn to liquid, so it would have to be cooled to its former state, especially if Gorden wanted it with chips. There was an abundance of fresh fruit and vegetables throughout Turkey and Iraq in all seasons from roadside traders, with everything imaginable east of Adana.

At times the heat was overpowering, with the cab resembling a furnace. The dashboard-mounted cooling fan only exacerbated the situation by blowing hot air. Late one afternoon I was heading towards Gaziantep when a truck travelling towards me suddenly started flashing his lights for me to stop. The pot-bellied driver from Ipswich was dying of thirst. Either he had caught too much sun or was coming down with a fever. It was bad enough for my twelve stone in the heat, so he must really have been suffering. Soon to be at Saxophone Joe's, I'd used all my cold drinks for the day. There was only some melted ice in the esky, but it was contaminated with dust. I had some warm orange juice but my East Anglian colleague was desperate for a cold drink. No sooner had I removed the esky from the cab than he lifted it to his lips, drinking non-stop, before pouring the remainder over his head.

He couldn't thank me enough, getting back in his cab a cool and contented man. I reckon he must have devoured half a gallon of dirty water, so for the next three days he'd be shitting through the eye of a needle. At least that would get rid of some of his belly. He was on his first journey, totally unprepared. I classed water, a kettle and even a small one-burner stove as essential tools. You could conjure up just about anything, the simplest instant meal being a pot noodle.

A perennial question amongst drivers is whether it's better to be too hot or too cold. The extremes of cold and heat were found at Erzurum in winter and Baghdad in July. Personally I prefer the cold, at least you can light a fire or conjure up some form of heating. If you're working in high temperatures without the luxury of shade everything is hot, including the ground, water, tools and possibly the brain. The Aussies have a saying for people that have gone bush crazy in the hot tropical conditions – "gone troppo."

It was rumoured that a driver, travelling to Jordan, had driven from Munich to Istanbul non-stop, apart from time spent at border controls. I wondered what medication he was taking to keep awake during the 1,100-mile journey. In late summer at the National Hotel I met up with another northern driver going to Iraq, so it was only natural we run together. He was keen to eat up the road, some days exceeding 500 miles. This fella was driving virtually non-stop from dawn till dusk. When we finally did make camp, two or three beers would rapidly affect him, and I would have to put him to bed. At first I put it down to fatigue, but by the time we reached Baghdad I began to wonder.

We were in the British Club, when without warning he suddenly fell asleep, resting his head on the bar top. Finding it impossible to wake him, I summoned a cab to take us back to the park, making excuses that he must be coming down with a fever. While he was snoring away I carried out a search of his cab, my suspicions confirmed by the hordes of Phylosan tablets on the shelf above the windscreen. No wonder he could drive for hours on end, filling himself with pills. It didn't matter about the poor fucker following him, whose eyelids were feeling heavy after fifteen hours of heat and dust. Months later I heard he'd been robbed in a bar in Germany, probably after falling asleep. Popping pills wasn't a problem I was aware of, even though the schedules were punishing on both mind and body.

Travelling in pairs could be ideal. One would cook while the other transferred diesel and checked the vehicle's mechanics, but you had to know how each other ticked. Two of Taffy's previous drivers, Ted Hannon and Andy Anderson, had run together for years. I preferred travelling alone for the majority of the journey, enjoying my own eating and resting rota. My relationship with Gorden was only moderate, but we ran together several times and had no choice but to make the best of it. My employment situation was totally different to Gorden's. For him it was a career, for me a long holiday with free travel. Occasionally he would inquire when I was moving to Oz, after all, nine months had passed. I assured him I was going when all the formalities had been ironed out. One night we had a slight altercation. Returning from the Anbar hotel in Baghdad, I was driving. After crossing the 14th July Bridge, I travelled straight ahead at a roundabout instead of turning left. Gorden started screaming that I was going the wrong way. I said I wasn't. It resulted in us having a minor bout of fisticuffs in the glare of the truck's headlamps, much to the amusement of a passing taxi driver. Gorden was right and I was wrong, but our disgreement was soon forgotten.

One hot afternoon, I was relaxing with a few drivers outside the National Hotel when I was alerted to someone wanting the Davies driver. A bearded stocky chap of around forty strode across to the table, dressed in t-shirt, shorts, baseball cap and shades, beaming from ear to ear.

"Hi, you must be Kevin. I'm Errol, pleased to meet yer," a welcoming hand accompanying his broad Scots accent. Finally I was meeting the man I'd read and heard so much about concerning his Iran adventure, swashbuckling Errol Flynn. He didn't exactly portray the image of his Hollywood namesake. He was neither tall, nor of athletic build, nor did he even have the looks of a lady-killer, so why the name? There was only one other possible explanation – the size of his manhood.

In January 1979, amid the political turmoil in Iran, Errol had been marooned in no-man's land between the frontiers of Iran and Turkey for five weeks. The Shah had fled the country, resulting in the borders being closed, while people awaited the return of Ayatollah Khomeini. The Turks wouldn't let him enter their country, bayoneting his tins of food when he protested. The Red Cross eventually provided some sort of nourishment. At least he could gaze on Mt Ararat, thankful that snow was falling instead of incessant rain, or Noah and his Ark would have to come to the rescue. When the borders finally re-opened the Turks conveniently mislaid his trailer's paperwork, refusing to let it pass through customs. They were after his trailer with its tanks of diesel, due to a shortage in Turkey. Taffy managed to relay a message to Errol, telling him to set fire to the trailer, thus ensuring nobody benefited.

When Errol finally arrived home he was hailed a hero, with the newspapers proclaiming that swashbuckling Errol Flynn had lived to fight another day. However, almost immediately, there was a falling out between him and Taffy, resulting in Errol departing to drive to Spain and Italy. He was keen to get back on the Middle East run, which meant more money, so he patched up his differences with the Welshman.

Errol was driving an immaculate two-year old Volvo F88 in Davies Turner's livery of green and white, one of the last made. On arrival at Istanbul we were both desperate for a shower, keen to be rid of the dust and sweat of the past fourteen hours. The truth would now be revealed, with my curiosity by now getting the better of me. I was expecting to see something to make my eyes water, but besides witnessing a fine specimen of a man, he was nothing out of the ordinary. I had to know. As soon as we were ready to go to the restaurant I asked him point blank.

"Errol, I've got a problem that's bugging me. Why the name Errol Flynn?" "One moment, Kevin," chuckled Errol. He climbed back into his cab, returning to ground level almost immediately.

"The reason I'm called Errol Flynn, is because that's my fuckin' name," at the same time handing me his passport, which I gazed at for a few seconds before bursting into laughter.

Even though Errol was born in Prestwick his mother hailed from Errol in Perthshire, naming her son after her roots, but I reckon the flamboyant lady's man must also have had some influence. Whatever it was, it caused Errol more than his fair share of problems growing up, with him regularly reflecting on the many times that his name had caused embarrassment. They still continued, especially at Dover, where Customs officials would have sly digs at the man who bedded thousands of gorgeous dames. Three cheers for Errol, with whom there was never a dull moment.

When I had the buses at Etherley, there was elderly chap called Sherlock Holmes living in the village. Apparently his father had been an avid reader of early writings of Conan Doyle, never thinking for one moment that his books, later his films, would enjoy world-wide acclaim. I guess carrying a famous name was more of a curse than a blessing.

Many of us do things we are not proud of or later regret, as happened with me one time in Baghdad. On arrival at the Haswa Customs park the mood was quite sombre in the Blighty camp. One driver was in a distressed state. He'd been manhandled by the military in eastern Turkey, resulting in him shaking uncontrollably from head to toe. The experience had shattered his nerves so badly, that his boss had arranged to fly him home later that day. This left his Volvo F88 rig at the mercy of others. For the past three days my alternator had been overcharging the batteries. I had to remove a fuse at regular intervals to prevent further problems. The Mercedes workshops in Baghdad checked the alternator and wiring before giving it the all clear, but during the drive back to Haswa the smell of acid fumes signalled the problem was still there. I had hoped to make the Zacho border by midnight but it was pointless. Losing my headlamps was not worth contemplating.

Back at the park a dismantling process was well underway on the abandoned Volvo. The good tyres were removed and replaced with damaged, worn or punctured

ones. The excuse was that the truck would be there
forever, and the owner could claim the loss on his
insurance. I decided to exchange my batteries for those on
the Volvo. A few minor alterations and the switch was
completed.

Next morning I was just about to move out, when a
solitary figure strode across the park for a chat. He was
easy recognisable by the large black tattoo on top of his
right hand. It was a driver I ran alongside a couple of
times, a cheerful lad in his late twenties, who at the time
was working for Duxbury's of Charnock Richard. I was
under the impression he'd finished driving Middle East,
so I asked him what was he doing there. "I'm finished
Kevin, but a firm back home asked if I'd fly out here and
drive a rig back for them, but it appears the vultures have
had their pickings."

You could have slain me with a feather. I never felt so
embarrassed since the time I got caught in Australia
trying to "shoot through" at Mrs. O Neil's. I hadn't a clue
what to say. My guilt was plainly obvious as I headed for
the border seconds later, my blushes spared by the sun
tan. On arrival at the depot Taffy's first greeting wasn't to
tell me to steam clean the vehicle, but to get in the office.
His face was like thunder. A haulier from Burnley had
been on the phone complaining that I'd replaced six of his
good wheels for six with faulty tyres, but with no mention
of the batteries. Naturally I denied switching the tyres. I
explained the electrical problem, but £40 worth of
batteries was nothing compared with the £700 it would
take to replace the tyres.

Taffy phoned the nearby Tyre Services depot, and
asked them to check the serial numbers on all the tyres.
Tyre Services had fitted ours six months earlier. I then had

to phone the haulier to try and calm the waters. He accused me of stealing the tyres, and said he had witnesses. Taffy tried to explain that all the tyre serial numbers tallied with his invoices, but the haulier was still full of hell. Davies vehicles always had good tyres, and Volvo wheels could not possibly fit on a Merc, but it seems that once I'd left Haswa I was termed the Thief of Baghdad. I could quite easily have spilt the beans about the southern firm whose drivers not only took the wheels, but also the wing mirrors, headlamps and wipers. It wasn't my style to grass on others, but they found it easy to shift the blame onto absent brethren.

I never did get to see the Lancashire driver again, only hoping that his judgement of me wasn't too clouded. It's just a pity that the rig hadn't been left at the airport, with only the "long vehicle" signs to go amiss. Did I get a thank-you from Taffy for nursing his vehicle home? Did I fuck! Some described him as being OK in small doses, but I reckon that was much too flattering.

I joined up with Taffy and Errol in July 1980, on a journey that enjoyed its own brand of humour. As usual I was travelling at the rear, with Taffy classing my tool kit as an insurance against the unforeseen. Being at the back meant I was constantly playing "catch up," the lead truck always had the advantage at traffic lights and overtaking manoeuvres. We arrived in Aksaray around nine, having covered 420 miles, during which time Errol and I both sustained a puncture. It was dark, we were dusty and sweaty, so we made do with a quick body-wash out of the bucket before tucking into a kebab. At five-thirty next morning Taffy knocked on the cab door signalling it was time to roll. I clambered out of the bunk feeling stiff, but within seconds pandemonium broke out when Taffy tried to rouse Errol. They went at it hammer and tongs.

"Fuck off yer Welsh bastard!" shouted the Scotsman, clearly annoyed at the early-morning call.

"Errol, I'm telling yer, get ready to go," snapped Taffy.

"And I'm fuckin' telling you, I'll leave when I'm ready," returned Errol, "don't try running my schedule. Now fuck off."

Their raised voices were an alarm call to the other truckers, with the international audience enjoying every second of the action.

The tempers of the two men soon reached boiling point, with Errol determined not to be railroaded out of his routine. Later that day Taffy and I pulled into Saxophone Joe's at Gaziantep, Errol arriving half an hour later. That was the only disagreement I witnessed between the two, but the sheer ferocity of the argument suggested it went deeper than that. The three of us became guest members of the Belgrade American Embassy employees recreation club, whose superb facilities would keep us occupied during the weekend driving bans. As things turned out I only visited twice, with Oz calling and Saddam desperate to show his might against the Iranians.

On my last get-together with Errol, I was the lead truck travelling through southern Turkey. At Birecik the ciggi boys were waiting as usual, having observed us for the past three miles. Some were barely out of nappies. They lived in small houses dug into the hillside, which explained why they were always in attendance, whatever time or day. To encourage your benevolence even more, one of the older youths sat on a horse at the top of the hill, twirling a sling above his head.

When we stopped for a brew, Errol was furious at the hole in the passenger side of his windscreen, inflicted by the lad with the sling, He was adamant he gave them some cigs. The stone he retrieved from the cab floor measured about two inches in diameter. Whatever the reason, Errol was lucky not to be injured, with the sling youth naturally thinking he was left hand drive. I never did get to ask Errol if he got off his horse to fire the thing. This was another advantage of laminated glass, whereby the screen would crack, chip or even take a direct hit without shattering. Eventually the screens were replaced. Suttons of Valley Street, Darlington, would renew the Merc's flat screen for £70. According to Mercedes, it was still possible to drive normally, or even smoke with the windscreen missing, due to the aerodynamic design of the cab.

Gardner engines may have been the driver's best friend for many years on the home front, and the showman's answer to driving generators at funfairs, but they certainly weren't at home in Turkey. They'd even proved their worth powering boats in the waters around Hong Kong and Shanghai, but Ted Hannon's evaluation of them for Middle East operations wasn't the most complimentary. In severe arctic conditions they couldn't generate enough heat to warm the cab, whereas in summer they were totally the opposite, forever overheating on long ascents.

Ted was often quoted as holding the record of 16 days for the Bishop Auckland to Tabriz (Iran) return journey, being rather fortunate that the spring climate and customs controls were in his favour. He also returned from Tehran to the depot in six and a half days, including loading in Austria and delivering to York. Ted was a top-quality workshop man, but driving through foreign lands made a welcome change to restoring commercial vehicles. Like most geniuses of their craft, he was partial to lubricating the tonsils at regular intervals, besides the occasional flutter with a fair maiden.

His artistic talents came from his Italian roots, as did his love of Alpha Romeos, although I would be hesitant to suggest any connection with Michaelangelo. Ted was appointed to paint a mural for the British club in Baghdad, but almost immediately the Iran crisis boiled over, and Ted opted to work in Saudi. He also had his regular clientele at home for the famous Tabriz Persian carpets and rugs.

Chapter Seventeen

Women of the Road

With twelve hours to kill in Koper before the ferry weighed anchor, I settled for a club buzzing with local "talent" and ended up with the star prize. She wasn't going to break any hearts by even the remotest stretch of imagination, but as the saying goes, "any port in a storm." On arriving back at the truck she asked for forty dollars, finally being grateful for twenty. There was nothing for nothing, just the risk of a dose of clap. Ten minutes later there was a knock on the cab door. Who the fuck's that, husband, boyfriend?

She was holding a forefinger to her lips as I slowly edged out of the bunk and peered through the curtains. Two policemen dressed in waterproofs were standing in the sudden heavy downpour. I lowered the window enough to get my head through, with us conversing as best we could about someone fitting her description. I got the feeling they were interested in her sex-for-sale activities, but I just denied all knowledge and with that they disappeared. Whatever she was up to I wasn't interested, as long as she didn't flash a blade or point a gun.

Females were always in evidence at the roadside diners and the less glamorous parking areas of Yugoslavia. These places were popular with Commi-block drivers and Turks, many of whom were chauffeuring for Dutch companies such Rynart transport, who had offices in

Istanbul. One afternoon near Zagreb I called in at a truck stop for a quick nap, only to encounter a fridge trailer with its rear doors wide open. Its cargo comprised of half a dozen Turks, enjoying a gang-bang with some of the local bottle-blonde girls. No matter what language you spoke, everyone knew the expression, bodily or otherwise, for engaging in lust.

Late one Saturday afternoon Gorden and I parked up at Incirlik. We topped up with fuel, showered and ate, before wandering across to Groovy Hasan's. In the store we met a USA military man from the nearby base. He asked if we were interested in going to a dance that night. Of course we were. The only stipulation was that we take some drink. He arranged to meet us at the entrance gate at eight to arrange security clearance. We spruced ourselves up in our best togs and took the short walk to the base, armed with a crate of beer. Eight o'clock came and went with no sign of our party invitation. Security on the gate was sceptical as to our intentions, especially when we didn't know our host's name.

Our tales of driving from London to Baghdad did little to convince the Oklahoma security guard. At nine we gave up the ghost, sending our American cousin to hell. After returning the beer to the trailer locker, we took a cab into Adana. We ended up in a club, where we tended to be the main focus of attention, along with the belly dancer. Later, in the toilet, a chap in his thirties, sporting plenty of jewellery, surprised us with his command of the English language. He asked if we fancied his sister and her friend. I could smell a rat, much the same as Gorden, a wink and a nod signalling our departure. Sister my arse. He would have been a pimp, with us probably ending up having to pay dearly for the privilege. The Yanks were probably his best customers.

Apparently a good time with the ladies of Istanbul could be had at Pig Alley. This was a rather crude interpretation of the name Pigalle Plaza, the red lamp district in Paris. The brothels were situated on the hill leading from the Galata Bridge to the Galata Tower. One such place was enclosed, fortified with two large iron gates, with entry and exit accessed by a wicket door in one of the gates. Burly Turks carrying various forms of weaponry policed the inside, ensuring that everyone got their money's worth. There was also the Kasbah close to the Londra camp, but even they were reluctant to accept Turkish lira. For the Iran drivers, the eastern Turkish frontier towns provided plenty of brothels and choices of nationalities. The girls were mainly from the bordering countries of Armenia, Georgia and Azerbaijan, offering far better comforts than the cab heaters.

When travelling through Greece towards Turkey, I'd usually park-up around dusk at Kavala. I'd stay on the edge of town, close to the beach and the football stadium, ready for an early morning start to Ipsala on the Turkish border. The fine damsels of Austria and Bulgaria were a source of comfort from time to time, but in Kavala it was no-go, simply because of the timetable. It wasn't normally part of the return route, unless you wanted to mix business with pleasure during the weekend driving ban.

The Bulgarian drivers weren't too keen on our western standards and morals, preferring their communist status and more sedate lifestyle. As far as morals were concerned, the young ladies at the steppes had no qualms about exchanging their bodies for wrangler garments or Pretty Polly stockings. There weren't many females who would be willing to share your bed for the night for £3.

That was the price I paid for wrangler waistcoats, counterfeit of course, from a market trader near Frankfurt.

With the temperature well over the hundred, my Kojak headline wasn't taking kindly to the sun's continuous rays, so after unloading I popped into the British Club for a dip in the pool. Friday afternoon was always a hive of activity, but for some reason it appeared busier than usual, with lots of females swanning around. Indeed they were a tasty bunch, inquiries revealing that they were part of a dancing troupe, staying at the nearby Carlton Hotel. They were at the start of a six-week tour of the oil-rich states, performing for various high-profile dignitaries throughout Arabia. By early evening I was well acquainted with one of the fairer species, with my accent, or hairstyle, having tickled her fancy. Karen jumped at the suggestion of viewing the landmarks, with us starting along Saddoun Street before taking a cab for the rest of the city tour.

Next morning I awoke with one of Karen's earrings in my left earlobe. I couldn't remember how it got there. There was still a mark from the original piercing so I guess she must have done the rest, even though the ear was left slightly bloodied. After removing it and placing it on the dressing table I wished her luck, along with a goodbye embrace. We would both continue our poles-apart ambitions, whether it be dancing, driving, loving or adventure. The only buzz better than travel, was the all-night company of a female, but even that had its drawbacks from time to time.

Two steel erectors from Sheffield were regular visitors to the British club, working on a variety of new building projects that were springing up all over the city. Their gross wage wasn't much more than that in the UK, the only advantage being that it was tax-free, along with other perks. One of them was cock-a-hoop about returning home, having achieved his aim of paying off his house mortgage. He was sick of working in a shit hole, as he termed it. He could now take a job back home for less money, instead of being away from his wife and kids for long periods. At thirty-years old he was lucky to have a new house paid for, so after a farewell drink it was only a case of bon voyage. Two months later I was surprised at seeing him again, only this time his mood was that of a sombre broken man. On arriving home another family had settled in his house. His wife had forged his signature to sell the property, before eloping with the new man in her life. I didn't know what to say, other than be apologetic, but that was scant consolation to a man who was left without a roof over his head, and no wife, kids or money. He worked in Baghdad a few more months, before drifting back to the UK to drown his sorrows even further.

I never reckoned that being apart for long periods from your wife or girlfriend was a healthy state of affairs, with the saying "absence makes the heart grow fonder" not always ringing true. If you were a young couple you wanted each other's company regularly, not two days a month, or two weeks every six months. You chased the big bucks at your peril, with always someone lurking in the shadows, waiting for the opportunity to warm your bed.

Chapter Eighteen

Return to Oz

When I decided to return to Australia for a second, and hopefully more successful, attempt at earning my fortune, I had no idea how much paperwork I would have to produce. Australia House wanted to know what I'd been doing in the fourteen years since I left their shores. In particular, they demanded a statement from my former employers with exact dates of my employment and training:

So that your occupational classification can be finalised, you are requested to forward the following:

1. A statement of service from Smiths Prompt Service Depot Ltd giving;

(a) Exact commencement and termination dates of employment.
(b) Exact commencement and completion dates of training.
(c) Trade classification in which trained.
(d) A full description of training given and work performed.
(e) Exact date first recognised and paid as a skilled worker.

Also details of employment subsequent to training, giving:

Employment or trades classification.
A detailed description of work performed in that classification.

(h)   Tools and equipment used.

2. Originals of any certificates awarded at a Technical educational establishment e.g. City and Guilds etc.

(b)   Original E.I.T.B. certificates, if applicable
(c)   Original Indenture of Apprenticeship endorsed as completed

Note: A personal statement covering present employment may be submitted if you are reluctant to approach your employer for a reference. This statement will need to be officially confirmed prior to final classification.

The following must be observed in relation to all statements of service. They:

A.   Must be on the official headed paper of the firm or firms concerned and/or bear the firm's stamp.

B.   Must specify the trade in which you were trained.

C.   Must include the correct, full and specific dates of commencement and completion of training and subsequent employment.

D. Must include a detailed description of the training received and work involved and the work performed after training.

E. All documents forwarded must be originals and be accompanied by one copy of each.

Note: All original documents will be returned by recorded mail.

This was another kick in the balls I could definitely have done without. The problem was, where to start? Smith's Garage was now under the control of former salesman George Dunleavy, he having risen through the ranks to the hot seat. My last meeting with him and Geoff Smith hadn't been the most amicable, so maybe he would ignore my request. There was also the question of my activities in the bus sector for the past eleven years, but who would give me a reference for that? I very much doubted if they would accept my version of events, so I would have to contact the Northern Traffic Area office for some sort of clarification. Time was also a problem, with only a couple of days to sort things out before heading east again. Finally I decided to draught two letters for Smiths and the NTA during my next trip.

It was proving more difficult to return to Oz than I'd ever imagined, with young married couples with skills taking preference. I had the skills, whereas marital status was against me, my plus points being sufficient funds. However, the biggest stumbling block was proving to be the divorce.

We were into July before I got time to visit Smiths garage. I got a cool reception from George Dunleavy, but at least he afforded me the courtesy of agreeing to my request. It seemed a long time since our first meeting in October 1959, our paths having taken totally different directions. I still had visions for the future, whereas George, by now in his late-fifties, was in the comfort zone. The workshop was as I remembered it, apart from a few minor additions, but lots of water, joy and heartache had passed under the bridge since then.

Next stop was Australia House in Newcastle. I informed them of my latest role as maintenance manager for an international freight company, with Taffy prepared to confirm this at a later date. Even though the application process was dragging its heals it suited me also, with the overseas expeditions still creating a buzz. At the Northern Traffic area office I outlined my future plans to the chief mechanical engineer, who obliged with a reference.

Northern Traffic Area, Westgate House, Westgate Road, Newcastle upon Tyne   NE1   1TW Telex   53351 Telephone Newcastle 610031

30 July 1979

TO WHOM IT MAY CONCERN

Mr K J Noble has owned and operated public service vehicles in the Northern Traffic Area for the past eleven years. I have known him in this capacity for the past four years, during which time his record has been entirely satisfactory.

Signed: Wm G Liversidge, Area Mechanical Engineer.

A letter from Australia House bore the news that all future correspondence would have to be addressed to their Edinburgh office, besides requesting more details of apprenticeship workshop experience. Apparently the Newcastle office was shortly to close. I found this rather surprising, considering it was housed in the monstrous-looking Swan House that had barely been in operation for ten years. Maybe the Geordies preferred the Tyne to the Swan. I classed them wanting more work details as a joke, total bullshit. I seriously considered calling the whole thing off. I would jump on a plane for a holiday in Oz, and then disappear. I had two current passports, so I could afford to relinquish one to the Oz authorities. A few hours later, after cooling down, I went to see George Dunleavy for another favour. Could he broaden the scope of my reference? He'd have been perfectly within his rights telling me to fuck off and not come back; after all I didn't mean a thing to him. I'd never been a greaseball, but now was the time to start pissing up his back.

In mid-December I finally received confirmation from the Australian authorities that my application had been successful. At the same time I got my divorce papers. I didn't know whether to laugh or cry. I wasn't quite sure what to do regarding the date of departure, with my next journey to Iraq taking in the festive period. My main priority was to give Taffy adequate notice to find a driver. The ideal time to go would have been there and then, with sun drenched beaches definitely more appealing than the prospect of fitting snow chains,

While tucking into a meal in snowy Graz a few days before my thirty-sixth birthday, Taffy returned to the table with some devastating news. "Kevin, I'm sorry to have to tell yer this, but yer Dad's died suddenly. They're going to delay the funeral until Thursday, giving you plenty of time to get back, so I suggest you get pissed to help you sleep." Apart from feeling numb with shock, I was just thankful I was on the return journey and not in Baghdad, or indeed Australia. He'd passed away the previous night at five, having had a heart attack after marking his pool's coupon. There were four of us present, including two Swindon subbies, all loaded and ready for next morning. My cargo was for Hereford, Taffy's being for Scotland, so we would change trailers and paperwork, with my instructions being to drive straight to the depot.

I loved the man, not because he was a high-flyer or Jack the lad, because he wasn't any of these. Dad was just an ordinary working-class chap who would give his last to help anyone. He'd lived three score years and ten, so at least he'd reached the average goal predicted by the statisticians. As the night wore on the drink started playing its own tricks, proving once again to be a temporary saviour. I finally surfaced next morning around ten, accompanied by a throbbing head, before heading for Salzburg and reflecting on what might have been. My conduct throughout the years definitely wouldn't have helped his cause, with guilt gradually giving way to tears.

I arrived home with just enough time for a quick wash and brush up, before donning the darkest of clothes for the requiem mass. According to the priest Dad was going to a better world, a world of eternal life and happiness ever after, where we would all be reunited again on the last day. At least it was a comforting thought knowing that I'd see him again, only to achieve that I first had to die. Years earlier Mother had bought a double burial plot, so for the foreseeable future he would have the place to himself, with the peeling of the church bells on the quarter-hour to keep him company. To me he was as famous as anyone I'd read or heard about, but to the rest of the world he was just a number passing through.

Afterwards we reminisced over old photographs, with the bungalow resembling a crowded bar, minus alcohol. Accompanying Lynda were my ex-wife and in-laws. Later that night Ann and I had a brief liaison, mainly discussing what might have been, and also that by sheer coincidence I was once again on my way to Australia. In the days following Dad's death my judgement was somewhat clouded by a number of issues. Mother was my biggest headache. Even though we hadn't seen eye to eye for the majority of my thirty-six years, should I really be moving to the other side of the world within days? After all the rigmarole, and months of frustration with the Oz authorities, I was left with no choice but to delay my departure.

As luck would have it I retained my job by a cat's whisker, after agreeing to finish at the end of February. Taffy was in the process of buying another rig, so it was a case of deja vu. On top of all this, Ann's affair with her fancy man had temporarily hit the buffers, so we enjoyed a spicy flirtation from time to time, even toying with the idea of setting up home again. In early spring she flew out to Belgrade, enjoying life on the road for a few days on the return journey. Sadly, we were unable to rekindle the magical spirit of earlier years, with us once again facing the reality that our paths lay in different directions. We were both in our thirties, with my outlook pretty much the same as it had been in my teens. The previous two years had seen Ann develop a more serious side to her personality. Unlike me, she seemed more content with life's offerings.

Summer came, so did autumn. Mother was finally back to her old ways, with bingo, whist drives, neighbourly visits and church commitments to keep her occupied, so in that respect I was happy. At least I could return from Oz at the drop of a hat if anything untoward happened. It was time to let someone else take over the reins, even though Taffy had "kinda hoped" that the Australian thing would fall through. The job I'd intended as a stopgap for two months had dragged out tenfold, but what a marvellous adventure it had been. There was a war imminent between Iraq and its neighbour Iran, so I guess in one sense I couldn't have timed it better. In the event of being killed in a war zone the insurance companies were only willing to pay £100 compensation. That put life's worth into perspective.

My last visit to the Anbar Hotel was on Sunday 7th September 1980. There were around eight drivers present, including Taffy, with everyone expecting a farewell piss-up. Even though it had been a hot day I just wanted to be alone with time to gather my thoughts, wondering for once if I'd made the right decision. I downed a couple of beers before shaking everyone's hand, with "good luck" wishes and "see you again" promises. When it was Taffy's turn, I also thanked him for giving me a lift with Lloyd's kennel, opening another chapter in my life. Then it was tally-ho towards the border, amid the many military machines preparing for action. Saddam was praised throughout the land as a fearless leader, with the people convinced that a new Iraq was about to rise from the ashes. The park at Gaziantep was empty, after all it was only 2pm, but I gave two long blasts on the air horns as I passed for the final time. Goodbye, Saxophone Joe. It was also thanks for the music, with the cassettes from the Tartous café keeping me company for countless hours and miles. Three days after I returned home, the Iraq-Iran war started.

I was finally returning to Oz after months of anguish and uncertainty. This time I was better prepared, confident that for once things would go as planned, with no bombshells regarding the fairer sex. The details of my departure were strikingly similar to those of fourteen years earlier, but there would be no tears at Durham Station. I was also better equipped for the climate. There was no chance of me getting off the plane in Perth dressed in a three-piece suit and an overcoat draped over my arm.

Farewell to Lynda. Farewell to Mother, Farewell to the fair frauleins of Graz. Farewell once again to the land of my fathers.

On October 5th, two days before leaving for Oz, fate once again played its hand in deciding I embark on a different course. It also ensured that I would have to wait a long, long time before getting the soles of my feet burnt on Cottesloe beach – but that's another story.

Chapter Nineteen

Never Look Back

The words of Saddam Hussein were nothing but hollow promises. He reversed the ideals of the legendary Ali Baba, taking money from the poor to give to the rich. Three wars in twenty-three years put the country on its knees. Instigating the 1980-88 war with Iran showed his lack of judgement, and his use of chemical weapons against the Kurds his lack of humanity. The "Supergun" scandal was just another example of his determination to cross swords with anyone he disagreed with. Not only did Saddam persecute and humiliate his own folk, but his actions also caused endless misery to the people of southeast Turkey. Their cross-border trade with Iraq disappeared virtually overnight. Many have to resort to selling fuel as a means of survival, with almost a thousand tankers daily crossing the Zacho/Habur frontier.

It's sad that such hard-working people should become victims of a dictator's lust for glory, or the invader's quest for oil. In a further twist, it's reported that the Turkish government is looking at the possibility of claiming the oil fields in Northern Iraq, which were ruled by them during the days of the Ottoman Empire. That announcement is bound to ruffle a few feathers. Now it would be suicidal even to contemplate driving to Iraq. The execution of two Bulgarian drivers is just one of a seemingly never-ending sequence of daily atrocities. The great explorers of the past were lucky to be able to travel the world without hindrance, but that luxury appears to have evaporated.

The number of migrants travelling to Australia and New Zealand dwindled in the seventies. That, coupled with a boom in oil prices, meant that the majestic ocean liners could no longer function economically. The Galileo then operated as a cruise ship, changing hands and names several times, before catching fire and sinking in 1999, during a voyage from the Thai resort of Phuket to Singapore.

The ship I missed from Australia to Southampton, the ill-fated Achille Lauro, had a rather chequered history. During its role as a cruise ship she suffered two fires, besides colliding with a cargo ship. In 1985 she came to the world's attention when she was hijacked by Palestinian terrorists, the murder of an elderly American disabled passenger causing public outrage. The incident was made into a movie, "Voyage of Terror – The Achille Lauro Affair," starring Burt Lancaster. In 1994 the ship caught fire yet again en-route from Genoa to the Sychelles, her final resting place being a watery grave 150 miles off the coast of Somalia. By sheer coincidence, the leader of the 1985 hijackers, Abul Abass, was captured in Iraq in 2003.

Port Hedland is now a thriving iron-ore town, even boasting an international airport, besides ranking with Dampier as the highest tonnage ports in Australia. The population has jumped from a mere thousand to 15,000. I'm afraid that I would be well out of touch with the way the one-horse town has progressed in the past forty years. The weathers still the same – hot – with Cyclone Rachel also venting her anger on its residents in January 1997, uprooting trees and disrupting power.

Besides its huge iron-ore output, Dampier also exports over three million tons of high quality solar salt annually from nearby pans. The specifically-constructed company town, along with neighbour Karratha, now have a population of 14,000 between them, with palm trees gracing the beach and harbour areas. I can only imagine that it looks very pretty, compared to the time of my brief stay, when there was nothing but scorched earth on one side and the Indian Ocean on the other.

Another important addition is the 1,700-mile tarmac northern highway from Perth up to the Kimberleys, compared to the mere 300 miles to Geraldton in times past.

Europe has totally changed since 1980, when there were only nine members of the then EEC. Even our passports are similar in design and fabric to the former eastern bloc countries, who supposedly lived in the backwoods. On May 1st 2004 the European Union opened its doors to a further ten members, making twenty-five in total, with Slovenia of the former Yugoslavia one of the latest. Much the same as Iraq, Yugoslavia has also been involved in a bitter war of race, religion and one man's craving for power. Turkey, Romania and Bulgaria are waiting in the wings to join the EU. Turkey's acceptance is a mere formality, especially with a little push from Uncle Sam, desperate to increase his foothold in the Middle East. Baghdad will then be only 330 miles from the EU's eastern border – a rather bizarre situation.

In future years, the EU could expand even further, by bestowing honorary membership on all countries bordering member states. That would allow us to bask in the sunshine of the Caspian Sea and Persian Gulf resorts, which would then be featured in the European holiday brochures. I cannot imagine Britain ever being fully integrated with the rest of Europe on a social level, simply because that twenty-five mile strip of water seems at times like a million miles. With communism seemingly a thing of the past, democracy is the word sprouting from everyone's lips, irrespective of race or creed. It makes you wonder if the shift to the new-world order is becoming too rapid. While it might be good for trade, many workers from the poorer countries and beyond are chasing the highest bidders, borne out by the growing influx of travellers heading west. I don't subscribe to the idea of letting people roam the continent at will. This alone encourages drug traffickers to peddle their supplies of heroin unhindered, from the cesspool of Afghanistan to all corners of Europe.

Package holidays are now as commonplace as a saunter down the local pub, with the latest craze seeing people jetting off to New York for a few days shopping, or hosting weekend parties in Prague, Dublin, or Paris. Twenty-one million people enjoy holidays abroad each year compared with two million in 1980, when exotic locations such as Mexico, India or the far east were only associated with the wealthy. Since then Turkey has joined the gold rush, even though the currency rate appears to have gone somewhat haywire, with a glass of chay now costing 150,000 lira compared with my last purchase of ten. Iraq has also gone crazy, due to war not tourism, with one US dollar buying you 1,471 new Iraqi dinar.

Besides adopting the Aussie dress code we've also developed their love of eating outdoors, prompting huge sales in barbecues. Not so long ago the wearing of shorts would have caused laughter among the 10 to 80 age groups, but they now appear to be the in-thing among all ages and sexes. Even in Spain, Greece and Italy, traditional long black trousers are taking a back seat, with the older generation accompanying their grandchildren in baring their legs. The weather experts seem to be of the opinion that due to global warming we can expect the summers to be longer and hotter, with sunshine the tonic we all crave for. Suntan parlours litter the high street, offering that all-year-round Mediterranean look, to add to the masses of gold chains, earrings, tattoos and body piercing.

Mercedes now have a commercial vehicle assembly plant in Aksaray, central Turkey, serving the requirements of all the Middle Eastern states. Instead of Mohammad going to the mountain, they have taken the mountain to Mohammad, ensuring work for the Turks in their homeland. Many of the hair-raising sections of highway have been updated in recent years, with the Pozanti-Adana-Gaziantep motorway just one example. Once the sovereignty of Cyprus is ratified, holidaymakers will be only a few hours ferry-ride away from Tarsus and Adana.

Adventurers and backpackers the world over now have the luxury of computer technology, plus the added assurance of mobile phones. Modern day electronics and tracking systems has also ensured that the trucker's activities can also be closely monitored, even in the house of fun!

It's now more than half a century since my Irish grandfather died, along with the many traditions and beliefs that he and his fellow countrymen brought across the water. If by chance he returned today he'd be gob-smacked. Not only would he witness females parading around the Church altar, he'd be unable to smoke his pipe in his beloved homeland whilst enjoying a glass of Guinness.

The motor-car is running our lives more than ever, resulting in many towns and cities entirely losing their character to make way for the four-wheeled monster. Some analysts are of the opinion that, at the present rate of car and population growth, Britain's roads will be gridlocked by the year 2030. Turbo-charged engines are now commonplace, in contrast to the seventies and eighties when it was mainly confined to commercial applications. Sadly, our truck, bus and car industries appear to have slowly extinguished themselves. The names of AEC, Gardner, Standard, Hillman and Triumph have long gone from the manufacturing sector, whilst many others are being influenced by out-of-town partners. Swedish and Japanese vehicles have stood the test of time, so perhaps they were aware of something we weren't?

Computerised high-horsepower trucks are seeing a return of eight to ten mpg for 44-tons gross, a figure that would have been inconceivable a quarter of a century ago. Hi-tech engine technology is also seeing engines lasting considerably longer, besides being more reliable. Its quite feasible in the not-to-distant future, that cars up to 1600cc will have a maintenance-free power unit, with the complete vehicle being recycled after five years. Contrary to what the geologists predicted in the early sixties, we are still being supplied with oil out of the ground. No doubt plenty of alternatives are waiting in the wings, with electric or hydrogen power seemingly the way ahead.

Even with no hold-ups at the now defunct EC's border posts, Ted Hannon's return journey from Bishop Auckland to Tabriz in 16 days will take some beating. This is due to more countries enforcing tachograph regulations, weekend driving bans and re-routing of journeys due to recent conflicts.

One thing that's puzzled me over the years about government transport policies, is why we've never copied the German piggy-back rail system throughout Britain to accommodate road haulage, similar to that used on channel tunnel crossings. We have an excellent national rail network, whose potential could surely be maximised during off-peak hours. One excuse is that UK rail bridges aren't high enough, which puts the Germans planners of yesteryear on a very high pedestal indeed. The advantages to the haulier would be the elimination of three of his major headaches:

More flexible driving times.
Less wear on vehicles.
No congestion on rail network.

Looking at the government's perspective, why bother doing anything? Do they really care about traffic jams in towns, cities and on motorways? The more vehicles on the road, the more taxes to the treasury. Cutting down on the mileage of trucks would also put a strain on the chancellor's coffers, due to less fuel tax revenue.

Joining the Euro is inevitable, with another possibility in the years ahead being the change from right to left-hand drive. Impossible, many would say. Sweden did it in 1967. The advantages would be enormous, mainly because it's cheaper to make vehicles with the steering-wheels in the same place. Other benefits would include a huge European market place to buy your autos at the keenest of prices. You could then board a cheap flight to Budapest, Barcelona, Naples or Athens and drive your left-hooker back home. The gallon is slowly fading into obscurity, much the same as feet and inches. Will we ever accept the pint of beer being replaced with a slightly less half litre, and will the spirit measures be as generous as those we get on holiday?

In recent years I've been in involved in the reconditioning of commercial diesel engines, although I must admit to being just a little workshop weary, even though it acts as my therapy. What drives me on, besides the need to earn a crust, is thinking of how my father toiled away at bricklaying without so much as a moan. An age-old saying is that hard work never killed anyone. Maybe it didn't annihilate the human species, but it killed horses and knackered engines. The legacy of hard work and long hours was reflected in aching joints and painful bodies in later years. I still live in Crook, but a totally different Crook to the one in the sixties. Grassland has replaced the areas that the town's prosperity was built on, leaving only the names of the pubs as a reminder. It now serves mainly as a commuter town, with many new homes servicing the needs of the city workers, along with the latest BMWs.

I always make time to play with the grandkids, whether it's games, riding bikes, or splashing around in the water. They are the future, the ones who'll grow up in a computerised world where leisure time is given top priority. My Dad was born not long after the motor-car took to the roads, whereas Granda witnessed the birth of aviation. My great-grandfather would have experienced the age of steam, which took the ordinary man beyond local boundaries and into the unknown.

Besides the many photographs, I also have a 1976 Volvo F88 truck, the same type used on the Middle East run. I keep it as a memento, along with two 1960s guitars. The Seiko calculator watch I bought in Tartous still keeps excellent time, even though its place of residence is now on a bookshelf. Until recently I could watch "Top of the Pops", now taken off the telly, with the Fender and Gibson guitars still belting out the tunes from their fifties-designed instruments. It makes me realise only too well how my parents must have felt at the first sounds of rock'n'roll.

If I'd opted for college lecturing in motor engineering I would now be retired, enjoying the benefits of a bumper pension. Instead I chose to do my own thing, instead of working within the confines of four walls for forty years. How quickly time has passed, making me realise that the good things in life certainly don't last a lifetime. One thing I don't have is any regrets as to my actions throughout the years. It's no use thinking otherwise, because yesterday is gone forever. Had I been a good boy and stayed in Australia, who knows what the future might have held? Had I been a faithful husband, then my visits to the kingdom of Ali Baba would still be an unfulfilled dream.

I can honestly say that driving to the Middle East was the most enjoyable and satisfying job in my entire career. Experiencing too many of life's ups and downs is not necessarily good for the constitution, but they are the only ones I have to ponder over. Without them there'd be nothing to put pen to paper.

Mother died in1996, but nothing ever changed in our attitudes towards one another. Even though I lived with her during the latter years, her famous words would ring out from time to time, especially after I'd spent a night on the tiles. On the day she died I went to the nearest bar and got drunk. Her death hit me harder than

I thought possible. While she lay in the Chapel of Rest I kissed her on the cheek, wishing her well on her way to the promised land.

One thing I neglected to mention, because I didn't think it was relevant to my experiences, was that Mother had a port wine birthmark on the right side of her face. Even though she covered it with special cream, she always seemed conscious of the fact that people were staring at her. It must have had a devastating effect on her early life, probably explaining the reason for her cold sombre attitude and her hatred of good-looking women. A few years before her death, I took her to a private clinic in Newcastle for a few sessions of laser treatment, the latest technology for alleviating the problem. I never noticed any difference, but it made her feel better and more confident about her appearance, which was the whole objective of the exercise. As long as she felt happy I was happy.

It's highly unlikely that I'll be chosen to offer spiritual guidance to others, with the thought of ending up a pauper not even worth contemplating. But who knows what the future holds, with that little bit of luck, sometimes the only difference between success and failure.

It is a wonderful thing, a mother. Other folks can love you but only your mother understands. She works for you, looks after you, loves you and forgives you.

Anything you may do she understands you. And then the only bad thing she ever does is to die and leave you.

This story was originally intended as a legacy for my grandchildren, when they reach an age to appreciate it. It was to give them an insight into the lives of their Granda and great-grandparents, without having to research into the archives or rely on second-hand gossip. Family trees unearth a wealth of information, but I've added a bit of spice and adventure, which I hope they will find entertaining.

Have an interesting life, enjoy yourselves, and take full advantage of that slice of good fortune that comes along occasionally – because tomorrow never comes.

Chapter Twenty

Facts & Figures

Expenses (August 1980)

Belgium   nil

Germany   nil

Austria

Transit tax (two ways)	3000	
Border overtime payment	106	
Schenkers (border agent)	170	
£1 = 30.00 Austrian schillings	Total 3276	£109

Yugoslavia

Transit tax (two ways)	2100	
Motorway tolls	612	
£1 = 46.7 Yugo dinar	Total 2712	£58

Bulgaria

Transit tax	Total 20USD	£8

Greece

Transit tax (two ways)	600	
£1 = 85 Greek drachma	Total 600	£7

Turkey

Transit tax (two ways)	974 DM.	£224
Telegram and Telex	1000	
Parking (six nights)	4800	
Punctures (two)	1000	
Bosporus crossing (return)	1250	
Habur border agent	1500	
Fuel (outward).		
Aksaray (366 litres)	9516	
Birececk (400 litres)	10,400	
Fuel (return).		
Birecick (350 litres)	9100	
Ankara (300 litres)	7800	
Istanbul (200 litres)	5200	
Truck wash (Londra camp)	750	
£1 = 190 Turkish lira	Total 52,316	£275

Iraq

Transit tax.	61	
Fuel.	24	
Alternator repair.	30	
Hotel (Baghdad, two nights).	22	
Taxi (return journey to Babaians office).	8	
Fuel tax (Zacho border).	70	
Backsheesh		£20
One Iraq dinar = £1.35.	Total 215	£290

Grand total £991

Fuel prices

England (diesel): 1979 £1.13/gall; 1980 £1.36/gall.
Turkey (mazot): 1979 £0.55/gall; 1980 £0.62/gall.
Iraq (mazot, naftta): 1979 £0.08/gall; 1980 £0.09/gall.

Distances from London

	Kms	Miles
Cologne.	610	384
Salzburg.	1370	863
Graz.	1630	1026
Belgrade.	2030	1278
Sofia.	2420	1524
Istanbul.	3010	1896
Ankara.	3448	2172
Adana	3934	2478
Gaziantep	4149	2613
Zacho	4741	2969
Mosul.	4806	3027
Baghdad.	5202	3277
Babylon.	5292	3334
Basra.	5782	3642
Thessalonika.	2682	1689
Volos.	2902	1828
Kavala (via Sofia).	2790	1758
Mt. Ararat.	4571	2879
Tabriz (Iran).	4839	3049
Tehran (Iran).	5363	3379
Tartous (Syria).	4031	2540
Damascus (Syria).	4270	2690
(Syrian mileages via Volos).		
Aachen – Salzburg.	810	510
Cologne – Frankfurt.	190	120
Frankfurt – Munich.	440	277
Munich – Salzburg.	130	82
Zagreb – Belgrade.	380	239

Turkey to Iraq (feet above sea level):

Edirne (border)	131
Istanbul (coastal)	33
Bolu	2,374
Ankara	2,787
Aksaray	3,215
Pozanti	2,552
Tarsus (mountain pass)	4,000
Adana (coastal)	75
Gaziantep	2,620
Urfa	1,800
Kiziltepe	1,560
Zacho (Iraq border)	1,706
Mosul	730
Baghdad	111
Basra (coastal)	62

Turkey to Iran (from Ankara):

Sivas	4,257
Erzincan	3,946
Erzurum	6,386
Tahir pass	8,122
Agri	5,371
Bazargan (Iran border)	5,730
Tabriz	4,257
Tehran	4,750

By way of contrast: Ben Nevis – Scottish Highlands 4,490 ft. (highest UK peak); Snowdon – North Wales 3,560 ft.; Helvelyn – Lake District 3,116 ft.; Madrid – Europe's highest city 2,400 ft.

A few of the many British Hauliers: Astran International, Axwell Inter. (Broxburn), B.R.S. overland, Carmans Transport, Cavewood, Duxbury, Eric Vic, Essex International, Evans International, Falcongate, Funston, Hicks, Radclive (Berkshire), Welsh International, White Trux, Whittle trucking.

Some North East Hauliers: A-Line, D & A McRae, Jimmy Keith, Maurice Gray, Ray Pearson, Simmons (Darlington), Stirk International, Van Hee.

A few of the Davies drivers who took the plunge: Andy Anderson, Bob Anderson, Mick Brennan, Alan Bryant, Frankie Cavannah, George Coyne, George Gann, Mel Hall, Ned Kelly, Frank Roach, (Geordie) Phil, John Lowther, Mack, Bob Metcalfe, John (the Baptist) Patterson, John Pennie, Arthur Ridley, Ronnie Seymour, Davey Storrs, George Sykes.

The Authors

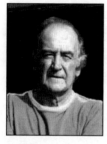

Kevin Noble was born on 26th February 1944 in the coal-mining town of Crook in North East England. His father was a bricklayer, a true Geordie born on the banks of the River Tyne. Apart from his time abroad, Kevin has lived in Crook for most of his life. He trained as a mechanic, before setting up his own coach hire business on his return from Australia.

A chance meeting saw Kevin become an international truck driver and experience "the most exciting time" in his life. "Baghdad Trucker," the true story of Kevin's adventures as a truck driver, is his first venture as an author. Kevin joined Northern Writers in 2006. He and co-author Chris are working on a novel, also based on Kevin's experiences. Kevin is married to Susan. Between them they have seven grandchildren.

Chris Foote Wood was born on 15th December 1940 in Prestbury, Cheshire. His father Stanley Wood from Manchester was a successful author, scriptwriter, musician and playwright. Chris's youngest sister, comedienne Victoria Wood, has often been voted the UK's funniest woman. Chris was brought up in Bury, Lancashire, and settled in Bishop Auckland in County Durham (six miles from Crook) after three years at Durham University, 1959-62.

After first working as a civil engineer, Chris set up and ran his first publishing business, Durham Free Press, 1968-71, pioneering commercial free press newspapers in the north east. After another spell in engineering, Chris became a freelance journalist and broadcaster, running his own North Press Agency for 30 years, 1974-2004, when he sold NPA to set up Northern Writers

Chris is married to Frances (nee Foote), adding her name to his on their marriage in 1977. They have no children, but Chris has three children from his first marriage and two grandchildren. In February 2006 Chris had his first biography book published, "Nellie's Book" (Sutton Publishing), the story of his mother's early life, with a foreword by his sister Victoria Wood.

Acknowledgements

I would like to thank Eric Sheen, Colin Wise, Richard (Chip) Hillary and Wayne Peacock for their help and assistance in teaching me computer skills. In preparing material for this book, fellow truck driver Ted Hannon has been particularly helpful. Ian Fothergill, Craig Dixon and Lee Nyland of Lintons Printers have done everything possible to guide us through all the production stages, remaining cheerful and positive throughout. Lee is to be congratulated on his excellent cover design. My wife Susan has given me much encouragement and support.
Kevin Noble

Most of the photographs in this book were taken by Kevin Noble. In addition, several were supplied by the following, to whom we are most grateful.

Ferdy De Martin truck@toprun.ch; www.TOPRUN.ch

Ian Taylor at46katie-fam@yahoo.co.uk

Namik Colpan and Adem Colpan, the Pudding Shop and Blue House Hotel, Istanbul
puddingshop@puddingshop.com;
www.puddingshop.com
www.bluehouse.com.tr

The Northern Echo, Darlington
www.northern-echo.co.uk

Chris Foote Wood, November 2006

Three "Trucker Books" of the 1980s:

"Cola Cowboys" (Franklyn Wood) W H Allen 1982. Trucking to Saudi Arabia with Astran Trucks. 14,000 miles on the world's toughest route.

"Juggernaut" (Robert Hutchinson) Heinemann 1987. Trucking to Saudi Arabia with Whittle International Freight of Preston.

"Danger – Heavy Goods" (Robert Hutchinson) 1988. Middle East run with Whittle Trucks. Driving the longest, most dangerous roads in the world.